AF560662

GANDHIAN EDUCATION

GANDHIAN EDUCATION

Dr. Joseph C. Mukalel
M.A., M.Ed., M.A.(U.K.), Ph.D.
School of Gandhian Thoughts and Development Studies
Mahatma Gandhi University
Kottayam (Kerala).

DISCOVERY PUBLISHING HOUSE
NEW DELHI

Published by:
Tilak Wasan

DISCOVERY PUBLISHING HOUSE PVT. LTD.
4383/4B, Ansari Road, Darya Ganj
New Delhi-110 002 (India)
Phone : +91-11-23279245, 23253475, 43596065
E-mail : discoverypublishinghouse@gmail.com
sales@discoverypublishinggroup.com
web : www.discoverypublishinggroup.com

First Edition: **1998**

Reprinted: **2020**

ISBN: 978-81-7141-214-3

Gandhian Education

Printed at:
Infinity Imaging Systems
Delhi

CONTENTS

Introduction VII

1. Gandhian Studies : A Rediscovery 1
   1. A Rediscovery of Mahatma Gandhi.
   2. Evolving a National Policy on Education
   3. An International Consensus
   4. Gandhi and Ultramodernism
   5. Scope of Gandhian Studies

2. Foundations of Gandhi's Educational Thoughts 34
   1. Education in Ancient India
   2. Education in Medieval India
   3. Western Education in British India
   4. Influence of Christianity.

3. Goals of Education in Gandhian Thought 60
   1. Education for Spiritual/Moral Development.
   2. Education for knowledge.
   3. Education for Social Development
   4. Education for Self-discovery
   5. Education for Life-experiences

4. Gandhi's Experiments in Education 85
   1. Gandhi's Experiments with Truth.
   2. Phoenix settlement and Tolstoy Farm
   3. Experiments in Champaran schools
   4. Nationalist Experiments in Education
   5. Gujarat Vidyapeeth
   6. Wardha Education conference

5. Educational Idealism and Pragmatism in Gandhi 110
   1. Aspects of Educational Idealism.
   2. Idealism, the Fundation of Gandhian Thoughts
   3. Gandhian Idealism and Educational practices.
   4. Aspects of Educational Pragmatism.
   5. Pragmatism in Gandhian Education - 1.
   6. Pragmatism in Gandhian Education - 2.

6. Satyagraha in Gandhian Education 135
   1. Foundations of Gandhian Satyagraha
   2. Satyagraha and Educational Goals.

3. Satyagraha as the Method of Education.
4. Satyagraha as the Content of Education.
5. Satyagraha as Providing directions in Education.

7. Vocational Education 165
1. Gandhi's Basic Education - 1
2. Gandhi's Basic Education - 2
3. Need-based Education in India
4. Rural Reconstruction
5. Vocational Education in the 1986 National Policy.

8. Holistic Education in Gandhism 189
1. Aspects of Holistic Education
2. Traditions Vs Modernism in Gandhi
3. Character Formation in Gandhism.
4. Education for Balanced Development
5. Liberal Education in Gandhism.

9. Education and Spiritual Values 213
1. Nature of Gandhian Morality
2. Spritual Values in Gandhism
3. Spritual Values in Education
4. Developing Spiritual Values in Education - 1.
5. Developing Spiritual Values in Education - 2.

10. Education for Peace and Tolerance 237
1. Gandhi and World Peace
2. Tolerance in Gandhism
3. Educational Goal of Peace and Tolerance
4. Educational Concepts of Peace and Tolerance
5. Methods of Peace Education.

Bibliography 257

Index 267

INTRODUCTION

Gandhian thoughts have a comprehensiveness that usually eludes the attention of the casual Gandhian student or observer. Gandhism has emerged today as one of the most potent vehicle of understanding the contemporary religious, socio-economic, political and educational problems the country in particular and world in general are facing. What is most basic and characteristic to Gandhism is that it provides orientations to every one as part of our life in this country as individuals and as a nation. Gandhian thoughts as a system has proved itself to be so encompassing as to contain basic directions for our individual, social and national life. This comes from the fact that "Gandhi was one of the deathless few across the centuries who have lifted human character to immortality ...... who made humility and simple truth more powerful than empires".[1] This perfection and encompassing nature have made Gandhian thoughts a system that will constitute the very foundation of our individual, social and national life, provided we desire so.

Gandhian education as envisaged in the present work comes exactly within this framework of Gandhian thoughts on life as such. Education, for Gandhi, is not relative, peripheral or superficial phenomenon. Education has resonances that lead us directly to the Supreme Truth and to the step-by-step realisation of this truth. Here lies the vital distinction between the Gandhian education and modern views on education that are based on behavioristic, materialistic and pragmatic concepts. Gandhi's views on education becomes most unacceptable to the contemporary empirical mind precisely because it is God-oriented and truth centered.

Gandhi's educational thoughts have an eclectic basis. Any one who undertakes the study of this aspect of Gandhism needs to bear this fact in mind that in developing his thoughts on education Gandhi was not attempting to fit his thoughts into the framework of any particular system or philosophy. Gandhi had his eyes consistently fixed on one and the same set of goals: Education for truth and non-violence, and Education for National Development. Truth and non-violence were the principles of self-realisation, and National Development for Gandhi meant emancipation of the suffering rural masses of people. Education for him was means exclusively for the realisation of these goals in thus proximate as well as ultimate dimensions. Because of this Gandhian education as he himself expoused it becomes eclectic in the sense that it receives several apparently dichotomous viewpoints from different schools of educational thinking. Hence we find in Gandhian educational thoughts elements that belong to educational idealism as well as pragmatism, traditional Vedic education as well as modern child-centered and life-centered viewpoints on education. This makes Gandhian education unique in its texture.

Gandhi achieves a synthesis of Spirituality and education. It is not possible in any manner to effect of segregation of the two in the Gandhian system of thoughts. The two are sides of the same coin. In Gandhism the goals of both are one and the same: "Self-realisation is the Summum Bonum of life and education".[2] Education is thought of strictly as a process for the development of the Spiritual personality of the individual. If education does not achieve this aim, then such an education does not become worthy of its name. Development in personality becomes a process of Spiritual development based on the principles of truth and ahimsa. This development is realised chiefly through the phenomenon of prayer in personal and social life.

The Gandhian principle of Satyagraha becomes the central framework in Gandhian education. Satyagraha is conceived of in the present context as the most comprehensive principle in Gandhism. The foundations of Gandhian Satyagraha becomes the very foundation of Gandhian education as developed in the present work. Education functions within the framework of a set of goals or aims that determine all the directions the process of education takes in its entirety. Satyagraha becomes the very goal of education in the Gandhian Sense. Education thereby aims at helping students adhere to the principle of truth in ways which are possible within the framework of education. Education, again, functions within the framework of the content which is put across to students in the form of knowledge, skills or experiences. Satyagraha, again, becomes this content of Gandhian education. Truth and ahimsa would permeate every bit of knowledge, skill and experiences that Gandhian education puts across to students. Education, thirdly, functions within the framework of a set of methods that control and determine the actual process. Satyagraha becomes the very method of Gandhian education. Here Satyagraha assumes most concrete dimensions in the delineation of the Gandhian educational ideals.

Gandhian education is holistic and universal in its perspectives. Education in the present context aims at the total, holistic development of all aspects of the human personality. Gandhi's own definition definitely points to this characteristic:

"By education I mean an all-round drawing out of the best in child and man-body, mind and spirit".[3] Gandhi was not willing to compromise any one aspect of the individual's personality for the development of any other. This uncompromising position Gandhi takes renders Gandhian education controversial to the contemporary mind. Gandhi does not find it contradictory in any way to develop a creative and does not find it contradictory in any way to develop a creative and productive yet humble personality. Gandhi does not want us "to be overpowered by the glamour of the West. We must not mistake glamour for true light".[4] Gandhian education does not wish to produce a glamorous personality in the sense modern education understands it. For Gandhi, "the thread of life is in the hands of God", [5] and he does not want us to forget this reality even for a moment. A holistic personality is not a glamorous personality, instead, a personality well-grounded in God-orientations.

Gandhi's thoughts on education became crystallized in his scheme of basic education. Basic education consists of not merely a scheme of vocationalised pattern of education but contains orientations for a most systematic vocational education that can bridge the gap between the resources of this country, human and material, and the country's manifold problems. Basic education is only a framework in which Gandhi envisages a solution for the growing problem of rural alienation in a developing country. Gandhi's fundamental aim in this regard is a systematic reconstruction of rural India for bringing relief and development to the rural masses. Basic education and other segments of Gandhi's educational views together provide the necessary directions for the right pattern of vocational education the country can adopt. Basic education, in this sense is not an outdated scheme but contains Gandhi's aspirations for a thoroughly need-based education.

Gandhian education is a symbol of peace. Education in its very fundamentals promotes peace and tolerance as part of the development of the individual, society and the nation. Peace and tolerance become the keynotes of Gandhian education which is founded on the principles of truth and ahimsa. Gandhi was martyr of world peace : "In his devotion to peace and tolerance of the brotherhood of man, the Mahatma was one of those rare spokesman for the conscience of all mankind".[6] Gandhian education represents Gandhi's aspirations for World peace in its efforts to inculcate the values of peace and tolerance as part of the development of the individual. Tolerance is a fundamental Gandhian value and one of the pillars of non-violence. The very survival and progress of the individual, society and the nation depends on the magnitude of tolerance practiced at each level. Education can orient its goal of peace in co-ordination with other educational goals towards the development of the nation in the framework of peace. Peace in the Gandhian sense can highlight the preparation of the curriculum of education and become the focus of educational experiences at different levels. Gandhian education for peace and tolerance will be embodied in the concepts of education at different levels. Educational concepts for peace become the content of educational experiences especially as part of the information and skills that form part of education. These concepts can be organised in such a way as to heighten the peace awareness of individuals. Peace education will be imparted through a large variety of specific methods which education can adopt as part of its curriculum.

Gandhian education focuses on education for social welfare. Gandhi never diverted his attention from his fundamental goal of rural reconstruction for the salvation of the rural masses:

"My mind is living in the villages. They are calling me to bury myself in them".[7] Education for Gandhi is a primary means of reaching out to these suffering millions in rural India and lifting their lot to the human level. Gandhian education is built on the concept of service and he spares no word to exhort students to take up the cause of Social Service as part of their education especially during their vacations.

Gandhian education as outlined in the present work in a most comprehensive system. The tentacles of this system reaches out every aspect of the life of an Indian in particular and a world citizen in general. Gandhi's vision of education did not develop in isolation as it happened with several other world visionaries. Gandhi's education becomes an integral constituent of the total Gandhian system for the holistic welfare of man. Gandhi's perpetual search for the refinements of truth and ahimsa manifests itself magnificently in the framework of Gandhian education and becomes a consistent response to the contemporary knowledge explosion that seems to threaten us.

References

1. Vandenberg, A.H., In Norman Cousins (ed.), *Profiles of Gandhi*, New Delhi 1969, P.97.

2. Bhatia, B.D., *Philosophy and Education*, New Delhi 1957, p. 126.
3. Gandhi, M.K., *Harijan*, Ahmedabad, 14 July 1937
4. Cousins, Norman (ed.), *Profiles of Gandhi*, New Delhi 1969 p. 52.
5. Gandhi, M.K., *An Autobiography*, Ahmedabad 1966 (repr) p. 186.
6. Marshall, G.C. in Norman Cousins (ed.) p. 96.
7. Tendulkar, D.G., *Mahatma* Vol.4, Bombay 1960, p.40.

1

GANDHIAN STUDIES : A REDISCOVERY

1. A Rediscovery of Mahatma Gandhi

Paying tribute to Mahatma Gandhi on his 75th birthday, Albert Einstein wrote : "Generations to come, it may well be, will scarcely believe that such a one as this ever in flesh and blood walked upon this earth."[1] Gandhi today has become a universal symbol more than anything else of the supreme principles of truth, love, non-violence, justice and human brotherhood, The world is found more and more lacking in these values to collossal degrees and we are being overcome by a realisation that these values alone can redeem the world from a state of increasing degeneration. No other techniques are found to be more potent than the Gandhian techniques generated from these principles of human conduct, and this realisation is leading Gandhi to ever greater recognition.

E. Stanley Jones calls Gandhi "the voice of the dumb millions."[2] Gandhi has become for us Indians not a mere national hero as the Father of the Nation, but a living voice exhorting us and inviting us to renew our commitment to build a nation of physically and spiritually free persons. Increasing problems leave us in ever greater bondage and Gandhiji's voice is a liberating voice, provided Indians and the world at large are willing to renew their commitment to truth and brotherhood. We are rediscovering Gandhi as the powerful light that is capable of shining over the whole modern world with the potent rays of spiritual integrity and spiritual revolution. One of the most valuable legacies Gandhi has left to posterity in his life and teachings are crystallised in satyagraha and non-violence. These great principles are envisaged to help modern world contemplate and practice truth and love penetrating all life's activities.

Mahatma Gandhi is rediscovered today in his intense devotion to world peace and political and religious tolerance based on the brotherhood of man. As George C. Marshall says, Gandhi "was one of those rare spokesman for the conscience of all mankind".[3] He has become again the voice of mankind for a livable world of peaceful co-existence that is facing nightmare threats, Gandhi is the need of the day, not only for Indians but for the entire world on the face of overwhelming problems. He saw the redemption of the world through the weapons of humility and simplicity and showed Indians that these values can be more powerful than empires.

Gandhi's vision was most comprehensive. This was manifested in all his teachings and actions. As a man of great principles every minute detail of life was significant for him from the view-point of his principles. He possessed an all pervasive spirit that encompassed these details of life no matter how insignificant they meant to the onlooker. This included everything right from dieteties to the vision of the Supreme Reality who is identified with Truth in all his teachings. All these Gandhi developed through a life-time of hard-core experiments and reflections. Edmond Taylor says : "The present Gandhi is the result of years of rigorous concentration on a few simple, emotionally significant ideas, of strict self-discipline and intense training,"[4]. This comprehensive vision of Gandhi includes first of all religion and spirituality and elucidates set of spiritual values for his posterity to believe, practice and profit from. His vision of religion was solid, unshakable, complete and perfectly down to earth. Gandhi says on several occasions : "What I want to achieve is self-realisation, to see God face to fact and to achieve

Moksha."[5] In the very core Gandhi confessed that he was an aspirant of Moksha. John Gunther says, "His approach to every thing is religious, but aside from Hinduism it is difficult to tell what his religion is".[6] John Holmes says, "His whole life was an obedience to God. He had no personal ends to serve."[7] This vision of religion, and spirituality formed the very foundation of Gandhian thoughts in politics, economics, education and international relations. He could not for a moment forget that he was committed soul and body to truth and love, the two great epitomising embodiments of all religious conceptions. Gandhi firmly believed that "without an unreserved surrender to His Grace, complete mastery over thought is impossible."[8] Gandhi would never for a moment conceive of a pattern of education delinked in its essence from spirituality and religion. Gandhi's vision of God, religion and spirituality was highly personal one, in the sense that he never agreed with the idea of an institutionalised religion : "Real religion should radiate from the individual the attitudes of love and service".[9]

Gandhi's vision includes a comprehensive system of moral principles. His religion is often called an ethical religion for a variety of reasons. We are often surprised at the way Gandhi speaks of morality. He resorts more to moral principles in the explanation of religion, hence the label : ethical religion. Gandhi says, "When morality incarnates itself in a living man, it becomes religion, because it binds, it holds, it sustains him in the hour of trail."[10] Owing to an exclusive and intense concern for the moral perspectives of life, Gandhi speaks in terms that sound categorical and leaves the impression that he is speaking in a defining manner. But a loser look at his perspectives and beliefs in religion shows that he was equally concerned about God, religion, prayer, ascetic attitudes, sense of sacrifice, heaven and everything that makes a phenomenology religion complete to the very details. Hence it will not be correct to say that it is mere ethical concerns that makes his religion. When Gandhi says, "Prayer is the heart and soul of religion. Therefore prayer should be the core of human life and no one can live without religion",[11] his spiritual concerns are no less than that of any one with professed religious attitudes. With his deep concern for prayer and his constant thirst for an intense encounter with God, he was far from what he is often thought of : one who identified religion with morality.

Gandhi is in several ways rediscovered by Indians and the world at large. It may be called a rediscovery because the spirit of interest and enthusiasm in everything related to Gandhi has come to be a recent thing. The Gandhian thoughts and trends, and all the values that he held as precious for himself, for the Nation and the world lay hidden in the annals of decades without receiving adequate recognition, when he lived he reached people through direct contact, action and example, coming down to and moving in the midest of the people for whose freedom he dedicated himself. After his death, independent India almost transformed Gandhi into a myth, a legend and a classic example of national heroism. The country found not much worthy of practicing in its march to sophistication and modernism. That was indeed a great tragedy.

Today we are witnessing a real spirit of interest in Gandhian thoughts, values and practices. We are trying to left the Father of the Nation from the state of being a legend. Today Mahatma Gandhi is becoming for the Indian, and for the matter for the world, a living figure whose message is no longer a classic example of heroism. We are rediscovering him for all that he was. We have begun feeling "the spiritual presence of an infinitely loving and lovable man".[12] This spiritual presence of Gandhi is exercising a rejuvenating influence on modern India and we are now slowly willing to recognise this presence. The totally materialistic attitudes and business mentality coupled with all the hypocrisy that we have will not take us very much ahead. Gandhi is recognised as our real guiding spirit and the light that is showing the nation the way. It is difficult for us still to accept this as a fact. We have been trying to build a nation without a spiritual, moral and religious basis, a nation devoid of God. Gandhi presented before us his life experiments: Richard B. Gregg says, "The result of his incessant experiments was an unshakable belief and trust in God, and in the power of God acting in all men, and hence in the power of non-violence."[13] Gandhi attempted to share with India and the world the experiences of his life freely and fully. We are now more willing to listen to him in a spirit of openness. Gandhi has become ever more relevant to problem -bound India. He has taught the country to search for the solutions within our own resources just he has taught us to search for the solutions of our own problems in our own souls.

We have also begun feeling that Gandhian political theory and solutions in particular have far reading consequences in a world of ours in which politics is most often deprived of all moral foundations. It was impossible for Gandhi to envisage the two as separate : religion and politics : He says, "I felt compelled to come into political field because I found I could not do even social work without touching politics."[14] Gandhi goes to the extreme of saying that "politics bereft of religion is absolute dirt, even to be shunned."[15] The whole thing was an entirely new approach to the question of politics. This approach demands a bit too much of politicians. Today we are more prone to see and accept Gandhi as the unique symbol of unity between personnel morality and public action. This personal morality which Gandhiji demands from politicians makes these job more difficult than they would imagine. Gandhiji envisages and defines politics only as a technique to generate soul force to refashion the personalities of millions of our country mere for specific collective ends. This synthesis of politics and religion is characteristic of India with reference to the problems and temperaments peculiar to this country.

Most important of all, Mahatma Gandhi is rediscovered today as the champion of the down trodden and the poor masses of India. This characteristic makes him all the more relevant to contemporary India. Gandhi's entire concept of religion is built on the service of the poor. He says, " I had made the religion of service my own, as I felt that God could be realised only through service."[16] Gandhi advised the students of our country to dedicate themselves to the service of the poor : "Students should be familiar with the poverty and the problems of the common mass,"[17] and further, "students should learn to sacrifice the things that the poor in India cannot afford for themselves."[18] Service of the poor was all in all for Gandhi. His 'Experiments with Truth' radiates in its length and breadth with his dedication and rededication of the poor. Love of the poor in India drove him to fight untouchability. The extent of his dedications to the cause of eliminating untouchability was evident when he said, "I was wedded to the work of extinction of untouchability long before I was wedded to my wife."[19] We know that Gandhi even resorted to fasting a number of times for the cause of Harijan welfare.

Love of the poverty-ridden Indian masses remained to be Gandhi's primary concern throughout his public life in general and during the heightened freedom struggle in particular, K.L. Gauba says, "Gandhiji became their (the poor) most important champion, much as he had espoused the cause of the weaker sections of the communities all his life."[20] He was driven to consider education, as mentioned above, as a vehicle of service to the poor. His concept of basic education aimed at equipping every student in the villages and the towns with a means to earn his or her daily bread. Every aspect of education for Gandhi one way or other envisaged the welfare of the common man in India. This was a concern that permeated all aspects of Gandhiji's public life.

India in particular and the world at large are rediscovering Gandhi. This is a lingering and slow process, but an inevitable one. The vision of Mahatma Gandhi is a vision of salvation for the country. The greatness of the Gandhian message has been tested on the anvil of decades. Gandhiji's greatness is not supposed to be mummified for the sheer pleasure of keeping it. It is a living greatness and living and evolving message. The most characteristic aspect of Gandhi's teachings is that he did not merely preach his message for the world but he lived it every moment of his life. As K.L. Gauba says, " Gandhi, the man of destiny, born to emancipate his country first emancipated himself by the conquest of desire and fear."[21] Eleanor Roosevelt paid her tribute to Gandhi where she said, "the hungry people of India were won by Gandhi's life of voluntary renunciation and service and they followed him as long as they lived."[22] We are rediscovering him after his death. His was not a life to have ende with temporal death but one to the evolved into the ve breath of modern India.

2. Evolving a National Policy on Education

Education in India is as old as history itself. Right from the known and recorded pre-Vedic period upto the present day problems of education in India have had a uniqueness of its own because of the sociological and religious complexity of this sub-continent. We have always confronted the major problem of arriving at a synthesis of the traditional Indian educational values that were held to the most precious for centuries, and the modern western educational values and systems that were introduced to and developed in this country by the British. The question was always whether or not to reassert the traditional educational values in a ways suitable to take case of the problems of modern India after Independence or to further strengthen the already well-established British system of education in this country. This much debated question has everything to do with the New Education Policy of 1986 introduced by the government of India.

In this context more than ever, Gandhian thoughts and practices on education have assumed a new dimension and gathered a new momentum. Mahatma Gandhi's ideas on the educational practice in this country were well known and to a great extent tried out in several quarters especially with reference to vocational education. But Gandhi is more than all that. Those who sneer at his basic education are not aware that Gandhian thoughts penetrate deeper layers of present day education and touch more intensely the problems of Indian education than is usually conceived of. It is an area where a rediscovery of Gandhi is taking place to make the knot left by the synthesis of traditional Indian values and western modern education.

Education is India has had a chequered history. The earliest known and systematically rewarded educational system in India was Vedic education. Vedic education that stretched up to the early period of the Christian era concentrated on the teaching of sacred Indian scriptures and of the rudimentary sciences. Care also was taken to train the pupil in a variety of arts and skills. Medieval education in India was more Islamic education under the patronage of the Muslim rulers. Modern India witnessed the rise and fall of the British empire. The very foundations of modern Indian education were laid by the British. India derived great benefits including Western scientific and technological knowledge. The Vedic spirit of Indian education, all the same, gave way to a more pragmatic progress oriented Western education imparted through the medium of English. This was a major breakthrough in Indian education. At the same time it came to be reorganised more and more that the British system of education in India during the initial, medial and final phases of the British empire aimed at a perpetuation of the British interests in this country. What was predominantly absent was a National Policy that aimed at the exclusive benefits and progress of this Nation and at an education that would solve the concrete problems of this country.

This was a major educational preoccupation of our policy makers after independence. It became so urgent to recognise and define our problems, recognise and define our resources, establish a link between the two, and give shape a national policy on education within the framework of the Constitution of India. The educational demands posed by the Constitution are to be realised in concrete and avoid collossal stagnation and wastage that is currently happening in our country. Gandhi had a comprehensive vision of national schools and national education : "National schools should be capable of spreading the message of Charka, unite the Hindus and the Muslims, educate the untouchables and thus remove from schools the cause of untouchability".[23] Mahatma Gandhi's educational thoughts and reforms have been evoked as an answer to the present crisis of educational values. In the wake of a New National Policy on education Gandhi's thoughts and reforms have gathered a new importance and significance.

The National Policy on Education has several fundamental characteristics. Shriman Narayan in his 'Towards Better Education' says, " Integration and proper coordination between our developmental and educational plans require our most urgent attention."[24] National development schemes should intelligently and with foresightedness integrate educational plans with a view to achieving one coordinated policy towards progress. Educational planning and reconstruction have become catch words of the day. This has become key to the new policy on education. The highest resource of a nation for development is the human resource. Until and unless the potentials of this mighty resource of our country can be adequately tapped for the betterment of the nation, our developmental plans are bound to fail. This would in the last resort mean putting the highest premium on education. As Rajiv Gandhi himself says, "It is high time that we stop regarding over population as a burden to the nation, but over population is our strength and a great resource. Education is the foundation of our human resources development."[25] It is fundamental to the New Policy on Education that education is to be viewed with reference to the greater needs and problems of our country at large. The new term 'human resources development' itself shows in what manner human resources are fundamental to a nation in the path of advancement. Educational reconstruction to suit and accommodate our problems and resources in the bridged manner is to be achieved through the kind of educational planning that would integrate first of all the traditional educational values that were held as dear for centuries. It is on the basis of the same values that our Constitution is framed. This Constitution enunciates the educational rights of our citizens which are most basic to our national life.

Such an educational reconstruction is a fundamental Gandhian notion. Gandhi continually, on every available occasion, bewailed the contemporary British system imposed on India. He wished by any means to eradicate that system and introduce a policy on education to suit our needs and uphold our values. Gandhi wanted "to convert every school into a community where individuality is not damped but developed through social contacts and varied opportunities of service."[26] Cautioning against the dangers of knowledge centered education imparted in schools and colleges Gandhi exhorted students : "your education should be built on the foundation of truth and love. Unless this is done your education will be rendered useless."[27] The conflict is more of ideological whether or not to reorient education to the creation of mere intellectuals. Gandhi could never succumb to this idea. Education, for him, has the noble aim of generating human individuals perfect in character. Dr. Radha Kumud Mukherjee says : "The mere intellectual development without the development of character, learning without piety., proficiency in the sacred lore without its practice's, will defeat the very end of studentship."[28] Gandhi conceived of education as the awakening of the soul, of the inner voice, and consequently to the fashioning of the character attuned to the service of God and of man. For this reason Gandhi defines education as "the all-round drawing of the best in the child and man-body, mind and spirit."[29] With this in mind Gandhi proceed a reconstruction of contemporary education in India articulated in all his speeches and writings.

The National Policy on Education within the framework of the Indian Constitution aims at a new synthesis between knowledge and information centered education and a vocation to solve the acute unemployment problem the country is facing. Gandhi was obsessed with the idea of reorienting all education to vocationalisation of one kind or other. The chapter on 'Vocational Education' will focus on this aspect of Gandhian education'. The quintessence, of Gandhian education is his 'Basic Education' which is the nerve centre of an education for character formation. The entire concept of his basic education came as a revolutionary approach as a reconstruction of the established educational tenets of the British days. Gandhi says, "I had long been impressed with the necessity for a new departure."[30] The need for a new departure, a new scheme, and for the synthesis between education and vocation was clear in Gandhi's mind. The New Policy on Education is thus a national requirement to enable teachers, educationists and policy-makers to see things in a new perspective and to create a brain-storming national consciousness about present day education. Education reconstruction can effectively be achieved only through constant national debates creating national awareness of the problem and prospects on a long term basis.

The new policy on education shifts attention to rural India in a way envisaged by the education commissions from time to time. A policy on education in India that does not cater to the needs of rural India can never be considered a national policy to suit our needs and utilise our resources. This shifts in focus is exactly what Gandhi wanted us to take care of. In this numerous speeches Gandhi bewailed the drawbacks of present day education. He says, "there is no relation between today's education and our family and village life,"[31] Again, "at the end of today's higher education, students arrive in an environment totally different from their own original world."[32] This process of alienation was alarming and most destructive to the socio-economic structure of our country.

Mahatma Gandhi loved rural India. It was noble for him to restrain and restrict the ordinary wants of life and uphold the basic virtue of sacrifice and renunciation. He says, "Civilization in the real sense of the term consists in the deliberate and ordinary restriction of wants. This alone promotes real happiness and contentment and increases the capacity for service."[33] Rural reconstruction for Gandhi was not meant to transform all Indian villages into cities or towns and make the village sophisticated. Rural reconstruction was a comprehensive process for Gandhi and that had a special meaning for him. The village was the focal unit of the swaraj for Gandhi. As a great American economist once said, "In India there is some richness in the poverty... they (the poor in India) stand up and possess a spirit of self help and self-respect."[34] In an age automatisation of everything where man is losing all dignity of being a person, this fundamental notice of self-help and self-respect is of great value indeed. Gandhi earnestly wished to integrate this value into his swaraj in general and education in particular. Gandhi has much to say about the future of Indian villages: "Given the right kind of teachers, our children will be taught the dignity of labour and learn to regard it as an integral part and means of this intellectual growth and to realise that it is patriotic to pay for this learning though this labour."[35]

A national policy is not a static but an evolving thing. The British failed to schematise education in India to evolve such a national policy. That was a major drawback and left a wide gap between our needs and problems and our great resources. No system of education in India can be thought of as separated from the great Indian tradition and the great values attached to this tradition. Our duty today is to rediscover, redefine and reintegrate these great values for which Gandhi sacrificed his life. He tells us in a thousand and one ways what these values are and how he expects these to constitute the goals of our education. Today's education aims exclusively at increasing the prospects of life, creating a craze for material comforts and totally leaves and the dimension of character formation to the disaster of the entire system. Character formation has become the willo- the- wisp of present day education because there are no ways of making any provision for this. Chester Bowles says, "for all his determination not to live better than the masses of his people, for all his opposition to what he called the West's craze for material luxuries, he always added, but neither do I want poverty, penury, misery and dust in India."[36]

The primary task of our education at the national level today is recognise and train the human potentials from the very grassroot level. The national policy that is being evolved and formulated has great potential to receive the basic guidelines from the store of Gandhian thoughts and values. Our priorities and national objectives are to be examined and formulated. If the priorities are not agreed upon, a national policy is bound to end in confusion and disaster. Many regard basic education as the only gift of Mahatma Gandhi to the field of education. The Gandhian vision on education in the swaraj was adequately comprehensive provided we see it in the right perspective. The depth of the Gandhian vision came from his experiment with life and the dedication to truth and love.

3. An International Consensus

Mahatma Gandhi not a legacy of India but the world. He was a world leader of magnificent dimensions. The world watched the freedom struggle of India with great interest for a large variety of reasons. On the one side the sprawling sub-continent of India ruled over by the mighty British empire. On the other side there was Gandhi and his associates : the most humble and insignificant man the world has even seen on the political platform. That was a thing to be watched for its progress. Gandhi had already caught world attention with his political activities in South Africa on the one side fighting the British for the cause of Asians in south Africa, and on the other with unparalleled enthusiasm manifesting loyalty to the British. Gandhi himself confesses, "Hardly ever have I known anybody to cherish such loyalty as I did to the British constitution."[37] He became well known for his humanitarian service in South Africa and for his services during the Boer War of 1906.

Here was a man who stood and fought for his principles and for his own people, but with a great difference : he was fighting not the person of the enemy but their attitudes and what they did. The British and Americans have constantly bore testimony to the great friendliness of Gandhi during the freedom struggle. Louis Fischer writes, "Gandhi retained their (the British) respect, often their love through his softness, tenderness and patience."[38] Herbert Mathews pays homage to Gandhi's "genuine national kindness and humour which endears him to children and adult alike."[39] The world watched the development in India with great interest because that struggle was unlike many that the world had witnessed thus far.

The world watched not only the event of freedom struggle as characteristic of the modern era, but also watched the person of Gandhi for what he said and did. With Gandhi's involvement and leadership India's freedom struggle assured a new dimension because Gandhi's was not a mere political leadership. The world knew that. It was possible for thoughtful and sensible men and women around the world to see in Gandhi a revolutionary of a characteristic kind. The revolution was not meant to destroy an existing system because it merely did not work. The revolution was geared to encompass a whole range of values that the world tend to forget. The revolution was a comprehensive one, spiritual one, a universal one.

The voice of Gandhi reflected for the world the voice of great world leaders and masters : Christ, Buddha, Thoreau, Tolstoy, and Ruskin, and at the back of all the great Indian Vedic scriptures. It was with a difference. The situation in which Gandhi presented himself was a most concrete one; there was a great urgency, and this was fact by the world. That was a period of great potential for transition : from colonialism to independence, not merely for India but for the entire third world, from drastic mechanisation of greater humanisation, a control that world always needed and appreciated. This situation made Gandhi a voice to be heard by the entire civilised world. No one could easily turn a deaf ear on Gandhi. Louis Fischer says, "Gandhi had radiated his influence to the friends of a disunited country and to every corner of a divided world."[40] This influence was generated by more than anything else the personal aura he succeeded in building around himself by his personal life: "Gandhi was the symbol of unity between personal morality and public action."[41]

Gandhi proclaimed for the world the universal hope of social redemption. The world has seen great social reformers who one way or other desired to uplift the tragic lot of the suffering masses of humanity. Each of them succeeded in bringing about changes in his contemporary scene and left behind for posterity a legacy of a very limited scope because of the one-sidedness of his doctrine. It became different with Gandhi. He proclaimed for the world the saga of satyagraha as a principle and the spiritual concept of non-violence that made a revolution acceptable even to the opponents. Satyagraha and non-violence were not mere political weapons of a limited scope. These were comprehensive, encompassing to include a whole range of values right from religion upto social welfare. Using these weapons " Gandhi fought an eternal struggle against nature and his own environment."[42] Frederik Ficher says," Gandhi the man, the living, breathing, loving, serving, repenting, triumphant Gandhi who is my friend."[43] These are all tributes paid to Gandhi by those who did not necessarily belong to this country. They groped for words to describe the qualities of this great world leader, and they were in loss.

Gandhi shared with the world a vision enriching politics with ethics : "I felt compelled to come into political field because I found I could not do even social work without teaching politics,"[44] and "politics bereft of religion is a corpse and fit to be buried."[45] For the first time the world witnessed "person and an event of this rare synthesis. No less a person than Albert Einstein remarks, "Gandhi's work on behalf of India's liberation is a living testimony to the fact that man's will, sustained by all indomitable conviction, is more powerful than material forces that seem unsurmantable."[46] This indomitable conviction was unique to Gandhi for whom it was possible to speak of 'self realisation' and 'the Supreme God' from the political platform. This vision was not one-sided, instead attracted to himself anyone who applied his mind on it in all sincerity.

Gandhi taught the world how to liberate truth and innocence from the bandage of modern civilization. That is of great significance. Modern civilisation come to be so organised and conducted that these great values because obscured and darkened. History paid the price for this through the two world Wars. Gandhi was the first person in modern period to recognise the role of truth and love with reference to the progress of human civilisation in all its details. Gandhi presented truth, love and ahimsa to the civilized world in an entirely new garment. Gandhi's life was a manifestation of truth to the modern world. He showed and proved to the world as Pearl Buck says, that "truth is more fundamental than the atone itself."[47] The world saw in Gandhi a man who could combine the forces of truth with the practical, day-to-day details of life. That was unique to the Gandhian way of life. Truth and ahimsa for Gandhi became a way of life not only ideals to achieve. Erik H. Erikson, the famous psychoanologist after analysing Gandhi's personal life writes, "Gandhi's personality is one of a minute and concrete interplay, perfect in every step of a long life of a craftsman like series of "experiments" with historical actuality in all its potential and existential aspects."[48] Gandhi's success as an experimenter of life principally lay in his minute attention to the details of human life. The manifestation of truth and love came through such details and he was not willing to spare any moment of life from the influence of these principles. He was like a great craftsman figuring out and shaping every details of his day-to-day life to the goal of his perfection and sparing no energy from this final end.

That revolutionary who went about in loin clothes proved to the world that like truth and innocence, humility and simplicity are like atom bombs capable of exploding the shells of modern mechanised civilisation. Gandhi became for the modern world the messenger of the values of humility and simplicity, values that have become alien to the modern world. Americans and the British who one way or other came in contact with him were fascinated by his personal perfection and homeliness as the political leader of a developing world. John Holmes says, " To see and talk with Gandhi, even for a few and hurried moments, was to be over. whelmingly impressed by the gentleness of the man, together with his dignity and authority,"[49] and "alongwith this came humility which was manifest in every quality and action of his life."[50] Norman Thomas writes paying tributes to Gandhi, "he was a saint with a humility, a sense of humour and love of human beings which appealed to the West and to the East,"[51] It was all part of the Gandhian search for the refinements of truth and love.

Humility and simplicity became catchwords Gandhian movement in all aspects of life as contrasted to the great absence of these virtues in the modern times. Gandhi proclaimed that "service without humility, selfishness and egotism."[52] Simplicity, again was the core of service in Gandhian context. We find him exhorting time and time again that a simple life is the panacea for all our economic problems in the country. Foreigners marvelled at the humility and simplicity Gandhi exhibited. Nobody escaped noticing the greatness of the simple man in loin clothes. Gandhi's personal life radiated to the world values which the world found to be the only means for redemption in an age of deteriorating personal commitments.

The world is thus eager today to rediscover the whole impact and weightage of Gandhian principles and thoughts. To know Gandhi has became a need because he has become most relevant in an intellectually, emotionally and morally turbulent world. The world has been watching Gandhism and its development in India with considerable interest and appreciation. Martin Luther King was among those foremost international figures for whom Gandhism meant a new message. Gandhism was, for Dr. King, a message freedom from colonial bondage to be achieved using a weapons more powerful than the atom bomb, satyagraha, enlivened by the great force of non-violence. It was a message of universal brotherhood between the Whites and the Negroes in the United States. Gandhism became the most forceful theory for King to apply to the conditions that prevailed in the States.

The universality of Gandhian thoughts, especially of non-violence and satyagraha was so great that King did not find it difficult at all to apply Gandhism to the movement that he led in America. Martim Luther King became fascinated by the teachings of Gandhi primarily because he found great analogy between the teachings of Christ and the thought of Gandhi. He writes, "Gandhi was probably the first person in history to lift the love of Jesus above mere interaction between individuals to a powerful and effective social forces as a large scale."[53] King recognises the Gandhian values of suffering and sacrifice for a personal and national cause as fundamental to any freedom movement : "The way of non-violence means a willingness to suffer and sacrifce."[54] Without these elements a movement for a national cause turns out to be one of deep ego-centricism. This is true of all occasions and all times when leaders clamour for social and economic justice without they themselves willing to suffer and sacrifice. Dr. King held these values close to heart until he became a martyr himself for the cause of the Negroes in America.

The world needs Gandhi and nations are finding him. But it is our duty to present to the world the right Gandhian perspective. Gandhism has an integrity and a holistic nature of its own. These are part of the very system that has been emerging as Gandhism. We have the responsibility to develop the Gandhian thought with reference to this integrity. Here we find the great scope of Gandhism studies. Gandhian studies are emerging into a holistic system. A development of Gandhism into such a system will redeem it from being a piece-meal affair. The world is waiting to give acceptance to such a system. Gandhism would amount to a theory and body of convictions. As a theory it generates an intellectual appeal and would satisfy to the intellectual thirst of millions who are grouping in the dark for answers that could not be discovered for themselves. As a body of convictions Gandhism is powerful to generate the soul-force Gandhi himself was so found of talking about. A theory left to itself becomes a matter for intellectual exercise. As a body of convictions the whole thing assumes a new dimension. The entire Gandhism is projected as a way of life. Gandhi like Jesus lived suffering and sacrifices and showed to the world the path of redemption to the modern world by living the very details of it. This is therefore Gandhism. We prove to the world not only that Gandhism is a body of knowledge, but a body of convictions to live through. With this Gandhian studies will assume new dimensions. It will not only have an integral nature but also the practical appeal. Gandhi never thought of making an appeal to intellectuals. He had always in mind the large masses of humanity that was India. The international consensus on Gandhism will depend therefore on how we, first of all, accept Gandhi and then how we present him to the world.

4. Gandhi and Ultramodernism

Gandhism stands for what may be called holistic development. Man is a complex being. He lives and reacts with a large variety of environments: social, economic, physical, psychological and religio-moral. Apart from the heredity that determines him, he is a product of these environments. The assessment of a man's integrity of personality, the value we attach to the strength of a man's personality depend entirely on the manifold way he reacts with these environments. Man is constantly on the search for happiness. In the ordinary sense of the term as applied to a common man's conception happiness too is the product of a man's personality shaped and developed against the background of these environments. Happiness in the right sense eludes a man who may possess any one of these environments in an excelling manner. A man having large wealth is said to be missing the finer joys of human relationship if he does not enjoy the company of society. Happiness too is the sum total of interactions in all these environments in an adequate manner.

If such is the background of the formation and development of human personality, one thing is crystal clear that moderation is the keynote of an integral person as well as an integrated society. A drive for happiness, in whatever way we may define it, should reach a stage where the pendulum tends to move to the opposite extreme. The success of an individual or a society lies in exactly knowing what this stage is, where one should stop and look back.

A moderate development of all dimensions of man's environments mentioned above is a central message of the Gandhian vision. I have labelled this as holistic development. This would amount to several things. This would mean checking all extremes of 'development' for their own sake. It means having the right knowledge of the dimensions and perspectives the environment consists of. It means keeping an eye on all the details of life and society that is capable of feeding into this environment. Ultramodernism is a dragon to be checked to secure this holistic development. All details of Gandhi's life point to this end. The modern dehumanisation is another dragon of the kind that needs to be driven out. Man must have the central place in all interactions in human society. Depersonalisation, that is sacrificing the worth of individuals, is another factor that needs elimination. Extravagant materialism, throwing God and religion for the sake of fashion or convenience is the death-kneel to a civilisation. It is all summed up in the life Gandhi showed us : simplicity, moderation rigorousness, self-control, love of poverty and love of humanity.

In order to understand the consequences of ultramodernism an analysis of it becomes necessary. Gandhi points to the civilization of the West as the best example for this. Ultramodernism amounts to, first of all, an approach to progress for the sheer sake of progress not for the benefit of the individual persons who are supposed to be beneficiaries of all progress and sophistication. Those who apply various techniques to progress are seldom aware of or pay attention to the consequences or the cost of these techniques to individuals or often to society itself. It becomes as if sophistication impressed on a society which may quite often deject elements of such sophistication. Numerous examples of these are known from the Western ways of life.

Ultramodernism, secondly, consists in perpetuating the weaker passions of the individual and society. An ultramodern society turns easily licentious by permitting the perpetuation and exercise of those passions which a traditional society like India does not go for such a society indulges in the make-belief that a progressive life in society becomes impossible in the absence of these exercises. The younger generation is far too early introduced to such situations: pornographic literature, censurable films, unrestricted access to reading, all possible contexts to free-exchange and expression of views, all forms of self-expression eliminating in undesirable fashion, introduction to and indulging in alcoholic drinks, drugs and smoking and a variety of involvements. These are labelled as sophistication and those who are not prone to indulge themselves into these are easily branded in progressive society.

Ultramodernism, again amounts to excess consumption of material goods of all sorts. Gandhi constantly warns us against this tendency of contemporary world. Modern education should aim at a liberation from the bondage to this excess need. "Education is that which liberates from extrinsic bondage on the one hand, and from intrinsic bondage to the needs of life."[55] Life in cities and loving especially point-out to this aspect of ultramodernism. People indulge themselves in excess consumption. This would mean the use of food without any restraint. For Gandhi food is meant to only to satisfy our hunger and it should never be a means to pleasure. But it has become a tendency like the ancient Romans, eating is done for its own sake. While the vast majority of our countrymen especially in villages are either in want of food or have just enough to satisfy their need, the more affluent sections of our society spend extravagantly on food. This is a conspicuous evil of ultramodernism : a life insensitive to the reality of one's surroundings.

This would mean, further, the use of clothes without restraint. Gandhi's life was an experiment in dietetics. This was done primarily to accommodate himself to the poverty sticken vast masses of India. He survived on minimum food.

In the same manner Gandhi warned us against the irrational and excess use of clothes. He did not say so much in words as he showed through his life. In order to become part and parcel of the poor in India and to identify himself with them, Gandhi resorted to the use of loin clothes, the simplest dress that a mass can possibly wear while preserving onc's civility. It was wearing this that Gandhi attended even the Round Table Conference in London. That was indeed remarkable considering the fuss Indians often make in identifying themselves with Westerners. Gandhi's whole life consisted in "experiments in living a simple life."[56] Devdas Gandhi said of his father, "Gandhi was one of the most refined persons in the world, refined in his scanty dress, in his speech and in his manners."[57]

Ultramodernism amounts further to an excess accumulation of physical comforts of all sorts. On the economic front such an excess use of material comforts chiefly in the form of modern gadgets would amount to possible opportunities of production and employment, this would on the personal plane result in great harm and again on the national front increase price spiral and decrease the habits of savings. Every family in Indian towns and cities compete with the rest in the locality in accumulating modern gadgets and household appliances for greater comforts and exhibition. Gandhi attaches great importance to emotional integration in his drive towards self-realisation. All the above mentioned attitudes and tendencies that we have seen as ultramodern are condemned by Gandhi as most dangerous to both the individual and the nation in their upward march towards perfection. Gandhi says, "Emotional integration helps a man to control his senses against the attractions of the world. Such a man will never wish others any evil and will desire the good of the enemy upto his last breath."[58] In the Gandhian scheme of character formation every one of these elements functions like the chips of the mosaic to produce the total effect on the personality.

Dehumanisation is a destructive tendency resulting from ultramodernisation. Both European and Indian renaissance placed man on a higher pedestal in world affairs and gave him a role higher than the one assigned to him by traditional religions. But beginning with the European industrial revolution machines assumed a far greater prominence in world affairs than man ever expected. Mechanisation, automatisation, in the modern period exercised such an influence on human affairs that even individual human beings began to be regarded and treated as automations. In all matters pertaining to politics, economics and commerce business attitudes predominated everything else. This business attitude in turn affected all works of life even religious and moral considerations.

Today the ultramodern society is heavily characterised by the treatment of individual persons as automations. People are no longer regarded as human persons. Behind all this is what is usually called the utilitarian attitude based on the philosophy of utilitarianism that engulfed the United States in the twentieth century. Other human beings, even members of one's own community and further members even of one's own family are regarded as means to one's own personal end. Nobody, man or woman, is loved for his or her own sake. This is the most dangerous attitude of utilitarianism that has amazingly pervaded our society and seem to engulf it in all affairs. Gandhi bewailed this automatisation, business and utilitarian attitudes of contemporary society.

The individual has a great role to play in the Gandhian social scheme. Perey Nunn says, " Nothing good enters into the human world except in and through the free activities of individual men and women; and that educational practice must be shaped to accord with that truth."[59] The great significance of the individual that the ultramodern society is prone to sacrifice is over and again stressed by Gandhi. He says, "To slight a single human being is to slight the divine and thus harm not only that being but with him the whole world, because when an individual gains spiritually, others who surround him cannot suffer,"[60] The individual is given a central place in the Gandhian social, economic, educational and spiritual thoughts. It is therefore a major evil of ultramodernism that the individual is more and neglected as the social system grows more and complex. In this se up the society and its manoeuvrings are exploited by a few individuals for thus own material and political gains by ansforming other individuals into mere automations. The individual in this context commands no respect, he has no forceful rights except those prescribed by the letters of the law. Everything becomes business and is judged by considerations of gains and profits for themselves.

Members of this ultramodern society against which Gandhi cautions us, live in a world of make-belief, of unrealism. They involve themselves in everything that is detrimental to the development of the kind of a personality that Gandhi envisages. It is a colossal unrealism priority because the ultramodernists way of life and utilitarian philosophy of life he follows do not in any way correspond to the ultimate goal of life. Everything that Gandhi did, everything that he believed was geared to the one ultimate goal, self-realisation and surrender to God : "What I want to achieve is self-realisation, to see God face to face to attain moksha, "[61] and as John Holme says , "His whole life was an obedience to God. He had no personal ends to serve"[62] Thus the only aim of people who are ultramodern is materialistic gains and pleasures.

Ultramodern tendencies are realistic, secondly, because it is dissipating in energy. The whole tendency is self-destructive for a variety of reasons. The over-consumers of this society take from the society and place greater demands on the society than they are in a position to give and contribute to. Subsequently the society becomes the overall looser, and becomes dissipating in energy and self-destructive. One is in a position to make significant or any contribution at all to society only if his demands are fewer, his consumption in minimum and needs few. For this reason Gandhi makes sacrifice and self denial a necessary condition for service. Gandhi says, "students should learn to sacrifice the things that the poor in India cannot afford for themselves."[63] As part of this principle Gandhi practiced all forms of self help: "My passion for self-help and simplicity ultimately expressed itself in extreme forms."[64] He exhorted students to wash their clothes, cook their food and do their work. All this was Gandhi's reaction to the ultramodern tendencies for self assertion, accumulation and over-consumption in a country like India where the problem of poverty was gigantic.

Gandhism is a living message for India and the world against ultramodernism and its evil consequences. Most problems of modern period can be one way or other traced back to this. Lack of self control and an absolute harshness to self denial coupled with the tendency to grab everything and all opportunities of oneself are at the root of all the problems. Gandhi leaves no stone overturned to impress upon the world how significant this principle is. Unless we are willing spare all efforts to brings our needs under control the needs are going to govern every pulse of ours. Gandhi preached this message and lived every bit of it until death to show Indians how marvellous this principle of self control and self denial is. We are able to fight ultramodernism only using this single weapon which is a constituent of the great satyagraha.

5. Scope of Gandhian Studies

Gandhi and his teachings are today assuming new dimensions of meaning and relevance as we have seen in the forgoing sections. The dynamic nature of Gandhian thoughts and practices is leading the whole thing to a new level of acceptance by the world community. Gandhism is thus evolving into an integrated and comprehensive discipline because of the great scope it offers for application to a variety of fields of knowledge, have the new term : 'Gandhian Studies'. The intention is not to evolve yet another field of knowledge for brain storming work in theory, but Gandhian studies is primarily an integrated, multi-pronged approach to present Gandhi to the world on the one hand and on the other, know Gandhi ever deeper with reference to the problems India in particular and the world at large are facing. Gandhian studies is an attempt in theory work and research into the holistic appeal Gandhi has made to the world in the renewal of the human spirit. It amounts, again, to a search for the solutions that have become characteristic to the present age of science and technology in an attempt to discover the system of values that are detrimentally forgotten.

Gandhian Studies offers considerable scope for us "to prove that Gandhi's entire scheme of action was to strengthens, organise and develop the potentials for good present in individuals and in society and thus defeat evil at all levels."[65] This fundamental aim of all activities of Gandhi to fight the forces of evil at all levels and nurture good sown in the sands and hearts of Indians is seldom understood in the right perspective. The aim of the present discipline therefore is to provide full scope in understanding Gandhi in this perpsective. Modern India must be concientised in regard to the Gandhian interpretation of the meaning of life and must develop an awareness of the full practical political o Gandhian thoughts and view points. Gandhi has a message for every one, belonging to all walks of life and this message should receive the full blossoming for the right understanding relative to the present day needs.

Gandhi wanted Indians to the fully conscious of the rural nature of our country. India meant rural India and all his thoughts rested with the working and agricultural populations of rural India. The greatest justice that we may do to him is to accept rural India as it is, study the problems of this vast population, recognise the potentials available at their disposal and thereby present rural India to the vision of the more affluent factions of the country. It was Gandhi's earnest desire to introduce students to the manifold problems of rural India and develop in them a sustaining love for them. Gandhi says, "students should spend every day of their vacation in the villages around their schools and colleges"[66] because "there is no relation between today's education and our family and village life,"[67] Gandhian studies incorporates a knowledge of and work in villages to develop in students a love for these villages. This will unable students to (a) acquaint themselves to rural India, (b) constructively study rural problems, (c) correlate such problems with their own personal life and views, (d) set out to investigate into aspects and areas for helping life in villages, and (e) develop schemes and plans of a comprehensive nature for rural upliftment. Gandhian studies can focus on such issues in a productive manner.

Gandhian studies offers scope for interdisciplinary learning and research. This discipline becomes highly interdisciplinary because of its very texture. It subscribes as many disciplines for work and development as covered by Gandhism itself. Gandhian thoughts cover a wide variety of fields due to its comprehensiveness and thereby relate itself to those areas of knowledge and practice as the stem of a tree to its branches. No study of Gandhi, for instance is possible without relating itself to the field of education because Gandhism gets itself rooted in educational goals, principles, values and practices. A presentation of and a training in the educational principles and practices Gandhi held as dear can be possible only by developing these within a more comprehensive study of education to avoid random and piece meal work. This approach makes it necessary to include as interdisciplines subjects within whose wider framework alone can Gandhian studies be developed.

Under this approach Gandhian studies includes *political science.* No understanding of Mahatma Gandhi can be possible without an analysis of Gandhi's political career that led to India's Independence. The Politician in Gandhi has received world-wide acclaim because of the unique way he conducted himself and developed his political philosophy. It is significant to see that Gandhi had no political philosophy separated from his central religious phenomenology. He says, "I was compelled to come into politics because I was convinced that without touching politics one will not be able to do any form of social service."[68] Especially in the circumstances in which Gandhi worked, he was convinced, that no spiritual or religious pursuit could be possible without entering into politics. Here we find already how the two fields of politics and religion are closely interlinked for Gandhi. A study of Gandhism would therefore amount to acquainting one self with the fundamental of political science that formed the basis of Gandhi's political involvements. That would also lead to the various influences on Gandhi's political thoughts including the people and ideologies that influenced Gandhi, the various political foundations of Gandhian thought, and the details of the political theory of Mahatma Gandhi. The student should have also an opportunity to critically examine the merits and relevance of the Gandhian political system.

Religious philosophy forms part of Gandhian studies. More than anything else Mahatma Gandhi's life and thoughts reveal an integral religious system. Gandhi never spared an occasion to show that his ultimate goals were primarily religious : "What I want to achieve is self realisation, to see God face to face, to attain Moksha."[69] B.D. Bhatia says, "The ultimate aim of Gandhiji is related to the ultimate goal of life—the aim of self-realisation, the knowledge of truth, and God in one's life."[70] Gandhi's whole approach to politics, economics, social questions and national movement was governed by religious considerations. Religion Predominated all his involvements, all the principles and values and penetrated every detail of his public life. C.F. Andrews says that Gandhi revealed himself "as a Saint in politics, a rare combination,"[71] Insisting are this basic relationship among the various fields of one's activities Gandhi says, "human life being an undivided whole, no line can be drawn between its different compartments...... One's every day life is never capable of being separated from one's spiritual being."[72] With undaunted convictions Gandhi declared his religious and spiritual viewpoints from any platform. Consequently the component of religious philosophy in Gandhian studies includes : the fundamentals of religious philosophy, truth and non-violence in religion, the various elements of religion, characteristics of religions, the concept of salvation in religions, Gandhi's ashram views, interpretation of Nishkama

Karma Yoga, Sermon on the mount and five pillars of Islam, a treatment of religion and secularism etc. All of these aim at acquainting students with the essence of Gandhian ethics and spirituality on the one hand, and on the other providing training in the spirit of Gandhian life.

Economics forms part of Gandhian studies, Mahatma Gandhi envisaged a free nation with the economic vision founded on truth, ahimsa and hard labour. He says, "We should develop a spirit of non-violence, because truth and non violence are the foundations of the system that I am envisaging."[73] Gandhi's economic views are not segregated from his view or philosophy of life. He was not willing to view economics as a water tight compartment and rationalize any form of injustice done to the poor on the basis of funny economic or commercial principles. For Gandhi there was no economics alienated from moral considerations. Morality strictly governed every aspect of the individual's and society's dealings with wealth.

Gandhi's economic ideals are built on the concept of labour. He says, That a life of labour, i.e. the life of the tiller of the soil and the craftsman, is the life worth living."[74] His speeches and writings vibrate with the ideals of physical labour for bread winning: "The economics of working for one's food constitutes the active means of life."[75] Gandhi visualizes physical labour as a technique to preserve and maintain freedom : "Manual work prevents exploitation and slavery."[76] Those who redicule Gandhi for his down-to-earth considerations of Indian economy overlooks the fact that Gandhi's eyes were set not on immediate, peripheral gains and progress, but on more ultimate, lasting and morally sound ideals. Consequently, in component of economics in Gandhian studies include the following aspects : 1. Sources of Gandhian economics, 2. Basic principles and concepts of Gandhian economic ideas, 3. Gandhian philosophy of development and planning, 4. Gram Swaraj and Swadeshi, 5. Gandhi's views on machinery and mass production, 6. Gandhi's concept of economic equality and 7. Economic ideas of Gandhi and Marx

Education constitutes part of Gandhian studies. Gandhi gave shape to his thoughts on Indian education in his numerous articles and talks directed to students and educationists in the country. He kept himself actively engaged in pursuing the goods and principles of education to provide India a system of education most fitting to his concept of Swaraj; These writings chiefly found in the journals of 'Harijan' and 'Young India' and talks given at various gathering of students contain a considerable courage of aspects and problems of education in India. Education, again, is not an isolated thing for Gandhi : "Self realisation is the summon Bonum of life and education."[77] Gandhi thoroughly integrates the ideals of education with the welfare of the nation, welfare of the individual and society, and with moral and religious goals and concepts. No other aspect of the Gandhian thoughts is so closely knit to the development of the human personality and the progress of the Swaraj as education. Gandhi understood the full import of education on the development of the individual's character and of society at large. Education aims at the Training of the whole mass, hence Gandhi's approach is holistic and integrated. He does not conceive of education as separated from the detailed development of the Swaraj, and it is vocational by nature. The component of education in Gandhian studies contains the following : 1. Historical and Social Contexts of Gandhi's educational thought, 2. Experiments as a basis for the Critique and philosophy. of educations, 3. Nai Talim or Basic education; 4. Major thrusts in Gandhi's is educational philosophy, 5. Implications for philosophical analysis, and 6. Gandhian crigne of educational policy and planning; a. Independence period, b. Post independence period, and c. New Policy on education (1986).

Peace science has become part of Gandhian societies together with *War and Disarmament*. Gandhi has been accepted today as one of the greatest champions of world peace because Gandhi's was not a haphazard attempt for peace but a well-lived 'revolution' carried out within the framework of total peace. Gandhi says, "If freedom for India means the destruction of England or the disappearance of Englishmen, I do not need such a freedom... My principle is that a nation should become free to fully dedicate itself for the world. There is no place for parochialism in it. Let this be our nationalism. "[78] In an atomic age such as our when the world is threatened with total destruction of mankind from the face of the earth, it is Gandhi's message of peace founded on truth and ahimsa that provides mankind a ray of hope.

Gandhian studies assumes a well-granted interdisciplinary role because of the multi-facial relevance of Gandhian thoughts that created, so to say, on epoch of its own and is evolved into a system by its own. All these manifold perspectives relevant to Gandhism enable the discipline of Gandhian studies to represent the great Father of the Nation in everything that he stood for, to develop this field in such a way as to encourage valuable research into the depth of Gandhism, to lead students and researchers to the concrete world of the rural population whose concerns Gandhi voiced, to instil in the hearts of Indians and those around the world a well-grounded love and concern for the values and principles Gandhi advocated, and lastly to prove to the world firmly and convincingly that the depth of Gandhian thoughts and principles of life is greater than what we have so far imagined. We say with Arthur H. Vandenberg, "Gandhiji was one of the deathless few across the centuries who have lifted human character to immortality.. who made humility and simple truth more powerful than empires."[79]

References

1. Einstein, Albert, in Norman Cousins (ed.) p. 164.
2. Jones, Stanley, In Norman Cousins (ed.) p.132.
3. Marshall, in Norman Cousins (ed.) p. 96.
4. Taylor, E., in Norman Cousins (ed.) p. 72.
5. Gandhi, M.K., *An Autobiography*, Intr.
6. Gunther, J., in Norman Cousins (ed.) p. 47.
7. Holmes, J., in *Profiles of Gandhi*, p. 172.
8. Gandhi, M.K., *An Autobiography*, p. 239.
9. Gandhi, M.K., *Harijan*, 13 April 1940.
10. Gandhi, M.K., *An Autobiography*, p.x.

11. Gandhi, M.K., *To the Students,* Ahmedabad 1949, p. 182.
12. Holmes, J., in *Profiles of Gandhi,* p. 122.
13. Gregg, R., in *Profiles of Gandhi,* p. 168.
14. Gandhi, M.K., *Harijan,* 6 October 1946.
15. Gandhi, M.K., *Young India,* 18 June 1925.
16. Gandhi, M.K., *An Autobiography,* p. 118.
17. Gandhi, M.K., *To the Students,* p.71.
18. Gandhi, M.K., *To the Students,* p.71.
19. Gandhi, M.K., *Young India,* 22 January 1925.
20. Gauba, K.L., *The Assassination of Mahatma Gandhi,* New Delhi 1969, p. 42.
21. Gauba, K.L., *The Assassination,* p.305.
22. Roosevelt, E., in *Profiles of Gandhi,* p. 159.
23. Gandhi, M.K., *Towards New Education,* Ahmedabad 1953, p.21.
24. Narayan, Shriman, *Towards Better Education,* Ahmedabad 1969, p.4.
25. Gandhi, Rajiv, *Educational Reconstruction,* New Delhi, 1985 p.2.
26. Bhatia, B.D. *Philosophy and Education,* p.130.
27. Gandhi, M.K., *To the Students,* p. 113.
28. Bhatia, B.D., *Philosophy and Education,* p.21.
29. Gandhi, M.K., *Towards New Education,* p. 35.
30. Gandhi, M.K., *Basic Education,* Ahmedabad 1962, p. 9.
31. Gandhi, M.K., *To the Students,* p. 97.
32. Gandhi, M.K., *Towards New Education,* p.32.
33. Bose, N.K., Selections from Gandhi, Ahmedabad, 1963, p. 37.
34. Narayan, Shriman, *Towards Better Education,* p. 95.
35. Gandhi, M.K., *Basic Education,* p. 44.
36. Bowles, Chester, In *Profiles of Gandhi,* p. 167.
37. Thekkinedath, J., *Love of Neighbor in Mahatma Gandhi,* Alwaye 1973, p. 59.
38. Fischer, Louis, in *Profiles of Gandhi,* p. 61.
39. Mathews, H., in *Profiles of Gandhi,* p. 142.
40. Fischer, Louis, in *Profiles of Gandhi,* p. 56.
41. Fischer, Louis, in *Profiles of Gandhi,* p. 61.
42. Fischer, Louis, in *Profiles of Gandhi,* p. 47.
43. Ficher, F., in *Profiles of Gandhi,* p. 21.
44. Gandhi, M.K., *Harijan,* 6 October 1946.
45. Thekkinedath, J., *Love of Neighbour,* p. 54.
46. Einstein, Albert, in *Profiles of Gandhi,* p. 100.
47. Buck, Pearl, in *Profiles of Gandhi,* p. 104.
48. Erickson, E., in *Profiles of Gandhi,* p. 187.
49. Holmes, J., in *Profiles of Gandhi,* p. 125.
50. Holmes, J. Ibid p. 124.
51. Thomas, Norman, in *Profiles of Gandhi,* p. 166.
52. Gandhi, M.K., *An Autobiography,* p. 298.

53. King, M.L., *Profiles of Gandhi*, p. 207.
54. King, M.L., Ibid p. 214.
55. Gandhi, M.K., *Harijan*, 10 March 1946.
56. Gandhi, M.K., *An Autobiography*, p. 159.
57. Gandhi, Devdas, In *Profiles of Gandhi*, p. 132.
58. Gandhi, M.K., *Harijan*, 28 April 1946.
59. Bhatia, B.D., *Philosophy and Education*, p. 21.
60. Bhatia, B.D., Ibid, p. 124.
61. Gandhi, M.K., *An Autobiography*, Itro.
62. Holmes, J., *Profiles of Gandhi*, p. 127.
63. Plllai, N.P. (ed.), *Gandhian Literature : Education*, Vol. 5. Trivandrum 1962, p. 46.
64. Gandhi. M.K., *An Autobiography*, p. 186
65. Pillai, N.P. (ed.), *Education*. p. 31.
66. Gandhi, M.K., *To the Students*, p. 31.
67. Gandhi, M.K., Ibid p. 97.
68. Gandhi, M.K., *Harijan* 6 October 1946.
69. Gandhi, M.K., *An Autobiography*, p. 159.
70. Bhatia, B.D., *Philosophy and Education*, p. 126.
71. Andrews, C.F., *Mahatma Gandhi's Ideas*, London 1931, p. 220.
72. Gandhi, M.K., *Harijan*, 30 March 1947.
73. Gandhi, M.K., *Charka*, Sabarmati 1924.
74. Gandhi, M.K., *An Autobiography*, p. 224.
75. Gandhi, M.K., *Harijan*, 7 September 1947.
76. Gandhi, M.K., *Harijan*, 28 April 1946.
77. Bhatia, B.D., '*Philosophy of Education*', p. 126.
78. Gandhi, M.K., *All Men are Equal*, Ahmedabad 1964, p. 109.
79. Vandenberg, A.H., in *Profiles of Gandhi*, p. 37.

2

FOUNDATIONS OF GANDHI'S EDUCATIONAL THOUGHTS

1. Education in Ancient India

The entire spectrum of Mahatma Gandhi's social, spiritual and educational outlook was primarily founded on the basic principles of Hinduism as practiced in Ancient India. The earliest recorded documents on these take us back to the vedic period, as early as 2000 B.C., stretching over to 600 B.C. That was the age of the *Vedas*, the *Upanishads* and the *Aranyakas* : the three Sacred Scriptures of Hindu religion and Indian philosophy. These constitute what we know as the '*Sruti literature*', the supposed to be divinely revealed scriptures of Hinduism, revealed to the ancient sages. The next important '*Smriti literature*' of Hinduism consists of the two world famous Epics : *Ramayana* and *Mahabharata*, the *Puranas* and the *Darsanas*. Among the sacred books of Hinduism that exercised the greatest influence on Gandhi the most important is the *Bhagavad Gita* that is known as "the quintessence of Hindu literature".[1] Every aspect of the Gandhian thoughts was permeated in essence by the teachings of Gita. The central religion message of the Gita is, "that Bhagavan, the highest God, is All and comprises all the perfections of the Upanishadic Atman and Brahman. He is the origin of all beings; he demands supreme devotion and the dedication of all actions of men to him".[2] The Gita has exercised such an influence on him that he says, "when doubts haunt me, when disappointment stares me in the face, when I see not one ray of light on the horizon, I turn to the Bhagavat Gita".[3]

Education of a variety of kinds imparted during the Vedic period is known as Vedic or Brahmanic education. A knowledge of the Brahman through the Vedic Scriptures and directions to the attainment of the Brahman through the practices of the Vedic injunctions were central to this period of education. Life and education were not conceived of as separate identities; the two were interwoven into one ultimate aim. The purpose of life and that of education were to attain the Brahman. Gandhi calls this the ultimate aim of education in all respects. According to Bhatia, "The ultimate aim of Gandhiji is related to the ultimate Goal of life - the aim of self-realisation, the knowledge of Truth and God in one's life".[4] Having this goal of salvation or self-realisation in mind, the vedic students were given training in learning the verses of the scriptures. The early Vedic period allowed only the brahmacharis of the Brahmins to receive education of the vedic scriptures. Listening to and recitation of the scriptures were their exclusive prerogative.

Education during the Vedic period was characterised by the Gurukula system. The pupils depended on the guru for everything. It was not a mere intellectual experience. It was an integral development of the pupil's personality. The teacher taught and guided the pupils. The pupils lived in the teacher's family and participated in his day-to-day life and rendered him the kind of help they could. It was learning by experience which Gandhi was so fond of advocating in his Swaraj. The gurukula provided not the modern school of anarchy, revolt, restlessness and aimlessness but "a Gandhian world of simplicity and harmony".[5] The gurukula searched for the refinements of truth and love which Gandhi later made the central principles of his life. It was a natural process of discovering truth in the details of daily life that the pupils learned from the teacher. The gurukula in all details emphasised the spiritual aspects of the pupil's life. This was a principle that Gandhi never ceased to drive home.

He always wanted students to keep their eyes on the ultimate goals of life even amist pleasures and enjoyment. He wrote in Young India, "The ancient conception of a student was that of a *brahmachari*, because the goal of thus learning and activities was the search for Brahman. Therein life was built on the foundation of self-control and simple life that all religions have advocated .... I do not mean that you should have all enjoyment and shut yourself in a room. But all your enjoyment and activities should have the nobility of a dedicated life".[6] In all involvements in the gurukula the students maintained the integrity of the brahmachari and kept the noble goal in mind.

Education in ancient India under the Vedic period was influenced and shaped by the Ashramas, the stages of a man's life : *brahmacharya* (as a student), *gruhasta* (as a householder), *vanapresta* (as a recluse) and *sanyasa* (as a religious mendicant). The four stages were integrally woven into a path to liberation or *moksha*. The foundation of this path consisted in the *brahmachari's* entire approach to life and God, hence the significance of his introduction to the vedic scriptures and all the learning he did of the brahminic mantras and sutras (sacred formulae and texts). Education was thus not a thing to end with the first stage but was only an introduction to the other stages of life. It was a gradual and lingering process of unfolding the spiritual personality to the ultimate goal of self-realisation. It is from the same point of view that Gandhi envisages education.

In the practical conduct of human life the four *purusharthas* or aims of life have a determining influence on the human individual. They are: *artha* (wealth), *Kama* (satisfaction of sense-desires), *dharma* (righteousness) and *moksha* (liberation). These *purusharthas* have become "the established framework of earthily existence".[7] The Ashramas and the purusharthas together provide the righteous direction for the common man to the ultimate goal of life. At the level of brahmacharya, education, the student under the teacher learns and practices the righteous and legitimate use of material wealth. Wealth is used as a means and not an end in itself. Gandhi's Autobiography bears constant witness to experiments in life to see material wealth in a totally disinterested manner. This is the message of the Vedas, especially the Upanishads. Again, the student is educated to make the righteous use the sense faculties and derive righteous enjoyment of life. Education meant providing guidelines to the individual in the ashram in the application of this *purushartha* in the detailed involvements of life. Much importance is attached to this principle in education by Gandhi because of the characteristic way this is related to the unmarried stage of the *brahmachari* whose eyes are set only on the nobler values of life at this stage.

The all-pervading and fundamental principle in the life of a Hindu under the Vedic injunction is dharma or righteousness itself: "Thus understood dharma designates the traditionally 'established order' which includes all duties, whether individual, social or religious. It puts men on their guard against the three great moral pitfalls : *kama* (lust), *lobha* (covetousness) and *Krodha* (anger)".[8]

Dharma is the all-powerful weapon against the fruits of 'Karma', the eternal law of action that controls rebirth in Hindu philosophy. The principle of dharma includes all forms of righteous thought and deed. Education of the Vedic period consisted in a painstaking training in the ways of dharma. It was the principal duty of the teacher to provide the students adequate awareness of the duties of dharma. Dharma thus includes fundamental virtues : "I will explain the good qualities of the soul. They are compassion for all creatures, patience, freedom from discontent, purity, earnest endeavour, auspicious thought, freedom from avarice, freedom from envy".[9] In the detailed involvements of daily life the teacher provides the necessary directions through life-experiences for the practice of : fearlessness, preservance in the path of knowledge and discipline, charity, self-control, sense of sacrifice, study of sacred precepts, ahimsa, truthfulness, gentleness, modesty and a host of other virtues that the Bhagavat Gita prescribes as constituents of dharma.[10]

Education during the Vedic period provided training in a definite set of learning methods. They are *sharvana* (listening), *manana* (memorising) and *dhyana* (meditation or reflection). That was a major contribution of the Vedic period to education. It was the primary duty of students to listen to recitation of the Vedic Scriptures. Shravana had special vedic significance. The vedic mantras and the sacred verses are recited with meticulous care. The fruits and the effect of the sacred rituals and sacrifices greatly depended on the nature of the recitation. Because of this sharvana required special training under the Vedic system. As reading materials were rare the principal learning technique was listening. The depth of learning and comprehending the meaning of the verses depended on the cuteness of listening.

Manana was the next method of learning during the Vedic period. As we have seen above learning materials were considerably limited as this early period of history and the principal medium for passing on knowledge was committing things to memory or memorization. The sacred verses recited to the group of students were intently listened to by them. The urgency to master these verses by listening perhaps increased the capacity to memorize. Manana was therefore the technique of retaining and storing the sacred verses on the one hand and interpretations of these on the other. This meant great labour on the part of the students because all this meant acute attention and on the spot learning.

The most significant method was *dhyana* or reflection. This was the climatic mental exercise needed as part of the process of learning. *Dhyana* primarily meant reflection on the meaning and applications of the sacred verses. At an advanced level *dhyana* would amount to meditation undertaken by more advanced ascetics. Training in *dhyana* provided to students was a unique opportunity for imbibing the sacred principles of Hinduism in general and of dharma in particular. Through constant reflection on these principles it was supposed that a greater sense of commitment to them would be developed. The great need and potential of this technique have long been forgotten but Gandhi made it a point to revive the method of reflection and meditation as part of the ashram life that he advocated and started. He says, "Without an unreserved surrender to His Grace, complete mastery over thought is impossible".[11] With this aim in mind Gandhi marched "through the solemn solitudes"[12] and often fell into deep thought on these mysteries of life.

It is important to see that vedic education consisted in not merely the learning of the sacred verses or religious rituals, but aimed at the development of the whole man, body, mind and spirit. It was a holistic attempt to educate the learner from different points of view of human life. When education grew out of the strict controls of the gurukula, and systematic efforts were made to coordinate learning on the basis rudimentary institutions towards the second half the Vedic period, we find a more comprehensive content of education emerging. This included the learning of languages of which Sanskrit was primary, arithmetics, geometry, history, nature science, medicine, engineering and architecture, fine arts such as painting, sculpture, music and dance. Most of these aimed at a disciplining of the mind and spirit. Knowledge was acquired for its own sake on the one hand, and for disciplining of the mind and development of the character on the other. Military training was introduced quite often and training of the body received attention as part of this early education.

More relevant for us to consider in this context is the training in craft and skills provided in the Vedic period. That was specially designed to develop technical hands for use in the community and to provide to students the necessary physical involvement as part of the formation of character. The later Vedic period taught guilds and crafts and equipped students for one occupation or other. In connection with Vedic education mention should be made of two most advanced centres of learning : Nalanda and Takshasila, two centres later developed into ancient universities. These universities of ancient India taught languages, arts and humanities, fine-arts of all sorts, medicine, architecture and astronomy. Students and scholars from all parts of India lived and studied in these ancient universities which received the patronage of kings of different ages.

Education in Vedic India as described above had a number of important charcteristics. It was idealistic by nature because the entire set up of education was founded on the philosophy of Hindu religion, just as the western idealistic education was based on philosophy of Christianity. Religion and education became so integrated that the two could not be separated with reference to this goals and principles. Education had the absolute and ultimate goal of self-realisation or liberation and union with the Supreme Deity. All immediate goals of learning, acquisition of knowledge and character formation and so on got well amalgamated with this one single ultimate aim of education. Under the idealist framework automatically Vedic education held on to the absolute principles of Hindu philosophy : Dharma and everything that went with it. This absolutism was again an idealist character. Gandhi was found attaching this absolute sense to all the moral principles and values that he believed in and practiced. This aspect is important in understanding Gandhian education in its full significance.

Discipline was an important factor in Vedic education. In fact discipline controlled the success of all other elements in the formation of the Vedic student's character. Gandhi considers discipline as the foundation of the Swaraj : "students require the drive for action. They should not be mere imitators. They should learn to think and act for themselves and at the same time behave with full discipline and obedience".[13] Discipline was the living pulse of *gurukula* system when the small group of dedicated truth-seekers conjoined themselves to their guru in complete self-surrender and discipline. The students considered it a privilege to be there surrendered to the teacher in obedience. Even after the dissemination of the *gurukula* education towards the end of the Vedic period we find discipline having still a major role in the formation of the student's character. Discipline was central also in the western idealistic tradition

Discipline in the vedic system was considered to be basic in the formation of the student's character for the development of the finer virtues of obedience, humility, self-control, sense of sacrifice and all those that a life of dharma aims at.

Vedic education was teacher-centered as all idealistic education were. The teacher was the focus of attention and in him was endowed the success or the failure of the education process. He was the giver of knowledge emanated from his experienced lips and students had to listen, learn and reflect. Discipline was the result of this dimension of education. The teacher had to give, show, and provide the examples. He could not afford to be like the teachers of the present-day classrooms who may teach one thing in the classroom and do the opposite outside. The principal learning consisted in the teacher's way of life, the teacher being "an experimenter in life". With vedic education the teacher-centered way remained beneficial to the students because learning took place not by mere provision of knowledge but by life-involvements and by living the principles of dharma. In the Western context of idealism education boiled down to mere provision of knowledge about the world, man and God, without concrete life-experiences giving the framework for learning.

An analysis of Vedic education as above become quite necessary and significant because Gandhian educational thoughts lead us all the way back from 20th century to the B.Cs. Vedic education constituted the very groundwork of Gandhian thoughts. Vedic education integrated the goals of life and education, and it was the same for Gandhi. He envisaged no education that had nothing to do with the religious goals one way or other. Even Gandhi's "bread and butter aim of education" came down to the spiritual foundation. No ethics or religion can be preached to the man who starves; the first thing is to show him a way to earn his daily bread before he can digest ethical or spiritual values for himself.

2. Education in Medieval India

The Hinduism of the Vedic India was characterised by

high speculation, intellectual mysticism and emphasis on the path of knowledge or *gnana marg*. Religious aspirations, mistical flights and the path of *gnana* were the prerogative of a few groups of sages and the vast humanity of the common man who belonged to all castes had little access to these aspirations. Consequently the religious reaction of around 600 B.C. gave rise to Buddhism and Jainism whose founders attempted to bring religion down to the common man, place greater insistence on morality, self-control and good works, give more rational interpretation to human life and satisfy the aspirations of all common man to believe in a personal God.

These religious reactions also affected education in medieval India. By this period the *gurukula* system began to be disintegrated with the result that several kinds of educational institutions of a formal kind came to be established. Buddhist monks became well-known in the field of learning, art and education. The greater insistence on the path of action or *karma marg* by the Buddhist monks compared to the contemplative and speculative flights of the early Hindu sages, gave rise to more of socially oriented activities. The Buddhist monks travelled from place to place founding their monasteries into which everyone was welcome. When the brahminic system of the Vedic period admitted only Brahmins to the study of the Vedic Scriptures and the mantras and the sutras for sacrificial rituals, the Buddhist monks to all irrespective of the caste or origins and admitted everyone to their monasteries. This was significant for education, because for the first time in the history of India education and learning were left open to the masses. When Gandhi advocated education for the masses in the country he was voicing the concern of the Buddhist monks of the reaction period.

The Buddhist monasteries developed into centres of learning. The monks dedicated their time in teaching the children and the youth of the community. Aspirants to these monasteries were initiated to learning and Buddhist way of life through the ceremony called 'pabhaja' or inititiation.

Education was a long process. It meant again a training for life and a well-disciplined formation of character. Austerity was essentially part of Buddhist and Jain training. In the Vedic system brahamacharya was only an initial stage of education, but the Buddhist aspirants vowed to a life of celibacy. the principal virtues the students practiced were austerity, renunciation and self-sacrifice. these were virtues so dear to Gandhi throughout his life and these determined his Ashram life. Even Gandhian education was highly characterised by these virtues. Any education which does not teach students to make sacrifices for himself, society and God, is not worthy of being called education, this was a major contribution to Indian education by Buddhism.

Buddhist education made use of a content of education which they tried to expand in course of time. This included primarily the regional languages. It was significant to see that the Buddhist as early as the 5th century B.C. and later made systematic attempts to learn the language of the local people and teach these languages in their monasteries and other institutions. They learned the regional languages as part of their drive to help the poor and the needy based on the 'Mercy of Buddha for all living creatures'. These monks became scholars in the local languages and enhanced the learning of languages as part of their scholarship. Apart from languages, Buddhists taught philosophy, elementary sciences, natural medicine, engineering and architecture. They gave much importance to fine-arts : the early Buddhist caves such as the Agenda-Ellora caves bear witness to the Buddhist love for painting and sculpture. Buddhist architecture and sculpture bear characteristic marks of the basic Buddhist philosophy of simplicity, austerity and love for all living creatures.

As part of the drive to help the local community the Buddhists continued the teaching of skills and crafts in their institutions. This enabled the local youths to find themselves as capable of taking up an occupation though everything at the time was still caste-bound. The ancient universities of Nalanda and Takshasila became in course of time Buddhist centres of learning. These centres produced great men of learning among Buddhist monks and the fame of these universities travelled far and wide even outside India to the then known world. Buddhists became remarkable for their concern for women's education. The Vedic period debarred Brahmin women from learning the scriptures and languages, but with the Buddists women's education saw the light of the day. They constituted monasteries for women monks and we have the history of several such groups who made contributions to learning and piety. It was significant that between the two extremes of the Vedic period and the later Muslim period which did not encourage women's education, we have the Buddhists who encouraged women's education. Buddhist education of the medieval period in several ways laid the foundation for the Gandhian concept of education.

The second half of the medieval period of Indian history witnessed the Muslim rule in India (1200 - 1757). Muslim rule in India became established with the occupation of the Delhi throne by Muhammad Ghori. The approaches of Muslim rulers to education were quite different. The policies and the processes became different. Muslim education in India brought to focus the teachings of the Koran. The spirit of Vedic education was that of the Vedic Scriptures. The spirit of Islamic education assumed that of the Islamic Scriptures, the Koran. The teachings of the Koran and the principles of Islam became the content of education during this period. The madrasas became centres of Muslim education. These were attached to mosques. The languages taught were chiefly Arabic and Urdu. Arabic and Urdu scholarship developed considerably during this period. It was left to Akbar to become sympathetic to the Hindus and to the great Indian tradition with the result that much encouragement was given to the learning of Sanskrit and to temple architecture.

Thus the major contributions to ancient Indian education at large were traced back to the Vedic-Brahminic period and we find a rather comprehensive system that emerged as a result of the deep religious and spiritual concerns of the period. As we have seen a right understanding on the Gandhian thought can be had only on the basis of the detailed religious concerns developed during this ancient period in the development of Hinduism.

Following the growth of Buddhism and Jainism during the Reaction Period of Indian history (600 B.C. - 300 A.D.) we find a spurt in the Hindu popular religion with focus on the bhakti cult (the path of devotion). This was in direct reaction to the earlier metaphysical flights (*gnana-marg* : the path of knowledge) of the sages, and the ancient ritualism of the brahmins (earlier notion of *karm-marg* or path of action). The rise in popular devotion compelled the ritualists and the metaphysicians to develop in course of time "a rational foundation"[14] from which were born the present systems of Indian philosophy. These systems or *darsanas* are : *Nyaya, Vaiseshika, Samkhya, Yoga, Purva-mimamsa, Vedanta Nyaya* is essentially a system of logic, which adopts an atomistic cosmology and admits a supreme Lord and cause of the World. The Vaiseshika system reduces all things to an atomistic cosmology of *patarthas* or elements. These are material elements of eternal atoms (*anu*) which differ from each other. The name comes from the word *visesha* which meant differing. The Samkhya system reduces the whole universe to one *Prakriti* and countless *Purushas*. The Purusha is the subject's pure consciousness. The *Purusha* is the later substitute for the Upanishadic Iswara for whose existence the Samkhya philosophers did not find sufficient evidence. The Yoga System is the most important in the present context because the belief in a Supreme Lord is central to the Yoga System. Yoga is a system of concentration of thought based on a set of techniques of breath-control, special postures and other disciplinary practices. The Supreme Lord is to be reached in a Supreme illumination of the mind called *Samadhi*.

The Purva-mimamsa provided rules for the right interpretation of the Vedic Scriptures and dealt with the conditions which had to be fulfilled to make the rituals yield full benefits. This system contain the old doctrine of Karma with its ritualistic and legalistic foundations. Like the Yoga system the Vedanta is most significant in the Gandhian context. The Vedanta is a remarkable harmonisation of the theories on nature, man, and Brahman-Atman. This has been accepted as the most advanced interpretation of the Vedantic theory of *Jnana*. Sankara and Ramanjua later developed this system into more comprehensive Vedanta theories of great standing. The Characteristic features of the systems are the following: the *Samkya* is absolubly dualistic, the old *Vaiseshika* is atheistic, the *Nyaya* is anthropomorphic (human elements projected on to the divine), the *Purva-mimamsa* is again atheistic and the Yoga as well as the Vedanta systems are truly divine-oriented.

Indian education of ancient period was deeply religious, spiritual, metaphysical and mystical. The purpose of learning was to achieve God and to develop a character that could truly follow dharma. Religious aspects, ritualism and principles of Hinduism formed a major constituent of learning. Education had a true spiritual orientation since the soul of the individual had to undergo the process of purification and have the right knowledge of its relation to Brahman. Prayer and invocations were a matter of constant preoccupation both in the early and late Vedic period as well part of the popular bhakti movement. This was part of learning. Education of the period was metaphysical due to the metaphysical nature of Indian scriptures and philosophy. The kjnana marg of the sages and the philosophers was truly metaphysical in character. Learning meant access to all these. Lastly education had the mystical over-tones. Self-realisation, and the Yogic samadhi meant mystical experiences of an exalted kind.

3. Western Education in British India

The history of English education in our country or what may be considered Western education may be said to have started on 31st December, 1600 when Queen Elizabeth I of England granted a Charter to the East India Company to trade with India. From Surat on the west cost of India where the British settlers established themselves for the first time, English as the language of the British spread to other parts of India and in course of a couple of centuries became the "associate official language of the country".[15] Originally the company's sole concern was trade. The educational activities of the few missionaries who accompanied the company in the 17th century could not have been very significant because they primarily ministered the religious needs of the company's officials.

The significant victory of the British at the battle of Plassy in 1757 enabled them to establish their supremacy in India after overthrowing the Mughal rule. The company was cautious in its policies as the new ruler. Persian was continued to be the language of administration; the British officials were asked to learn Persian and Sanskrit to administer the new land: "No attempt was made at this stage to introduce English as the language of administration".[16] Since the company did not wish to antagonise the people it had to rule, the company in 1783 prevailed upon British Parliament to stop the entry of foreign missionaries into India without a licence. Education in India then received encouragement of a characteristic type with generous support from the British in the study of Arabic, Persian and Sanskrit. The first educational institution in India came to be established in 1781 by Warren Hastings who started a madrasa (school) in Calcutta to teach Persian thorough Arabic. In order to revive interest in Oriental studies and to promote the study of Arabic the Asiatic Society of Bengal was founded in 1784. A Sanskrit college was established at Varanasi in 1791 to encourage the study of Sanskrit. In 1800, "Lord Wellesley founded a college in Calcutta to promote the study of Bengali and other Indian Vernaculars".[17] As S.H.Rudolph writes, the English in the early years of their rule "tended to prize Indian learning and attempted to master it through Indian language and thought forms; to rationalise and modernise it; and to introduce modern scientific ideas within its framework".[18] Many of them desired to familiarise themselves with the languages and culture of the land and all at their disposal to support and encourage Indian learning. That was only one side of the story; on the other hand, there were those who thirsted to introduce western education into the country through the medium of English.

Charles Grant and others in 1792 strongly recommended that English should be adopted as the medium of instruction to communicate to the Indians "western light and knowledge". The Charter Act of 1813 was important in this connection. Inspite of the company's renewed insistence on emphasising and promoting Indian Knowledge and Indian languages, the Charter of the company was renewed that year in which British Parliament asked the Company to set aside a large sum of money "for the introduction and promotion of a knowledge of the sciences among the inhabitants of the British territories in India".[19] In spite of this no serious move was made to teach English and the sciences to Indians in any quarters. Due to this lack of enthusiasm on the part of the company , a group of Indians under the leadership of Raja Rammohan Roy, David Hare and Edward Hyde East, took initiative to establish a Hindu Vidyalaya which was the first of its kind in teaching English in the country. The Vidyalaya was established in 1817 to instruct the sons of Hindus in the European and Asiatic languages and sciences".[20] The primary aim of the Vidyalaya was the promotion of Bengali and English language. This remains as the proof that long before Macaulay wrote his famous minute on English education, Indians had taken initiative in establishing institutions for teaching English having realised the great advantages of learning this language. Even at this stage the company was not keen on promoting English, but established in 1823 a Sanskrit college in Calcutta followed by colleges in Agra and Delhi.

The decision of promoting English education in India largely depended on the controversy between the 'Orientalists' and 'Anglicists' in the General Committee believed that oriental learning was the best for India while the Anglicists supported the spread of English education.

In fact the Anglicists among whom there were Indians also found themselves in a minority. The two groups strongly held their positions and tried to influence the decisions of the committee. To resolve the problems created by the controversy Lord Bentick appointed Macaulay president of the committee and asked to give a ruling on the controversial issue whether or not to encourage English education by using the grants of the committee. This resulted in the historically important 'Macaulay's Minute' of 1835 in which he gave his ruling which laid the foundation stone of English Education in India. Macaulay wrote "We are free to employ the funds as we choose, that we ought to employ them in teaching what is worth knowing, that English is better worth knowing than Sanskrit or Arabic, that the natives are desirous to be taught English, and are not desirous to be taught Sanskrit or Arabic....... that it possible to make the natives of this country thoroughly good English Scholars, and that to this end our efforts must be directed....."[21].

The first official policy decision on English education was then taken by Bentick on the basis of this minute: "that all the funds appropriated for the purpose of education would be best employed on English education alone".[22] Following this decision the committee of Public Instruction made 'extraordinary efforts' to promote the knowledge of English language among Indians. Thus schools and colleges began to be established for the teaching of English and science through the medium of English in various parts of the country. Lord Auckland who succeeded Bentick, stressing the importance of vernacular education "guaranteed the maintenance of institutions for oriental studies"[23] but declared himself in favour of English education.

The renewal of the Character of East India Company resulted in Wood's Despatch of 1854, named after Charles Wood who headed the committee for inquiry into the educational developments in India. The recommendations made by him is often called the Magna Carta of English Education in India. As result three universities were established in India, one each at Bombay, Calcutta and

Madras. English education received a new vigour as a result of the establishment of these universities. These functioned as examining bodies with authority to grant degrees, Wood's Despatch reasserted the view that "a knowledge of English will always be essential to those natives of India who aspire to a high order of education".[24]

The universities at this stage did not do any teaching and that responsibility lay with colleges. The European teachers in colleges began lecturing in English and English became the language of instruction in colleges. Admission to these colleges were restricted by the Matriculation or Entrance Examination conducted by the university. The university used English as the official language for all instructions and transactions. Subsequently all universities passed resolutions to the efforts that all papers in all subjects had to be answered in English. These developments compelled schools in India to introduce compulsory English from the very early stage.

All this consequently led to the creation of the English speaking elite. It was the historical necessity that gradually led to the creation of this elite and the importance that came to be attached to English. The responsibility of introducing English Education in India largely lay with Indians themselves who recognised its role in a developing world as the sole medium for western education. The British was in fact only responding to this need voiced by the educated Indian elite. Researches into this problem have made this point abundantly clear. English became thus the fashion of the day. Universities made English the medium of instruction at the college level and later by 1916 at the university level only when actual teaching was undertaken by Indian universities. English became basic to school education, and English medium schools got mushroomed. The response to the call of English education was great. Attracted by the prospects of learning English enrolment in colleges rose to surprising heights. In 1836 "more than 1200 students wanted to enrol in the department of English alone as against the 300 in the oriental department"[25] of the

Chinsura college at Calcutta. The language of the rulers provided the necessary natural attraction to the younger generation coupled with a foresight regarding the great prospects of English education.

In a short while English became the language of the educated professionals : doctors, engineers, lawyers, professors, teachers, business executives, and professionals of all kinds. This English educated elite found themselves privileged to discuss in English matters relating to their professional field and communicated with the British and other Westerners in English. English soon became an integral part of the communication matrix of educated people. This situation soon resulted in an alienation of the common masses of people, the large bulk of the country, from the English speaking elite. This is often called a hyber-Westernisation. These resulted not only the use of English the use of English forming a privileged class, but also this hyber-westernisation in which educated sections of society began a cheap westernisation of themselves. That was a tragedy for India. While the poor and underprivileged did not have means even to cover their nakedness, these educated or more affluent sections resorted to all kinds of 'modernisation' and sophisticated ways of life. There arose a tendency or rather a phobia to ape western society for cheap sophistication. This affected in turn the Indian economy as imported goods of western life began flooding our markets.

The educational situation resulted from the introduction of English as compulsory medium and the creation of the English speaking, hyber-western elite in India caused serious concern for the leaders of the Indian Nationalist Movement. Lord Curzon in his educational policy statements in 1904 had made it clear that English had no place in India's primary education. He did not favour India's slavish attitude to English models".[26] A national movement against English education resulted from the policy of the British to divide Bengal in 1905. This soon became a far cry for 'national' education. The Rowlatt Act 1919 which extended the wartime emergency measures individual rights to peace-time, and the Jallianwalla Bagh massacre converted even the loyal supporters of the British into national revolutionaries. Mohandas Gandhi, by then the undisputed leader of the Congress launched his first nation-wide Satyagraha. Gandhi called for a total boycott of schools and colleges as part of this movement.

Gandhi realised the urgent need for transforming Indian National Congress into a mass movement. To have access to great bulk of the population, their language i.e. Hindi, he thought was the only solution. Gandhi's became an anti-English education wave as much as it was nationalist movement. He held publicly and wrote that English could never become the language of Indians, "that English could not and should not become our National language"[27] Gandhi strongly argued out his cases against English education, and in favour of Hindi in his numerous public speeches and articles. In 1937, the elected representatives of the people of India formed ministries in the provinces under whose initiative regional languages became the medium of education in schools. When India became Independent, at the national level English was replaced with Hindi as the official language, and with regional languages at the state level. The anti-English education drive is still strong in the Northern States while at the same time English education at the school and university levels is receiving added emphasis at the national levels for a variety of practical reasons that are most obvious. India is attempting to evolve a national policy to suit the country's urgent needs and her great resources respecting the pulses of our national leaders.

4. Influence of Christianity

The teachings of Jesus Christ in the Bible were of a great source of influence and inspiration on Gandhi throughout his life. Several components of Gandhian thoughts manifest a clear synthesis of religious Hinduism and Christian concepts which amalgamated into a single system of principles. Gandhi knew Christianity from very early days and accounts of this are available in the Autobiography. For different reasons Gandhi had developed a dislike for Christianity until he left for London in 1883, at the age of nineteen, where he came in contact with the Bible introduced to him by his Christian friends. Gandhi became much impressed by the New Testament especially the Sermon on the Mount. He says, "the New Testament produced a different impression, a specially the Sermon on the Mount which went straight to my heart. I compared it with Gita. The verses, 'But I say unto you, that you resist not evil; but whosoever shall smite thee on thy right check, turn to him the other also. And if any man take away thy coat let him have thy cloak too' delighted me beyond measure..... My young mind tried to unify the teaching of the Gita, The Light of Asia and the Sermon on the Mount".[28]

Gandhi later in life developed an open mind to know all aspects of truth in religions. His pursuit of truth and constant dedication to truth enabled him also embrace in Christianity what he was convinced was truth. Gandhi became fascinated by the Person of Jesus. The Person of Jesus projected in the New Testament became for him an embodiment of Truth and Love: "His sacrifice is a type and example for us. Every one of us has to be crucified for Salvation".[29] Gandhi developed the concept of 'self-sacrifice'and 'self-denial' also with reference to those values in Christianity. Gandhi's life and action, goals and thoughts permeated with the concept of self-sacrifice and self-denial. These values are most central to the Gandhian satyagraha. No satyagraha could succeed except by rooting out the concupiscence of the mind "by intense self-examination, surrender to God and lastly, grace".[30] Gandhi valued greatly the role of self-sacrifice and self-denial in the process of education. Education as character formation meant the development of these virtues relating to the pursuit of truth: "A stranger to self-restraint could never teach his pupils the value of self-restraint".[31] In his exhortation to students Gandhi says, "Students should learn to sacrifice the things that the poor in India cannot afford for themselves".[32] He further says, "A student is like a rishi; he should be an embodiment of simple life and high thinking".[33] The basic Christian principles of sacrifice and simplicity ever so lacking in the life of an ordinary Christian were a fundamental attraction to Gandhi. This is also a central message of the Sermon on the Mount.

The person of Jesus was a source of great attraction to Gandhi as Gandhi himself lived every word of what he taught and every article of faith that believed in. Jesus went around doing good. Jesus' was a living faith, a faith that he lived in every detail. Jesus meant truth and love for him. He says, "Thus I say that Jesus occupies in my heart the place of one of the great teachers who have made a considerable influence on my life".[34] All the same Gandhi makes it clear that his view of Christ was different from that of a Christian: "I do not accept the orthodox teaching that Jesus was or is the God incarnate in the accepted sense or that he was or is the only son of God."[35] What mattered most for him was the content of what Jesus taught. The vision of Jesus as Love and Truth incarnate enabled Gandhi to arrive at the fullness of the message of Gita, Gandhi believed that if man cannot build his life on the law of love that Jesus embodied and taught, then the life and death of Jesus would be a waste: "Jesus lived and died in vain if he did not teach us to regulate the whole life by the eternal law of Love".[36] The text, 'but whosoever shall smite thee on the right check, turn to him the other also', provided Gandhi the greatest strength needed in times of suffering.

Christian education is an attempt to incorporate the basic values of Christianity in the field of education. Education aims primarily at the formation of character and the building of the individual's personality. Christian education inculcates the basic Christian values in the formation of the learner's character through a variety of means. Gandhi acquainted himself with Christian education in Britain as a student. He lived there amidst Christian friends, vehemently put up a personal fight against meat-eating habits among the friends, but imbibed several values that were characteristically Christian. Gandhi's days in South Africa put him in contact with numerous Christian friends for whom he had high regards. Gandhi has dedicated a full chapter, 'Christian Contacts' in his Autobiography.. The attempts of several of these friends to convince Gandhi of the need for a committed and active faith in Jesus and in Christianity did not at all succeed. Gandhi was left unmoved by those arguments developed by his friends.

It was Jesus and his teachings rather than Christianity as a religion that moved him. Jesus' teachings left a conspicuous mark on all the Gandhian principles. Truth is central to all Gandhian thoughts. For Gandhi Truth is an attribute identical to God Himself: "And nothing is or exists in reality except Truth. That is why *Satya* or Truth is the most important name of God. So it is more correct to say that Truth is God than to say that God is Truth".[37] The Person of Jesus became for Gandhi, as we have seen, the embodiment of truth and love. The whole of the Bible bears witness to Truth as the greatest attribute of God : "God is Truth". Jesus himself says, "I am the Way, Life and Truth". Jesus tells Pontius Pilate, "I have come to bear witness to truth." Gandhi believed that it is through the commitment to truth above all that the world could attain peace which is essentially a Christian message. He says, "For a happy and contented human life truth and non-violence are essential. The absence of these will inevitably result in anarchy, and their presence in peace".[38]

E.Stanley Jones says, "And there was Mahatma Gandhi, the leader of the New India, an ascetic. It gripped the soul of ancient India. But he gripped the soul of modern India by relating renunciation to the needs around".[39] Asceticism was the keynote of Gandhian Spirituality with prayer and renunciation forming the essential constituents. Asceticism is the very foundation religious Hinduism but Gandhi relates this asceticism to and enlivens that by the more Christian Spirit of Sérvice founded on the notion of 'love of the neighbour' in the New Testament: Gandhi imbibed the spirit of service of humanity in its full dimension as envisaged in the New Testament and tried to have the vision of God in the service of man in every detail and founded on the principle of service every spiritual attitude that he possessed. Gandhi says, "I endeavour to see God in the service of man because God lives not in heaven or on earth, but in the living beings with flesh and blood".[40] Gandhi identified the essence of religion with the service of man.

The Christian spirit of service is the very foundation of Christian education. Education has always been seen as the avenue for the Christian missionaries to put themselves at the disposal of the poor and the needy on the one hand and the illiterate on the other. Christianity down the centuries attempted to stand for the cause of the poor and the down-trodden. It is wrong to identify Christianity as a religion with forces of imperialism that have often used elements of the religion for their selfish ends. The Christ who was born in the poverty of a manger and died on the Cross is the Christ of Christianity. It was this Jesus that the Christian missionaries tried to bear witness to in their entire approach to problems of education. To serve the poor and the needy on the one hand and to impart education to the vast urban and rural population in a well-organised manner remained their urgent goal. To this end Christian missionaries began establishing schools and other educational institutions all over India. Christian missionaries are the ones most misunderstood and misinterpreted in their approach to education. They were most often accused of conversion, but except in very rare circumstances the missionaries did not mix conversion with education. They were two separate goals: to bear witness to Jesus through education was one thing and to draw others into Christianity quite another.

Education was a field of activity for Christians to nurture in the youth the Christian concept of love. The entire New Testament has its foundation, as we have seen in the concept of love. Gandhi never ceases to talk of love as the foundation and the goal of all his activities. For Christians love is the beginning, it is the means and it is the end. Love is an all-pervasive value on which all other Christian concepts are founded. The living and practicing Christian has not always succeeded in putting this concept, this principle of love, into practice. This does not alter in any way the true nature of Christianity and its principles. Education has been accepted as a major field of activity for the practice of Christian love. Education is meant for the Christian missionaries a whole net-work of activities. It meant occasions to dedicate themselves to the growth and development of the younger generation and occasions to help them imbibe the Christian values manifested in the community life of which the students become a part.

The net-work of activities generated by the educational activity of the missionaries included close contacts with the parents and the community for a variety of purposes. These contacts provided them with opportunities not for conversion as usually misunderstood, but for opportunities "to bear witness to Jesus" in their thoughts, words and actions in which could be manifested the principles and the things for which Jesus lived and died. Education was accepted as a field of great necessity and a field of great potential for putting themselves at the service of the people. This was the major impetus behind all the educational involvements of Christian missionaries down the time of the British in our country. The exaggerated enthusiasm that these missionaries often showed in education have caused concern and doubt in the minds of our nationalist leaders.

Gandhi's thoughts on education were thus permeated by the concepts, principles and from different ages, religions and systems. We have looked into these rather in detail because they serve as foundations, not mere sources, of Gandhian system of education that is elucidated in the present work. As we have seen Hinduism forms the heart and soul of Gandhian educational thoughts. Hence a major section is dedicated to Vedic education from which Gandhi draws most of his ideas on education to be developed in his swaraj. For Gandhi every component of education ought to be dedicated to a life that would properly develop the heart the mind, the soul and the body. The spiritual dimension is a major dimension of education for Gandhi, a dimension that is totally neglected for practical, materialistic reasons. For all these he has valuable historical foundation that we have examined.

References

1. Thekkinedath, J., Love of Neighbour, p.21.
2. Jesuit Scholars, Religious Hinduism, Bombay 1964 p. 225
3. Gandhi, M.K., Young India, 12 march 1925.
4. Bhatia, B.D., Philosophy and Education, p. 126.
5. Einstein, A., in profiles of Gandhi, p.99
6. Gandhi, M.K, To the Students, p.92
7. Jesuit Scholars, Religious Hinduism, p.28
8. -do- , Ibid p.114.
9. -do- , Ibid p.113.
10. Bhagaved Gita. (Swami Chidbhawananda) Ch. XVI.
11. Gandhi, M.K., An Autobiography, p.238
12. -d- , Ibid p.237
13. -d- , Towards New Education, p.31
14. Jesuit Scholars, Religious Hinduism. p. 26
15. Sechadri, C.K., English in India, Baroda 1977, p.14.
16. -do- , Ibid p.15
17. -do- , Ibid p.23
18. -do- , Ibid p.15
19. -do- , Ibid p,16
20. -do- , Ibid p.17
21. -do- , Ibid p.20
22. -do- , Ibid p.20
23. -do- , Ibid p.21
24. -do- , Ibid p.23
25. -do- , Ibid p.21
26. -do- , ibid p.24
27. Gandhi, M.K., Thoughts on National language, Ahmedabad 1956 p.3
28. -do- , An Autobiography, p.51
29. -do- , Young India 4 Sept. 1924
30. -do- , An Autobiography, p.248
31. -do- , Ibid p.255.
32. -do- , To the Students, p.71
33. -do- , Ibid p.266.
34. Thekkinedath, J., Love of Neighbour, p,26.
35. Gandhi, M.K., Young India, 4 September 1924
36. -do- , Harijan, 7 January 1939

37. -do- , Young India. 31 December 1931
38 -do- , Harijan, 29 September 1946
39. Jones, Stanley, in Profiles in Gandhi, p,134
40. Gandhi, M.K., to the Students, p.94

3

GOALS OF EDUCATION IN GANDHIAN THOUGHT

1. Education for Spiritual/Moral Development

Education is a system on the one hand a process on the other. As a system education is structured of definite and well-definable constituents each of which is susceptible to analysis and study for better development of the system. As a process education is functional, it has life and movement, it has progress in a direction, and it remains constantly dynamic. The dynamism of education is a significant factor because this dynamism is what enables education to deal with children as living and thinking beings. When education as a system and as a process combines into one integrated field of thought and activity, we have this field emerging into one with a set of definite aim or goals, methods and techniques of activity, materials on which to develop the educational process, as well as the realisation of the aims in a variety of ways.

Educational goals constitute a significant component of the system of education. John Dewey, a world famous educationist maintains, that "to have an aim is to act, with meaning, not like an automatic machine; it is to mean to do something and to perceive the meaning of things in the light of that intent..... the aim as a foreseen end gives direction to the activity, it is not an idle view of a mere spectator, but influences the steps taken to reach the end".[1] Possessing the right goal would thereby mean the thing half done. The goal is very significant in the Gandhian context. Gandhi was throughout conscious of the intimate but intricate relation between what he calls 'the end and the means'. Truth and Ahimsa are for Gandhi the end and the means: "Means to be means must be always within our reach and so Ahimsa is our Supreme duty".[2] The goals are gradually realised in means; the means for us is the process of education. In otherwords Gandhi teaches us not search for the goals outside the means: the wrong means are thus never justified in the Gandhian context. The two are "the sides of the same coin" and are therefore inseparable in conception and in process. This Gandhian notion is most relevant in the context of education : the goals are gradually realised in the means i.e. the educational process.

Education as conceived of by Gandhi and a advocated by him primarily aims at the formation and development of the spiritual and moral personality of the individual. He says, "Education is thus an awakening of the soul".[3] Without education attempting this awakening of the soul of the individual and without developing and strengthening the "inner voice" in the individual, education has no serious purpose to serve.

Gandhian education in all its aspects is founded on Spiritual principles. In this sense we shall talk of the 'Gandhian idealism', to be fully developed in a separate chapter. This is the most solid and character-based foundation from which to build education. In this sense, at the base of all we have concepts and principle drawn from one or more religions, developed into harmonious whole to which the goals of education are properly integrated. There should also be enough scope for the various components, processes and methods of education to build from. As we have seen Gandhian education is in all its details founded on the Vedic concepts and Vedic education. He says, "Truth which is the ultimate end which is all pervading can be realised only through a discipline of mind, body and spirit".[4] This was the essence of Vedic education. Brahman is Truth embodiment and the realization of Truth through a life-long process of disciplining of the body, mind and spirit was in face the essence of Vedic education.

This Gandhian idealism, in line with the western idealism encompasses all obsolute virtues and values. The principle of religion to which education in the is sense is oriented are all absolute and there is no room for loopholes and escapims and limpid excuses that would indiscipline the process of education as it happens today. The greatest absolutes that Gandhi embarks on are, truth and ahimsa. Gandhian education thus aims primarily and basically at a realisation of truth and ahimsa in the individual. As Louis Fischer says, "Gandhi faced such morning's issues in the light of eternal and universal values".[5] Gandhian education has in focus the development and inculcation of these values which Gandhi always held as most precious.

The universality and eternal dimension of Gandhian values render them a highly spiritual dimension. We are most often hesitant to speak of Gandhian Spiritually because Gandhi does not in any intimate way associate himself with any particular religious denomination, or to any professed manner of spiritual way of life. But Gandhian Spirituality is a wholesome attitude of the mind, in every detail directed to the supreme being, God. Gandhian education cannot be thought of a divorced from this spirituality. This would mean several things. Education should pave the background for, first, the practice of truth in every aspect of the individual's life. The maturation of the human soul and the practice of truth are intimately related. The Gandhian concept of the formation of character in education includes this. Education as a process develops the environment necessary to him with reference to the detailed experiences of life whose agents are the teachers, the parents and the community. Success at this level depends on how much these agents can influence the individual in the process of learning. Gandhi says, "If I was to be their real teacher and guardian I must touch their hearts. I must share their joys and sorrows".[6] Formation of the Gandhian character in education amounts to the provision of the circumstances in which truth can be nurtured in the individual. He told students, "truth will make you courageous".[7] This courage is a spiritual courage which Gandhi wants education to aim at.

Education for Gandhi as part of the Spiritual dimension means ahimsa reinterpreted as love. This would amount to another central component in the formation of the Gandhian character in the individual through education. Gandhi says, "I have no doubt that your teachers will repeatedly say the intellectual and literary education that you are getting will be rendered useless unless it is built on the foundation of truth and love. Truth will make you courageous and fearless, ... love will make your life bearable because love has the special potential to attract more love towards itself".[8] The process of education is organised in such a way as to nurture in the individual this courage to face the obstacles in the practice of ahimsa. Education aims at providing the necessary conditions for the individual to practice ahimsa in their attitudes towards all living creatures. Gandhi says, "Non-violence is the first article of my faith. It is also the last article of my creed".[9] The importance Gandhi attaches to this principle enable the educator to find out detailed ways and means to attach this principle to everything that he helps the individual to carryout as part of education. This would require a deep conviction.

Ahimsa is the most concrete value that education can help nurture in the individual as seen above. So far as education is concerned it is not the negative meaning of ahimsa that is more valuable ; "ahimsa means avoiding injury to anything on earth, in thought, word or deed".[10] This is the negative connotation of ahimsa or non-violence. In the English sense this would mean not to be violent in thought, word or action. So as to avoid hurt to oneself and others. This is ofcourse valuable to the process of education. At the same time education is capable of integrating more the positive value of ahimsa : the concept of love. In this sense Gandhi identifies ahimsa with love. He says, "The real love is to love them that hate you, to love your neigbours even thought you distrust them".[11] And again, "ahimsa consists in allowing others the maximum of convenience at the maximum of inconvenience to us, even at the risk of life".[12] This value is capable of providing education a totally different outlook, different from the way we conceive of present-day education.

Gandhian education in its spiritual sense aims at, again, developing in the individual a sense of self-denial and sacrifice. He says, "I have no doubt that all self-denial is good for the soul".[13] He further says, "I must reduce myself to zero. So long as a man of his own free will put himself last among his fellow creatures, there is no salvation for him".[14] Self-denial, suffering for others, the constant sense of sacrifice, everything that renders a movement of the heart to other in self-sacrifice are exalted as component values that education should nurture in the individual in the process of character formation. Gandhi is never tired of exhorting students to sacrifice for the poor and the needy in India. He says, "students should be familiar with the poverty and the problems of the common man".[15] There are a thousand ways for education to inclucate in the individual these habits that Gandhi thinks of as most essential qualities of character.

The development of the spiritual personality includes the all-important component of prayer. Education in the Gandhian sense remains no education if the individual is not trained to raise his thoughts in prayer to God. Gandhi has no place for atheists who do not possess faith in God in his educational system. Vedic education, Buddhist Education, Islamic education as well as Christian education do not in any way accommodate atheistic attitudes, or encourage such attitudes to develop. A brahmachari for Gandhi is one who is oriented to the Brahman. His prospects and development, his thoughts and deeds are not defined in any way separated from Brahman, God. The student is a traveller to Brahman; he is Constantly on the move on the path towards Him. The progress on his path is what we should call education. It is ridiculous, for Gandhi, to call education any knowledge that creates obstacles between the student and God. Education is the path in which knowledge becomes the content to the attainment of the ultimate spiritual goal of the individual. Gandhi identifies the life of a student and of an ascetic. He says, "Spiritually the life of a brahmachari (student) and that of an ascetic are identical".[16] Gandhi bewails and adds, "The life of the student who is a brahmachari has become contaminated at its very source".[17]

Thus prayer which is the movement of the individuals heart and mind to God has become a central concept in Gandhian education. Gandhi says, "Modern education has the tendency to turn away from the soul. Hence we are not excited by the powers of the human soul".[18] Prayer is the medium to thus excite those powers of the human soul. For Gandhi prayer is the heart of religion. He says, "Prayer is the heart and soul of religion. Therefore prayer should be the core of human life and no one can live without religion".[19] Through the process of intimate personal prayer education can train the individual to obtain for himself the richest personal experience. Prayer and the consequent peace of the soul that results are experiences that the student can otherwise never dream of securing in life. Gandhi says, "We are confused in not finding the peace, innocence, and the joy that are necessary in the life of a student".[20] This personal experience that we have lost can be rediscovered only in a life of enduring prayer. Prayer was the sole strength for Gandhi in his times of trial and problems. "Prayer has been the saving of my life. Without it I should have been a lunatic long ago. My autobiography will tell you that I have had my fair share of the bitterest public and private experiences. They threw me into temporary despair, but if I was able to get rid of it, it was because of prayer".[21] Gandhi put the firmest faith in prayer and exhorted students to develop the habit of enduring prayer.

Gandhian education aims at, lastly, an ethically upright life as part of the formation of the spiritual personality of the individual. Gandhian spirituality is most often interpreted in ethical terms because as we have seen Gandhi does not associate himself or identify his thoughts with any institutionalised religion. Gandhian concept of religion often gives the impression that leading a morally sound life is in fact religion. This is just one side of Gandhi's concept of religion. But Gandhi gives his religion a sound moral basis: "religion is to morality what water is to the seed that is sown in the soil".[22] Again, "as soon as we loose the moral basis we cease to be religious".[23] This ethical basis of Gandhian thought constitutes also the foundation on which, again, to build the individual's character. The process of education in the Gandhian sense aims at the creation of the environment for the practice of an ethical, a morally sound life.

Such a moral basis to the formation of character extends itself to all human involvements in life: political, economic, social, cultural and educational. Education has the responsibility, in the Gandhian context, to extend the moral precepts to the field of politics, for instance, and develop in the individual a sound moral basis for his future political involvements. It is the absence of such a moral basis, supposed to have been provided by education, that leaves present-day politicians entirely without morals. Such a predicament of politics without morals can be avoided only with an ethically sound education. Education is a period for such a training and not for active involvement in politics without the formation of such an ethical basis. Gandhi was very clear in this. "Students should never be involved in sectarian politics. They are students, investigators; and not politicians".[24] Before they actively involve themselves in politics what they require is not training in politics but a training in leading on ethically upright life as part of their education. The same is true of other aspects of life too. Gandhian education is oriented thus to the formation of a spiritually and ethically sound character without which no education will make sense.

2. Education for Knowledge

Education is defined as a process of bringing about changes in the human individual in desired directions, with a view to helping him live a socially desirable life. Education carries out these individual and social functions by directing, guiding, and reshaping the inmate potentials and impulses of the child, by helping the individual in the process of growth, unfolding what is within and preparing him to assume the responsibilities of adult life. But education carries out all these by introducing him to the total experiences of the human race classified into heads of knowledge. Historically speaking education has become a process of the individual's acquaintance with a large variety of classified information grouped under subjects. Much emphasis was given to the communication of classified knowledge to the individual in the idealist context. Western idealism attempted in a variety of ways to develop in course of a centuries these classifications of knowledge into subjects. These subjects as a whole carry the total experience of the human race to which the individual learner is exposed in the classroom.

Gandhi defines education with reference to the holistic development of man: "the all-round drawing of the best in the child and man - body, mind and spirit".[25] Gandhi gives adequate importance in this conception to the development of the mind. Education of the mind of the head, cannot be undertaken except in its wider sense by the provision of knowledge or rather by exposing the individual to the classified heads of knowledge or rather by exposing the individual to the will take different shapes. This can be a matter-of-fact information about the physical, geographical, social and a economic reality of the individual's own surroundings. From this base, such knowledge can range up to the most abstract philosophy or the science. Gandhi did not speak against the provision of knowledge as such, he spoke against education dealing with useless knowledge, the kind of knowledge proved useless to the child in the Indian village who had to earn his daily bread using the education he acquired.

Gandhi agrees that education should reflect the experience of the human race, and for us, Indians, the ancient culture and civilization that we have developed. He says, "Your only desire should be to enliven everything of our ancient culture that was great and enduring".[26] A knowledge of our culture and civilization becomes thus part of the education that we impart to the new generations. Several values will thus be attached to the education individual a love for the heritage of the country. This love ensures several other values in children. Such a knowledge, again, develops as part of education a sense of commitment to the values this heritages has presented to us. The primary among those values, as we know, are : truth, love, ahimsa, and the fine virtues of humility, sacrifice and renunciation, which Gandhi holds as most precious in the development of the individual and the progress of the nation. Such a knowledge of our heritage imbibed through education, again, enables the individual to undertake an evaluation of the pros and cons of western civilization that often looks so charming to us, Indians. Gandhi's voice against the civilization of the west was powerfully waring: "Today's manner of education does not in any way cater to the needs of our country........ The excess importance given to English has rendered the educated mentally handicapped, made it a burden for the whole life and made them foreigners in their own country".[27] This evil can be remedied by providing a through knowledge of the details and the greatness of our own heritage.

Education for knowledge, further, extends itself to introducing the individual to his physical and geographical environment. Gandhi's basic education begins with acquainting the individual with the working of the spinning wheal. The spinning wheal as a working tool becomes the starting point for a variety of knowledge-based learning. With such a drastic work-oriented and skill-oriented and skill-centered system as basic education, Gandhi could not help stressing the necessity for introducing the child to a system of knowledge : "It may be asked how the mental ability can be developed through spinning. If not done mechanically that is very much possible. His mind and the eyes are trained when you teach the child the reasons for each activity, when the mechanism of the spinning wheal is explained to them, when the child is led to the places where cotton is grown and when the history of cotton and its relation to civilization is explained to them".[28] The problem for Gandhi in this context is not whether or not knowledge is a must, but regarding the mode of introducing the individual to this knowledge.

Education can in no way neglect introducing the learner to a system of knowledge that encompasses the learner's own environment. This goes with the Gandhian basic concept of character formation as conceived of in modern education. Education has the function of helping the individual surroundings and of the environment in which one lives requires as much detailed knowledge of the events and objects there in as possible. Such an appreciation is a major part of the life of the learner. Education has thus the responsibility to help him achieve this appreciation through the knowledge that we are arriving at. This attitude of the individual forms part of his interaction with the environment. To have this interaction developed to the fullest extent, education needs to base itself on the communication of knowledge to the individual.

Education cannot possibly communicate knowledge in a haphazard manner. Gandhi's concept of primary education for instance, is an organised one. Using the spinning weal as the starting point, Gandhi was careful to classify knowledge into the traditional groups of languages, history, arithmetic, science and so forth. This classification was arrived at as a sheer necessity of the intellect because by virtue of its very nature knowledge cannot remain confused, it lends itself to classification and organisation. That is how historically we have knowledge classified into subjects in order to facilitate the presentation of it. This system enables a more productive and systematic communication of such knowledge to students.

Education for knowledge is also known as literary education. This would include the knowledge of languages, and literature and a variety of other arts-oriented subjects. Gandhi was not against such an education provided the goal of imparting such a knowledge stands justified in the context of the Gandhian goals of education. He says, "The scheme of education that I have recommended is meant for this year which is a time for self-examination and self-purification. If situations become normal, and if the Swaraj is already established, then only one hour needs to be spent for spinning. The rest of the time can be used for literary education".[29] The nature of education is such that character formation and all other training forms only the cost of it or its central tendency. The very flesh of education would constitute knowledge and without knowledge no process of education can be carried on far.

Communication of knowledge aims also at providing the necessary rationale of the individual's life - experiences. We do not want people to live an insensitive and irrational life. People should have the what and why or everything that they think, believe and do. This can be developed only as part of education. Animals have consciousness, they know that something is thus food or something is their enemy. They cannot on the other hand turn on to themselves and have reflection. This is the capacity only of man. Education is the instrument that helps us develop this ability to rationalise and reflect. This is what makes us responsible individuals. This responsibility constitutes the root of our social, religious and political involvements as members of the human race. This responsibility that Gandhi holds as a most essential quality for the educated comes with the ability to know fully why we do certain things in our lives and have the willingness to bear the consequences of our actions for ourselves. Education thus aims at knowledge in the Gandhian sense. Intellectual development is a condition necessary for the formation of character that Gandhi envisages.

3. Education for Social Development

It has been a traditionally debated question whether or

not education should focus attention on the development of the individual as such or society more. Should the efforts of education be directed to the harmonious development at different times. It is true that no body can emphasize one without taking into consideration the development of the other. For Gandhi, "individual development and social progress are interdependent".[30] Gandhi is for a synthesis of the two in its fullest sense. Gandhi wanted a society "in which all individuals have to play their part for the good of the whole without losing their individual character".[31] Every goal of education that Gandhi envisaged in fact harmonised with others. We have seen in the preceding sections how forcefully Gandhi pleads for character formation with its spiritual and moral characteristics. Gandhi was not developing a theoretical point of view but dealing with a burning practical problem. That gave his standpoints the acuteness that we may not see elsewhere.

Education in the Gandhian sense aims at the development of society. This aim of education primarily adds a great responsibility on the individual who is being educated as well as on the one after his education. The development of society is not an automatic thing; individuals have to be pressed into service for that purpose. This requires great training for the individual as part of education that enables him to commit himself on a permanent basis for the welfare of society.

Gandhi's educational thoughts attach great importance to this goal of education. Exhortations to students and educationists in the country to attach importance to the value of social service and social welfare in all aspects of education were common in his speeches and writings. Gandhi develops eight points in this regard: "1. There should be concrete Hindu-Muslim unity, 2. The disease of untouchability and caste differences should be rooted out of the Hindu community, 3. We should be convinced that there is no authority other than that of truth and ahimsa, 4. The public should develop a sense of cooperative service, 5. Young men and women should come forward in great number to dedicate themselves for the service of people, 7. People should wake up from lethargy and involve themselves in spinning or any other constructive work, and lastly, 8. Educated people should teach literacy to their illiterate brothers".[32] The very Gandhian norm of education became an orientation to the service of the people. He wanted education to turn itself to the needs of the people at the grass-root level. From this viewpoint he find out serious drawbacks in present-day education. Gandhi alleges that today's education does not in any way reach the povery and problems of the villages. It leves a tremendous gap between 'the have's and the have not's. it leaves such a gap between the educated and the illeterate. the gap that has been created among those who know English and those who don't had been a serious issue for Gandhi. Again, the country is compelled to invest huge amounts for higher education which benefits only the more affluent sections of India's popultion. Today's education from this viewpoint segregates the villages from towns and cause in influx of population from village to towns in search of greater prospects. All these Gandhi viewied with great concern.

Education to be worthy of its name should keep these drawbacks in focus and work towards bringing the student to the very heart of the people for whose sake they are educated. Education thus aims at creating in the individual a sincere love and concern for rural India. Gandhi says, "If we wish to provide such an education as to become oplimum beneficial to the needs of villagers, then our educational institutions should be moved over to the villages. We should convert them into schools of training in order to provide teachers practical education according to the needs of villagers. It is not possible to give practical education to teachers based on the needs of villagers from training schools in cities".[33] Education as imparted in most cases has become so sophisticated as to include no rural orientation. With seventy-nine percent of our people living villages, education has a great responsibility at the national level to have the right orientation to villages. We are today as if training all our students for white-collarred jobs.

Education for social development aims at thus creating in the education individual a number of socially-oriented values. First, education in schools and colleges should do everything at its disposal to nurture in students a love and concern for society and its needs. It should curb all ego-centric tendencies in the individual and develop in them a consciousness about the needs of others in Society: "Students should learn to sacrifice the things that the poor in India cannot afford for themselves",[34] and again, "they should identify themselves with the poor and the down-trodden in the country".[35] The goals, the content, the materials and the methods of education should be organised in such a way as to develop in the students a sincere dedication for the cause of society. It should be an enduring tendency to delimit, for example, one's own day to day material needs for the sake of those others living around, in the school, family and community.

Again, education in schools and collages aims at developing in the individual a willingness to spend a part of one's time for some cause of social welfare or other. Gandhi says,"If your education is a substantial one, it should spread its odour in your surroundings. You should everyday utilise a portion of your time in the service of the people around you".[36] This service can take different forms. It would primarily mean a constant awareness of the presence of the rest of the community and of the needs that the community usually experiences. It would mean remaining in contact with the people of different walks in society and trying to know how their presence in society adds to the increasing welfare in society. One who is willing to lend a helping hand to one's neighbor will be on the lookout for opportunities for doing so and such opportunities are bound to be plenty. Gandhi envisages several such concrete opportunities for social service by students : "Students will live in villages during their long vacations; they will organise adult education classes; they will teach the villagers principles of hygiene; ordinary ailments among the villagers can be treated by them. They will spread among them the use of the spinning wheal and teach them how to make every minute of their day useful".[37]

Education for social development ensures that the students imbibe the necessary qualities for undertaking such activities as part of their life. Gandhi says, "The qualification for such a service would be to have a generous heart and purity of character beyond doubt. It these two are possessed, then the rest of the qualities will necessarily follow". [38] Educational institutions should set for themselves the ideal of social service in all aspects of their educational activity. Gandhi recommended set of qualities for the type of individuals these institutions would aim at providing to be of service in society. He wants students and teachers alike to develop attractive social attitudes with genuine natural kindness" which endears the individual to children and grown up in the outside world. In order to achieve qualities like generosity and purity of character to serve one's people Gandhi recommends the education of the heart. He says, "Education of the heart can never be imparted through books, but only through the person of the teacher".[39] Gandhian education aims at 'liberating the individual' from all sorts of bonds. Such a liberation of the personality from environmental bondage would become possible only if education can also socialise individuals. As Percy Nunn says, "Nothing good enters into the human world except in and through the free activities of individual men and women; and that educational practice must be shaped in accordance with that truth".[40] Education should aim at helping individuals to dedicate themselves for the cause of society and social development through helping them generate free activities and involvements. The attractive social attitudes that Gandhi wants education to develop can narrow down in course of time the gap that now exists between the students and rural India and draw them to the development of villages.

4. Education for Self-discovery

Education for the development of the individual has been

central concern for all times: "Schools of every type fulfil their proper purpose in so far as they foster the free growth of individuality, helping every boy and girl to achieve the highest degree of individual development of which he or she is capable in and through the life of a society".[41] Inspite of all that we speak about social attitudes and social development education at all levels has to deal with the individual, begin its work with the individual and end it with the individual because he is the unique building blocks of all social tendencies. Percy Nunn, a famous educationist, tries to summerise the significance of the individual to education speaking of "the infinite value of the individual person".[42] According to him all educational efforts attempt to create conditions suitable for the complete development of this individuality and help the individual to make "original contributions" to society.

Gandhi attaches great importance to the individual's development as he does to society. The individual is the central entity and the focus of Gandhian thought for different reasons. In Gandhi the individual is conceived of from two viewpoints : the ultimate and the immediate. The individual is of divine origin : "We were born men in order to realize God who dwells in us. That indeed is the privilege of man and it distinguishes him from the brute creation".[43] This divine orientation makes great difference in the organisation and conducting of the individual's life. The ultimate aim of the life of the individual is thus the realization of the Divine Self : "what I want to achieve is self-realisation, to see God face to face, to attain moksha".[44] To this end Gandhi organised his entire life in a conscious chain of experiments with life : "To develop the spirit is to build the character and to enable one to work towards a knowledge of God and self-realisation".[45] So far as the individual is concerned this becomes the ultimate reality towards which his faculties are always directed. The ultimate self-realisation which occupies the Gandhian consciousness so powerfully is of totally spiritual dimension and becomes the concern of education only as the ultimate goal as we have examined it in the very first section of the chapter.

Individuality as we have seen above has yet another viewpoint or dimension, that is what holds the attention of education for all practical matters. When educationists like Percy Nunn and others talk of 'self-realisation' it means the step-by-step drawing out of the individual's "spiritual personality" and helping him to have a full flowering of his personality in the spiritual, social and psychological sense. If the ultimate goal is called 'self-realisation', we shall call the immediate goal 'self-discovery' with which also Gandhi is fascinated. He says, "Just as physical training is to be imparted through physical exercise, and intellectual through intellectual exercise, even so the training of the spirit was possible only through the exercise of the spirit".[46] So far as education is concerned this training of the spirit takes concrete forms and enables us to develop concrete paths for the process of self-discovery.

Education for self-discovery would thus include all the processes of the individual's development that would help him live the life of "an educated person" in the sense Gandhi understands it. Such an educated individual has the necessary "discriminative powers" that would help him see life in its proper perspectives. Gandhi says, "If teaches aim at developing the discriminative powers of the boys and girls under them, they will continually foster their reasoning capacity and enable them to think for themselves".[47] Education would mean coming in contact with literary material of all sorts that present to the student occasions to examine and analyse them and develop his reasoning capacity on the basis of those materials. These powers of discrimination are considered necessary for leading a 'liberated life' as Gandhi conceived of it. A life that is devoid of physical or intellectual bondage on the one hand, or exterior or interior bondage on the other was considered significant for that full utilisation of human powers. Gandhi was fond of the individual's holistic development; the full utilisation of the potentials of these powers become a pre-condition for the realisation of the type of a personality that Gandhi envisaged.

The discovery of the self would mean realising for oneself over serval years of hard training the attitude of humility and willingness to deny oneself for the sake of society. In this instance the individual development that we are discussing and the social development that we discussed in the preceding section coincides. The kind of humility that Gandhi considers and the spirit of self-denial that he requires of the student demand a considerable level of the purity of the heart. Gandhi says, "The state that you are an educated individual comes to an end the moment you are unable to bring your emotions under control and when your heart is not pure".[48] The process of the discovery of the self in the Gandhian sense is a slow and lingering one. Just as self-realisation is the ultimte goal of life and education in a global sense, self-discovery in the context that we are developing it also takes its own time and efforts. Gandhi set humility as a central virtue for the success in the pursuit of more ultimate virtues in life. Gandhi developed this virtue in his own life and set himself the best possible example . John Holmes remarks, "We had the spiritual presence of a loving and infinitily lovable man. Gandhi's attitude had the naturalness and simplicity of a little child".[49] Whoever came into contact with the person of Gandhi became fascinated by a man of most unassuming character: "Along with came humility which was manifest in every quality and action of his life".[50] Gandhi's son, Devdas Gandhi said of his father on one occasion, "Gandhi was the most refined person in the world, refined in scanty dress, in his speech, and in his manners".[51] It was this quality that he developed in his own life that he wanted students to possess through the process of self-discovery.

Service for Gandhi was central to the development of social attitudes. In the same manner Gandhi could not see any form of service without the foundation of humility and self-denial. He says, "service without humility is selfishness and egotism".[52] Again he says, "I have no doubt that self-denial is good for the soul".[53] Any form of service undertaken without the deep-seated humility and sense of self-denial turns out to be a form of hypocrisy. Those who advocate education to develop the opium forms of self-expression also tend to give themselves over to the service of others. Such a service whatever be the concrete form it takes is directed not to the exclusive benefit of society but to the benefit of oneself as a concrete form of self-expression. The traditionally understood self-expression and the Gandhian notion of self-discovery or self-realisation are two very different things. The former is directed to the other and turns back upon the self for its own total benefit. While the latter is directed to the other but rests uniquely upon the other for his or her own good. This difference is essentially based on the attitudes of humility and self-denial.

Self-discovery in the Gandhian scnsc is a uniquc notion, Gandhi proposes this as a goal in education and also recommends the methodology necessary for that. Self-discovery in the Gandhian sense assumes 'experimentation with truth' as the unique method. Gandhi's own life was a continuing experiment with truth. Gandhi reveals in his Autobiography, "I simply want to tell the story of my experiments with Truth, and my life consists of nothing but those experiments".[54] A reading of the Autobiography convinces us that he tried to validate every value putting it into continuous and painstaking tests in his life. Gandhi's was an experimentation in the process of self-discovery and development of the values he held as most dear to him. The foremost of these that he experimented in life was that of living a simple life: "In course of time I became an expert washerman so far as may own work went —— my passion for self-help and simplicity ultimately expressed itself in extreme forms".[55] Gandhi was never contented exhorting students to follow and develop in themselves the lesson simplicity, humility and self-denial in the process of discovering the self on the path to self-realisation.

5. Education and Life-experiences

Gandhi was greatly influenced by the American Pragmatic school of education whose details we shall examine in later chapters. John Dewey, the most outstanding exponent of pragmatic education in America developed a system of education based exclusively on the value of life-experiences, experimentation and activity centered teaching. The project method of pragmatists manifests education undertaken through well-organised, practical learning activities, "that would equip the individual with the knowledge and skills necessary to deal effectively with the situations of real life".[56] It was possible for the pragmatic school of education to undertake a detailed analysis of life-experiences that could form that centre of education and coordinate practical activities in order to re-create these learning experiences for children. Education became for them a matter of optimum usefulness. The only question they ever asked was whether or not a value or scheme or an experience is useful to the individual or society from its viewpoint of productiveness.

Gandhi too made life-experiences a central aim of education. There was, all the same a major difference - Dewey's value of practical usefulness was an end itself, while for Gandhi it constituted a major means to more remote ends and consequently to the ultimate end itself. Gandhi envisaged life and its experiences from a dynamic perspective and attempted to analyse and see life in all its completeness. The famous psychoanalyst Erikson remarks, "Gandhi's personality is one of a minute and concrete interplay perfect on every step of a long life of a craftsman like series of 'experiments' with historical actuality in all its political and existential aspects". [57] Gandhi did not wish to leave things to chance and looked at the events of day-to-day life with immense care and attention. Louis Fischer says, "He discovered a new dimension of action; he split the social atom and found a new source of energy".[58] That was a major achievement as this constituted a basis for the development of Gandhi's philosophy of life and action.

Education for life-experiences in the Gandhian sense aims at presenting to the individual the varied aspects of what we call practical life in which the individual is expected to make a life of his own. The individual is provided with opportunities to know for himself the intrinsic value of action. Unless this aspect is brought into focus, ordinarily education does not lay any stress on this. Right from the beginning of education the individual should be helped to undertake introspection, reasoning and analysis of his own action and those he sees around. Basically this is an ability that renders him quite different from the animals living around him. By stressing this aspect education is helping the individual to undertake something proper to man as man. He becomes able to exercise his rational mind on everything around him, accept or reject things and experiences that life ordinarily presents to him. This would mean the individual should learn to valuc every minute in his life : "It is to be emphasised that every minute of man's life is to be valued in a productive manner".[59] A link is established between the time that becomes available to oneself and the series of responsibilities and duties one is expected to carryout.

For Gandhi life-experiences constitute the primary means to achieve the full flowering the individual's personality for the sake of oneself, society and God. He says, "Through the vocation in which the student receives training the personality hidden in him or her should receive full development".[60] For this reason Gandhi strongly advocated the linking of a skill or a vocation to all forms of education, if possible at all levels. Education, apart from developing the aptitude for introspecting and reasoning on every bit of involvement the individual has, attempts to link the student's personality with these involvements. Of all these aspects for Gandhi the central one was the individual's spiritual / moral personality, all other aspects being subservient to this. Radha Mukerjee says, "The mere intellectual development without the development of character, learning without piety, proficiency in the sacred love without its practices, will defeat the very end of studentship".[61] This central concern of Gandhi alters the basic educational attitudes to life-experience in general and adds to them a new dimension i.e. spirituality.

Education for life experiences aims at developing in the individual, again, an attitude of self-dependency or independence. Gandhi considers this attitude most valuable in his individual and national aims. Gandhi wanted no individual in his swaraj to depend on anybody else in a way as to sacrifice his individuality and develop ego-centric attitudes: "It was possible to introduce the complete man by undertaking the scientific teaching of the handicraft. Attainment of self-dependency is a long process. Students cannot be helped to achieve this in a day or two. As part of a long training, using the tools of self-examination and self-reflection as mentioned above, the individual evaluates the level of his actions and involvements and the role he played in these actions. The individual may in several cases by totally dependent on the family, friends and community. In other cases the individual requires only partial help from these agencies and he is capable of carrying out several activities on his own. In the third case the individual receives such an education and training that he becomes exceptionally self-dependent for most things in his life.

In the first case the students is so dependent that he cannot even do a bit of shopping for the family for instance. In the second case the student is trained to be of help to himself in several of his day-to-day needs and he becomes considerably responsible. In the last case the student learns, as Gandhi envisages, eves to wash his own clothes and to help himself with some form cooking. This would mean an advanced level of responsibility on his part. Gandhi is cautious about the use of time in this process: "If the spending of time is strictly controlled, they can save number of hours of themselves".[63] The efforts the students make in this direction have a pervasive efforts on their personality: "Those efforts will increase their mental, moral and physical potentials.[64] Students will in turn be convinced of the self-dendency that arises from the logical result of their realisation that every one of the inherent potential is most useful in the development of their self-dependency. A conviction and realisation of this kind are most essential to the formation of this all-important characteristic in the Gandhian scheme.

Life experience aimed at self-dependency in the Gandhian line would amount to living a simple life in which the needs of life are drastically curtailed for the sake of one-self and society. Gandhi says, "In course of time I become an expert washerman so far as my own work went .... my passion for self-help and simplicity ultimately expressed it-self in extreme forms".[65] Gandhi wants students to develop a constant awareness of the need for acquiring these simple living habits and look at life from this viewpoint. Gandhi says clearly what painstaking efforts he make in order to pick up the art of managing things by himself. He recalls how he invited the ridiculcs of his barristcr-friends by washing his collar for the courtroom himself: "But I could not make my friends appreciate the beauty of self-help".[66] In the same manner in course of time as Gandhi freed himself "from the slavery to the washerman"[67] he "throw off dependence on the barber".[68]

The goals of Gandhian education cover a wide spectrum of values that relate themselves to the total development of both the individual and society. He does not in any way consider the development of the individual and the welfare of society contradictory. The ultimate aim of self-realisation, the immediate aims of self-discovery, the ideal of service to humanity based on the principles of Truth and Love, preservation and development of the moral values that are intermediary, and development of a harmonious personality centered on a spiritual core etc. have made Gandhian education a system by itself.

References

1. Bhatia, B.K. Philosophy and Education, p.14.
2. -do- , Ibid p.122
3. -do- , Ibid p.125
4. -do- , Ibid p.122
5. Fischer, Louis, in Profiles of Gandhi, p.60
6. Gandhi,M.K., An Autobiography, p.258

7. -do- , To the Students, p.113
8. -do- , To the Students, p.113
9. -do- , Young India, 23 March 1922.
10. -do- , Harijan, 7 Sept. 1935.
11. -do- , Ibid 3 March 1946
12. -do- , Young India, 2 Deç. 1926
13. -do- , An Autobiography, p.246.
14. -do- , Ibid p.383
15. -do- , To the Students, p.71
16. -do- , To the Students, p.56
17. -do- , Ibid p.56
18. -do- , Ibid p.172
19. -do- , Ibid p. 182
20. -do- , Ibid p. 57
21. -do- , Young India, 24 Sept. 1931
22. -do- , Ethical Religion, Madras 1930, p.49
23. -do- , Young India, 24 Nov 1921
24. -do- , To the Students, p.58
25. Bhatia, B.D., Philosophy and Education, p.125
26. Gandhi, M.K., To the Students, p.121.
27. -do- , Basic Education, p.17.
28. -do- , Ibid p.13
29. -do- , Towards a New Education, p.39
30. Bhatia, B.D., Philosophy and Education, p.129
31. -do- , Ibid p.129
32. Gandhi, M.K., Harijan 18 March 1939
33. -do- , Basic Education, p.13
34. -do- , To the Students, p.71
35. -do- , Ibid p.71
36. -do- , Ibid p.173
37. -do- , Ibid p.174
38. -do- , Ibid p.175
39. -do- , Towards New Education, p.31.
40. Bhatia, B.D., Philosophy and Education, p.21
41. -do- , Ibid p.21
42. -do- , Ibid p.21
43. Gandhi M.K., Harijan, 2 April 1938
44. -do- , An Autobiography, Intr.
45. -do- , Ibid p.255
46. -do- , Ibid p.255
47. -do- , To the Students, p.71
48. -do- , Ibid p.105
49. Holmes, J., in Profiles of Gandhi, p.122

50. -do- , Ibid p.124.
51. Gandhi, Devdas, in Profiles of Gandhi, p. 132
52. Gandhi, M.K., An Autobiography, p.298.
53. -do- , Ibid p.246
54. -do- , Ibid Intr.
55. -do- , Ibid p.160.
56. Bhatia, B.K., Philosophy and Education, p.134.
57. Erikson, in Profiles of Gandhi, p.187.
58. Fischer, Louis, in Profiles of Gandhi, p.61
59. Gandhi, M.K., Harijan 6 April 1940
60. -do- , Basic Education, p.19
61. Bhatia, B.D., Philosophy and Education, p.129
62. Gandhi M.K., To the Students, p.176
63. -do- , Ibid p.176
64. -do- , Basic Education, p.51
65. -do- , An Autobiography, p.160
66. -do- , Ibid p.159
67. -do- , Ibid p.160.

4

GANDHI'S EXPERIMENTS IN EDUCATION

1. Gandhi's Experiments with Truth

Of all the great world figures Gandhi emerges to be unique because of his approach to life. There has been no one who exercised such tremendous energy to arrive at a close synthesis of the ideals and principles of life and the practical, day-to-day living at the grass-root level. Gandhi says, "Experience of the soul is the richest and the only one that helps our development".[1] He was most willing to keep before his eyes the significance of right from the minute details of life up to the final goal of Self-realisation. Gandhi observed life and its movements like a magician observing his magic crystal for best results. Gandhi was an idealist and be proved himself to be a committed pragmatist. As an idealist he developed his concepts, values and principles in detail, examined, studied and criticised them for their validity, and he clung to them as most valuable entities in his life. But as a pragmatist Gandhi developed his life-experiences, examined their validity and results and used them for generating nobler and more valuable experiences.

Gandhi viewed life as the arena for the recognition and realisation of truth. For Gandhi "Truth is more fundamental than atom itself".[2] Truth is hidden in the vast reservoir of life which the individual is out to discover. Truth is like an ice-berg whose tiny edge alone is seen on surface; the individual is oriented to discover the gigantic portions of it hidden beneath the waters of life. Gandhi's unique method of discovering this vast reservoir and this gigantic ice-berg of truth constituted his experiments with truth and life. Gandhi was convinced that the more one searches deep into its realm the greater the discoveries one is bound to make. He says, "Truth is like a vast tree which yields more and more fruit, the more you nurture it".[3] Gandhi learned to judge the depth of an action and the spiritual and the social validity of it from its potential to generate further actions of greater truth value. This was the essence of Gandhian experimentation with truth.

As Truth, for Gandhi, is God, and the two realities are identical, the attainment God in one's life and the confrontation with Him means resorting to the unique way of Satyagraha i.e. "the way of life of one who holds steadfastly to God and dedicates one's life to Him",[4] or rather way of life holding fast to truth. Truth was accepted by Gandhi as a way of life in which the confrontation with God becomes a reality for the satyagrahi: "Satyagraha is a total and integral way of life based on truth and non-violence".[5] As a way of life truth became observable, analysable and tangible for Gandhi, and emerged as the unique content of the Gandhian experience of life as well as the material for the experiments for greater discovery. In this process of discovery Gandhi was most conscious of the impediments of evil and the surmounting problems that he would have to face. Gandhi writes, "I know well that I shall never realise God in my life without confronting and fighting against evil even at the risk of my life".[6] The confrontation and fighting against the forces of evil Gandhi consider to be fundamental to satyagraha.

This raises the problem of discrimination between these obstacles on the path of the discovery of truth and the refinements of truth and live manifest in one's life. Gandhi's unfailing dedication, keen observation and sense of commitment to the very caused helped him in this process of discrimination. This aspect was evident from Gandhi's experiments in spirituality and education at the phoenix settlement, Tolstoy Farm and Sabarmati Ashram. Gandhi never saw life as black and white formula with a single proposed solution. He accepted the too complex nature of the reality of life and attempted to respond to the problems of life keeping this complexity in mind. He was forcefully guided by his values and principles and these sustained in him an immense strength of conviction, one that was never lost inspite of the obstacles Gandhi had to face. He writes, "There should be an unbridgeable gap between one's ideal and one's practice. The moment the ideal becomes realisable it ceases to be an ideal. Happiness lies in the effort and not so much in the realisation".[7]

Gandhi was right in stressing the point that man requires a powerful motivation to follow his ideals, and the attraction of ideals needs to persist in order to keep his efforts going in the right direction. That was the strength working behind all his experiments. That was the strength Gandhi wants to work in the case of our experiments with life and education. In order to have things in the right direction Gandhi always kept his ideals most powerful, not too comfortably attainable, for instance drastic formation in character, dramatic alterations and innovations in education, as well as total ahimsa in life on the path to self-realisation.

Gandhi's experiments with truth took manifold dimensions as a way of life to confront divinity in worship and to confront his neighbour in live. Gandhi's experiments in diet-keeping lead to further and further simple food habits in which he reaped wonderful results. He writes, "Many such experiments taught me that the real of taste was not the tongue but the mind".[8] Gandhi's experiments with diet-keeping and those to develop self-denial went hand-in-hand. It was a powerful movement from the wants of the body and material life to the wants of the spirit and spiritual life: "Gandhi had a disciplined way of putting his soul to work, with results that were patent to all, but none the less hard to understand".[9] Training in self-denial became the essence of Gandhian experiments with food and he does not spare education from self-denial as a condition for the right success. He writes, "Education is the that which liberates from extrinsic bondage and from intrinsic bondage to the needs of life".[10]

Gandhi's experiments with truth became in course of time an experiment in simple life and a life of total self-dependency. That was Gandhi's antithesis to the over-sophistication of his own times. He was governed by the powerful conviction that self-restraint alone could redeem mankind from catastrophy and the nation from slavery. He exhorts teachers, "A stranger to self-restraint could never teach his pupils the value of self-restraint'.[11] In all his experiments the basic fact was the search for the truth content that as we have seen had to be uncovered as part of the huge hidden ice-berg. He says, "I am a searcher after truth. My experiments hold to be infinitely more important than the best equipped Himalayan expeditions. And the results? If the search is scientific, surely there is no comparison between the two".[12] Gandhi's greatness lies not only in his achievements but also the method and techniques he employed in every detailed approach to life. The very term 'experiments' he employed indicates how objective, scientific and convincing he wanted things to be for others to share his light.

2. Phoenix Settlement and Tolstoy Farm

At Johannesberg Gandhi made acquaintance with Mr. Polak in the vegetarian restaurant which Gandhi used to visit. Polak was the sub-editor of "The Critic". He was for a long while wishing to meet Gandhi to exchange ideas. Later Gandhi discovered to his delight that they two held very similar views on several essential aspects of life. Polak had a radical way of translating into his life what appealed to his mind and he liked to live a simple life. All this made impressions on Gandhi, and he took Polak into full confidence. It was Polak who gave to Gandhi Ruskin's 'Unto this Last' for reading during a journey to Durban.

The book left such a deep impression on Gandhi that

several of the Gandhian experiments later were based on it. Gandhi was determined to change his life according to the ideas contained in the book. The Book 'Unto This Last' became the basis of Gandhi's 'Hind Swaraj or Indian Home Rule' (1908) which contains the quintessence of Gandhi's thoughts on people's rule in the real sense of the term. Gandhi conferred that the first book of the kind to bring "to an instantaneous and practical transformation in my life was 'Unto This Last'".[13] It was a fresh discovery for him that some of his deepest convictions were embodied in this work. Gandhi was greatly captured by the following ideas of great significance that he thought was fundamental to several of his own experiments with truth : "1. That the good of the individual is contained in the good of all. 2. That a lawyers work has the same value as the barber's, in as much as all have the same right of earning their livelihood from their work. 3. That a life of labour i.e. the life of the tiller of the soil and the handicraftsman, is the life worth living".[14] Gandhi drew up a clear analysis of these principles and became ready to be translated into practice.

Based on Ruskin's ideas Gandhi drew up a plan for a settlement in which to run his" Indian Opinion' (Gandhi's Journal in South Africa) and where everyone had to labour, receiving the same pay, and attend to their work in the press. But there was the problem of everyone at the place i.e. all the workers agreeing to go to the new place, settle down and be satisfied with the bare minimum pay that would be given to them. It was therefore made an option for all either to accept their salaries and gradually become members or accept the new scheme of settlement.

Gandhi purchased the necessary land at Phoenix. Living under canvas sheds, the small group moved out in a week's time. Gandhi attempted to draw into Phoenix as many Indian settlers as possible but as most of them came in search of wealth, they were not willing to part with their business and join Gandhi. Of those who accepted Gandhi's invitation, he makes a special mention of Manganlal Gandhi who "by ability, sacrifice and devotion stands foremost among my original co-workers in my ethical experiments".[15] Phoenix Settlement was finally started in 1904 with "a small group of Indian and European idealists"[16] who had enough foresight to see and accept the path of truth Gandhi showed them. 'Indian Opinion' was transferred to the settlement.

Gandhi's first night at Phoenix Settlement in the company of his relatives and friends was an exciting one that proved the extent to which the Gandhian values were imbibed by the inmates of the settlement. The failure of the printing machine at night, the workers' labour with the hand-machine and the miraculous working of the machine in the morning helped Gandhi make an excellent beginning at the settlement. The initial experience "created an atmosphere of self-reliance in Phoenix ..... Those were, the days of the highest moral uplift for Phoenix".[17] In course of time Phoenix became a little village. The basic idea was to experiment as to what extent simplicity of life, harmonious living of people together, can be successfully and joyfully practiced: "The colony was to be as far as possible self-supporting and life's material requirements were to be reduced to a minimum".[18] Gandhi's concept of self-supporting education as well as his constant requests to students to strive towards a sort of life in recognition of the problems of rural India received grounds for development right from Phoenix itself. It provided the first grounds also for putting to test Ruskin's ideas in 'Unto This Last'.

Tolstoy Farm became the next arena of Gandhi's work. Friendship with one Mr. Polak was the beginning of Gandhi's inspiration for Phoenix Settlement while the friendship with a German architect, Hermann Kellenback was the beginning of the inspiration for the establishment of Tolstoy Farm: "We incidentally talked about Gautama Buddha's renunciation. Our acquaintence soon ripened into very close friendship, so much so that we thought alike and he was convinced that he must carry out in his life changes I was making in mine".[19] The land for the new settlement was donated by Kallenbach in 1910, to be used by the passive resisters and their families in South Africa. That land was named after Tolstoy and was called Tolstey Farm. The sellters came from all parts of India.

Gandhi and Kallenbach lived with the Indian families, called Satyagrahi families, which included young people and children. There were Muslim, Christian and Parsi youngsters whom Gandhi encouraged to follow their respective religions observances. It was considered a privilege to join others on the occasions of their religious fasts. Gandhi writes, "I explained to them that it was always a good thing to join with others in any matter of self-denial".[20] The inmates of the Farm welcomed Gandhi's work in Tolstoy Farm included comprehensive experiments. "To make sellters self-supporting, small industries were started on Tolstoy Farm".[21]

Gandhi found it necessary, as the farm developed, to make provision also for the education of the boys and girls of the settlers. There were children who belonged to various religions. Practical problems make it difficult to avail any qualified teacher to work on the farm. For Gandhi there was the genuine opportunity for experimenting his new ideas, as he was thoroughly disappointed with the existing system of education. There was his chance to try a hand on something new and what he was convinced as the true way of education. Under ideal circumstances the parents had the duty of imparting true education. Tolstoy Farm was a family and Gandhi its head, the father, and that he had to as far as possible shoulder the responsibility for training the young. Gandhi planned his own system with the available resources, what constituted the foundations his basic education to be later tried out the developed in his Swaraj.

As part of the education on the Farm, classes were held in the afternoon. Gandhi prepared a few young men to work as teachers. The entire process was thought of as a training for true character formation. Gandhi writes, "But I had always given the first place to the culture of the heart or the building of character, and as I felt confident that moral training could be given to all alike, no matter how different their ages and their upbringing, I decided to live among them all the twenty-four hours of the day as their father".[22] Gandhi's basic conception was that character formation was all in all in education and everything else could be achieved as a corollary of that by individuals themselves or with the help of others. Gandhi himself gave religious instruction which included the fundamentals of Hinduism, Islam and Zoroastrianism. Gandhi tried to drive home the concept of respect for all religions in theory and practice and taught them how to live together like blood brothers. It was based on those instructions that Gandhi developed and wrote his 'Ethical Religion' or Niti Dharma", published in 1912.

Classes were constituted with pupils of all ages, boys and girls from the age of seven to men of twenty and girls of twelve. Classes were engaged in two sections with the medium of Gujarati and English. Gandhi recommended the method of narration and reading to pupil stories of very productive and useful kind. Gandhi himself taught Tamil and Urdu. The curriculum included also the general knowledge of history, arithmetic and geography. In addition, Sanskrit was taught to Hindu students as a necessity to introduce to them the great language which embodied the vast domains of Indian culture and literature. Emphasis was given to writing and the recitation of prayer songs: "No textbook was used in this school. In education he gave the first place to the culture of the heart or the building of character".[23] It was a literary training organised to meet the bare needs of the children and given against the background provided by the Tolstoy Farm. Gandhi recalls, "But my love for the languages of my country, my confidence in my capacity as a teacher, as also the ignorance of my pupils, and more than that, their generosity stood in my good stead".[24] It was a training in the temperament to accept the simplicity of the physical and social climate on the Farm in a spirit of self denial and sacrifice keeping in mind the needy and the poor whom they wished to imitate in actual life. It was the same spirit of simplicity, self-confidence through self-denial, and self-supporting that Gandhi wished later to become the central values of basic education.

Gandhi later wrote in the Harijan (September 1937) about his successful work tolstoy Farm: "I had no difficulty in providing to the boys and girls under my care on Tolstoy Farm complete development. The central fact was that they were given vocational education for about eight hours. There was literary training for one or at the most two hours".[25] It was his intention to teach everyone of the youngsters some useful manual vocation. Gandhi sent Kallenbach to a trappist monastery and there he learned shoe-making. They also conducted classes in carpentry. Since almost everyone knew cooking no special training was needed for it. Students had the pleasure of doing only whatever their teachers actually did. That made learning an easy and pleasant experience. A teacher never asked the student to do anything that he himself did not do. That was an important maxim in Tolstoy Farm. That enabled them to develop a high degree of self- confidence which ordinarily education failed to provide.

Corporal punishment of all forms was strictly forbidden. Gandhi believed "that the training of the spirit was possible only through the exercise of the spirit".[26] The exercise of the spirit, on the other hand entirely depended on the life and character of the teacher whose life in fact became the message for the student as Gandhi himself exemplified. On occasions when Gandhi struck anyone with a ruler he was sorry for that. Gandhi also experimented with co-education where under his own supervision boys and girls lived and studied together. The duty of self-restraint was explained to them: "The experiment made from a belief that boys and girls could live together without harm did not always work very smoothly".[27] Yet it was an attempt to find out to what extent the refinements of the human personality could find development when suitable atmosphere was created for that.

The inmates of Tolstoy Farm, as in the case of Phoenix Settlement strived together to live a life of simplicity, and self-denial. The routine, the living habits and the food ware kept as simple as it was humanly possible. All become labourers and did a great amount of manual work. They wore the clothes made of coarse materials like prisoners' uniform made by the women settlers. They survived on simple meals and used wooden spoons for eating. Gandhi's vision of "the life of the tiller of the soil" boiled down to every minute detail in the life of those in Tolstoy Farm. The whole pattern of life became an education for adults and children alike. For everyone that as experiment with truth to discover, through the educative process, the finest sensibilities of the human personality in the spirit of service.

3. Experiments in Champaran Schools

Champaran was the land of indigo plantations. Indigo plants were grown and indigo was manufactured in Champaran at great hardship to thousands of farmers. Champaran was situated in Bihar. Accepting the invitation of the Champaran farmers to see for himself the anguish of those indigo farmers, Gandhi set out for the place in 1917. Gandhi realised that Bihar was a place of strict untouchability and he was deeply pained. Gandhi was touched "by the humility, simplicity, goodness and extraordinary faith".[28] Of those farmers whose problems overwhelmed him. Gandhi's aim, first of all, was to thoroughly inquire into the condition of the Champaran farmers and understand their grievances against the indigo planters. Gandhi was faced with difficulties chiefly from the side of officials and indigo planters whose vested interest in the affairs was a significant factor. Gandhi was ordered to leave Champaran and was threatened with arrest. But the officials soon realised that people were with Gandhi, that he did not have any personal grievances but only wised to offer civil resistance to their orders. Gandhi recalls, "The people had for the moment lost all fear of punishment and yielded obedience to the power of love which their new friend exercised".[29] All that was inspite of the fact that no one in Champaran knew Gandhi except a few of his close associates who led him to the place. They did not know the Congress and no political work was done among them. Gandhi says, "yet they received me as though we had been age-long friends".[30] For Gandhi that meeting with the Champaran farmers was a face to face confrontation with God. Ahimsa and Truth. Gandhi was finally permitted by the Authorities to proceed with his inquiry and they promised him all the necessary help he needed for the inquiry. The first stage of Gandhi's mission in Champaran ended successfully.

Gandhi's attempts first of all was to educate not the Champaran farmers but his own friends who were involved in his work. They had a curious way of life. Each had a servant and a cook with a separate kitchen in which vegetarian or non-vegetarian meals were prepared. They most often had their dinner late at night. Things were so irregular that I subjected them to friendly scolding and ridicule. Finally it was decided that some radical changes be brought about in their mode of living. The servants were sent away; and the numerous kitchens were dispensed with. They agreed to have a regular hour for their meal. Since maintaining two kitchens both for vegetarian and non-vegetarian was expensive, it was decided to have only a common vegetarian kitchen. An insistence on simple meal was also accepted. Because of this it became possible for them to record the grievances of large crowds of people with considerable case and greater enthusiasm.

Gandhi's acquaintence with the problems of Bihar convinced him that changes of a permanent nature was not possible with out adequate village education. Ignorance and poverty reigned supreme everywhere. The workers led a pathetic life with no possibility to rise above and understand their true plight. Their children merely roamed about or worked in plantations just "for a couple of coppers a day".[31] Everybody toiled for a meagre wage and it was just a matter of existence for the workers in the plantation. Gandhi made his own plans to improve their lot. He opened primary schools in six villages. The poverty in those villages was so utter that no money could be raised for the purpose of establishing those schools. The only thing they could do was to contribute grain and other raw-materials.

It was difficult for Gandhi to provide teachers for those schools, especially when they would have to work on a minimum salary or without remuneration at all. Gandhi never liked the idea of employing just ordinary teachers for doing a work which he knew was crucial to the development of those villages. What they required was strong "moral fibre" and not so much literary qualification as Gandhi envisaged it. In response to a public appeal Gandhi issued, there came immense response to a public appeal Gandhi issued, there came immense response from various quarters to have teacher sent to champaran for the work. Since the focus of training was not literary talents, grammar, reading writing and arithmetics, Gandhi made it clear to the teachers the objectives that he himself had in mind. The focus had to be on cleanliness, essential moral habits and good manners. In the primary classes the rudiments of the languages and a knowledge of the numerals were thought essential.

Primary education could be only a beginning. The whole village was wanting in education in hygienic habits. Wherever Gandhi went he was confronted with dirt and filth to unbearable dimensions. The homes were kept most untidy, the lanes full of dirt, wells which were the nerve-centre of the village could be seen surrounded with mud and filth. Skin diseases were most common with elderly people. It was necessary, therefore,, to approach the problem of education from a larger viewpoint and involve themselves with the life of the villagers in its totality. With the help of a doctor from the Servants of India Society Gandhi embarked his work among villagers.

Education could not be conceived of as an isolated thing in Champaran. If education meant the welfare of the villagers it had to be integrated with health and sanitation. The group launched a medical help-drive in all the villages under the supervision of the doctor in the group to meet the medical needs of the villagers and ensure basic health in them. Self-help even in this regard was a thing unheard of among them. They were willing to do nothing to improve their health and surroundings. That lethargy, found in backward areas of this sort, was the result of a sense of resignation to the lot to which they are as if condemned. It was Gandhi's firm commitment to raise them from that utter disregard for their own welfare. The medical relief given to them was a simple affair : "Castor oil, quinine and sulphur oinment were the only drugs provided to the volunteers".[32]

Education through village sanitation was proved a difficult affair. The children were given instructions about cleanliness and general sanitation in classes. But the problems lay with adults, They were not willing to do any thing by themselves. Even field labourers were not willing to undertake cleaning up their surroundings. The volunteers, therefore, concentrated on the village an ideal place to live in: "They swept the roads and the courtyards, cleaned out the wells, filted up the pools nearby, and lovingly pursuaded the villagers to raise volunteers from among themselves".[33] It was more an effort to conscientise the villagers and train in them a fair degree of self-help and self-dignity which had to become a permanent character in them, if education had to be complete.

At several place the villagers frankly expressed their dislike for the work Gandhi did. That was simply to be expected because of the dire habits the villagers had formed by living under adverse conditions. Inspite of that it was possible for the volunteers in Champaran to touch the hearts of the villagers with their work in schools, sanitation work and medical relief. Gandhi wanted a permanent group of volunteers to carry on the work he had started in Champaran. But that did not materialise for want of people. The educational work became a part of Gandhi's experiment in that direction. That was an attempt to challenge the traditional mode of literary education by imparting to little children facts about things which hardly come under their usual, day-to-day experience. The work in Champaran was an example as to how problems in typical rural India could be dealt with. It required courage and determination on the part of Gandhi to employ quite untrained and unqualified hands to take up teaching and training the rural folk in a way that could be subject to ridicule. Gandhi was clear in his total vision in Champaran as at other place as to the values he wished to stress. There lay his success.

4. Nationalist Experiments in Education

Gandhi and the nationalist leaders in the Congress expressed grave concern over the deplorable condition of education in India during the pre-independence period. They felt that "the present system of education does not meet the requirements of the country in any shape or form".[34] The British introduced English with a view to getting their imperialist ends fulfilled and hence English education did not serve any major purpose. Gandhi asked students in the whole of India to think whether the education they got was useful for the realisation of their ideals and develop the inherent potentials in their personality or was it just a factory that produced potentials in their personality or was it just a factory that produced government servants and employees" in business offices. He asked, "Is the primary aim of your education to secure a mere job in a government department or other fields?"[35] English education, it was said, endeavoured to introduce us to the western sophistication under which western civilization itself was groaning. Gandhi asked students if they themselves wanted to receive such an education. They had to think several times before accepting such a sophistication and education that had the potential to destroy our values and our heritage. British education, he said, was planned without in the least taking into consideration India's economic progress. The money spent on primary education was sheer waste: "Education directors have agreed that today's system of primary education is a collossal loss".[36] The present system of education and the budgetary provisions made for that affect and becomes beneficial to only a small percent of the rural population.

The education that was imparted only covered one aspect, literacy. It never attempted to harmonise the child's personality, by achieving a proper integration of the training of the mind, body and spirit. Our villagers put in hard labour like animals and slaves. The education that was planned could not come down to their level and redeems them from that bondage to hard labour and poverty. "They have gone down to the level of animals without obtaining any help to develop their mind and spirit".[37] Education is schools and colleges looked upon with respect because such an education was totally alienated from manual work and physical labour. Since some form of exercise for the body was necessary schools introduced quite artificial and uninteresting physical training whole thing is ridiculous beyond words:.[38] Gandhi bewailed the condition of a man emerging out of present-day education who have absolutely no capacity for suffering and self-denial or even physical forebearance.

Gandhi felt that as a nation we are so backward in education, and we have great obligations to the nation in this regard. He therefore in all force recommended that education should be made self-supporting. In the July issue of *Harijan* (1937) Gandhi drew up his definition of education: "By education I mean allround drawing out of the best in child and man-baby, mind and spirit".[39] Literacy is not the end of education, not even the beginning. Gandhi could not accommodate the idea that literacy was essentially education. He wanted to begin the child's education by teaching it a useful handicraft and by enabling it to produce from the moment it begins its training. Thus every school could be made self-supporting.

Gandhi held that the highest development of the mind and the soul was possible under such a system of education. Every handicraft had to be taught not merely mechanically, but in a scientific manner providing the necessary intellectual stimulation. The method was adopted and tested out at several places wherever spinning and weaving were taught to workers. Gandhi taught sandal-making and spinning on these lines with good results. That method also included a knowledge of history and geography. It meant all-round development all-round economy.

In the course of a resolution passed at Haripura at the time of a crisis in the Congress ministry in U.P. and Bihar, the following resolution was adopted on the issue of national education. The Congress emphasised the importance of national education ever since 1906. Several educational institutions were established under its auspices during the non-cooperation movement. Congress attached the utmost importance to a proper organisation of mass education. It was convinced that all national progress ultimately depended on the objective, the content and the method of education that was provided to people. The existing system of education in India was provided to people. The existing sÿstem of education in India was admitted to have failed. It was therefore essential to build up a national education seeking new frontiers and covering the larger interests of the nation. Using the influence and authority the Congress exercised in state education, it had privilege to lay down the goals and principles necessary for a kind of education envisaged by it. It was therefore recommended to have a basic education imparted at the primary and secondary stages in accordance with the following principles: "1. Free and compulsory education should be provided for seven years on a nation-wide scale. 2. The medium of instruction must be the mother-tongue. 3. Throughout this period education should centre round some form of productive and manual work and other activities to be developed or training to be given should, as far as possible, be integrally related to the central handicraft chosen with due regard to the environment of the child".[40]

On the basis of that resolution it was recommended that All-India Education Board be formed to deal with that basic part of education. Dr. Zakir Hussain and Shri Aryanayakam were authorised by the Congress to take steps, under the guidance of Gandhi, to bring such a board into existence in order to work out a programme of basic national education.

Addressing the newly created National Education Board,

Gandhi developed and elucidated the meaning and objective of new education. Concerning the establishment of schools for basic primary education Gandhi said, "We have to make of this training school a school for winning freedom and for the solution of all our ills, of which the primary one is our communal troubles. And for this purpose we have to concentrate on non-violence".[41] Gandhi recalled that Hitler's and Musolini's schools accepted violence as their principle and for the Congress it was non-violence. We should have a non-violence approach to all our problems. Gandhi envisaged the new approach in which all the school subjects would have a non-violent colour : history, arithmetic, and science. Instead of history being a past history violent conflicts and wars, "the future history will be the history of man".[42] That could only be non-violent. Then we could concentrate not on urban but rural industries. Gandhi hoped that if we imparted education through those crafts, then we could bring about a true revolution.

5. Gujarat Vidyapeeth

It was a committed aim of Mahatma Gandhi and other nationalist leaders to evolve a system of education that would produce students who were not mere administrators and clerks but real servants of the people of the country. Such an education would generate in the students a love of the poor millions residing in the Indian villages. Such an education would compel them to be at the disposal of the rural masses for their upliftment and they would never find rest without achieving that aim. Such an education would foster in them not material freedom but spiritual freedom with all that go with such freedom.

In order to realise such an ideal in the field of education Gandhi founded the "National University of Gujarat' called 'Gujarat Vidyapeeth' at Ahmedabad in November 1920. All aspects of education embodied in the curriculum and the syllabus of the Vidyapeeth finally aimed at the unique ideal of achieving a united India shedding all the caste and communal differences. In one of the National Education Conferences held at the Vidyapeeth Gandhi said, "All those studying in national institutions and connected with them must do all the things that the country has to go through for the attainment of the Swaraj, so that they may be ready to offer themselves willing sacrifices when the time comes".[43]

The Vidyapeeth fostered a considerable number of ideals in relation to the Indian traditions. Greater importance came to be attached to the study of Asiatic culture than Western sciences. Efforts were made to commit the students to enquire into the vast treasures of Sanskrit, Persian, Pali and Arabic. These were supposed to contain great sources of strength and inspiration for the nation. The Vidyapeeth aimed at building a new culture based on the traditions of the past, in such a way as to ensure each component culture its legitimate place without seeking its destruction. According to Gandhi literary training, scholarly research, linguistic pursuits, the study of English, Sanskrit and fine arts had to be given importance in the Vidyapeeth but 'take a back seat'. The very motto of the Vidyapeeth is: 'That is knowledge which is designed for salvation'.[44] The educational institution symbolised the highly value-oriented Indian Vedic culture and education. Material freedom is included in the spiritual as the logical corollory. All knowledge taught and learned in the Vidyapeeth and other institutions should lead to such freedom. For this reason every sincere student becomes a satyagrahi and every satyagrahi naturally undergoes perfect education and the ideals of both become identified.

Addressing the students of Gujarat Vidyapeeth Gandhi said, "The only loving tie of service that can bind these villages to us is the spinning wheal".[45] Gandhi attached the greatest importance to the kind of national education that he wanted to impart in educational institutions. For him the education is not 'national' that does not take into account the starving millions of India and devices no means for their relief. He wanted the Vidyalaya to make people workers who would give themselves up for the villages. Gandhi gave weekly lectures at the Vidyapeeth and he essured personal attention to the students of Sabarmati Ashram and Gujarat Vidyapeeth. When Gandhi met the students he took pains to explain to them the Gita, the New Testament and the Ramayana of Tulsidas.

The students discussed various topics with him. Gandhi exhorted them to shed all fear and resist violence with all their might. During the Dandi march in 1930 the Vidyapeeth suspended all academic activities. The staff and the students offered their services as volunteers for the forthcoming Satyagraha struggle. They were given emergency training. The students were sent to the site of the satyagraha to do the necessary preparations and assist site of the satyagraha. Gandhi said, "I am sure that every national institution will copy the example of Gujarat Vidyapeeth."[46]

Gandhi was most satisfied, with the working of the Gujarat Vidyapeeth. He said, "In my opinion the Gujarat Vidyapeeth by its supreme sacrifice has more than justified its existence, the hopes entertained by its authors and grants made to it by donors".[47] Gandhi wanted other national institutions to copy the example of the Vidyapeeth in its example of sacrifice. National universities in the form of Vidyapeeths were also established in Bihar and Kashi to pursue the ideals of national education. The Vidyapeeth became the source of strength in Gandhi's fight against the evils of untouchability and communal disharmony. Education for him could not isolated from all these evils that ransacked society. For this reason Gandhi attached great significance to the Vidyapeeths as well-organised national institutions that stood for the nationalist ideals.

6. Wardha Education Conference

Gandhi's new approach to education became craft-centered and skill-based, developed against the background of the concrete needs of the country. The new conception was based on primarily the principle of Rousseau who said, "Do as much as possible of your teaching by doing".[48] The new conception was also based on the educational principles of

John Dewey (See pragmatism) who defines the school as a place "where experiments in life will be carried on where other experiments in life will be read about and told about because of their result".[49] Gandhi was familiar with the pragmatist educational principle of "learning by doing or learning through one's experience".[50] Gandhi was thoroughly misunderstood as many thought that he was recommending sheer manual work as an alternative to all other studies. It became therefore a responsibility for him to discuss at length matters pertaining to his new concept of basic education.

Gandhi wrote in the *Harijan* answering a question as to what happens when a child may have no aptitude for weaving and may have it for something else. "Quite so. Then we will teach him some other craft. But you must know that one school will not teach many crafts. The idea is that we should have one teacher for twenty-five boys, and you may have as many classes or schools of twenty-five boys as you have the teachers available, and have each one these schools specialising in a separate craft-carpentry, smithy, tanning or shoe-making. Only you must bear in mind the fact that you develop the child's mind through each of these crafts".[51] Gandhi recommended a primary education covering a period of seven years in which all the subjects except English, and a vocation are taught. Such an education should be conceived of as self-supporting.

A session of the Educational conference commenced at Wardha on 22nd October 1937. Several distinguished members of the Congress including Dr. Zakir Hussain and Aryanayakam participated at the conference. Gandhi presented a review of his entire scheme of education in his presidential address at the conference. Gandhi claimed the scheme of education to be fresh and new, although based on his experiences. Gandhi's ideas covered education at the primary and college levels; he held, "but me will have to give special consideration to primary education".[52] He stressed the role it primary education that included in his conception the upper middle and the secondary also, because he had grave concerns for the people in Indian villages, and primary education pertained to the villages more. He said that he was convinced of the need to thus combine the primary and secondary education in just one stream to meet the requirements of rural conditions. Such a national scheme of education as what the conference had in mind had to be primarily for the villages. Gandhi tried to drive home the need for focussing on primary education and then easy solutions, he thought, could be arrived at for college education.

Gandhi bewailed the state of primary education as, he thought that it was "positively harmful".[53] The boys were alienated from their parents and from their traditional occupations. Education made them conducive only to picking up bad habits. The sole remedy lay in educating them by means of vocation or manual training. Gandhi had the background for vocational training of some sort on the Tolstoy Farm in South Africa. "The whole education should be imparted through some handicrafts or industry".[54] Such occupational and craft centered training of the Middle Ages did not serve any concrete educational purpose. The development of the intellect was never thought of.

Gandhi's scheme meant the teaching of the whole art and science as a craft and imparting the whole education as a practical training with orientations for adequate intellectual stimulation. Spinning becomes the starting point of a variety of subjects with elementary knowledge in them. "Spinning presupposes the imparting of knowledge of the various varieties of cotton, different soils in different provinces of India, the history of the rein of the handicraft, its political reasons, which will include the history of the British rule in India, knowledge of arithmetic and so on".[55] Gandhi was convinced that spinning was the only practical solution to out problem, considering the grave economic situation that prevailed in India. Gandhi wanted primary education to centre around the 'takli'. During the first year everything could be taught through spinning/ In the second year other processes could be introduced side by side. Gandhi envisaged that the cloth produced by children could meet the requirements of parents themselves. It was seven year course leading to a practical knowledge of spinning, weaving, dyeing and designing. This primary education included also "principles of sanitation, hygiene, nutrition, of doing their own work, helping parents at home etc".[56] There would also be compulsory physical education through musical drill.

The impact of that training, Gandhi explained, was enormous. "While the child will be encouraged to spin and help his parents with agricultural jobs, he will also be made to feel that he does not belong only to his parents, but also to the village and to the country, and that he must make some returns to them".[57] Children would be made self-confident by their paying for their own education by their own labour. Gandhi calls this his practical religion, the religion of self-help. Making education self-supporting was the true test of its efficiency. Gandhi failed to understand why there should be unemployment of graduate students. College education was thus fairly disappointing.

Gandhi concluded the address by inviting the attention of the conference to the fundamentals of self-supporting education: "If we want to eliminate the communal strite, we must start on the education I have now adumbrated. That plan springs out of non-violence".[58] Our students are to be made true representatives of our culture and our civilization, of the true genius of our nation. Gandhi stressed the point that the whole western civilization and its achievements were based on force and violence. India could not think of in terms of violence and exploitation as the West did, and India had no alternative other than the plan of education based on non-violence.

Dr. Zakir Hussain making observations on Gandhi's plan of education drew Gandhi's attention to the fact that the Gandhian scheme was not original in concept. The same method was called Project Method in America and Complex Method in Russia. The scheme was a failure in both the places due to several practical difficulties. Dr. Zakir

Hussain and others reiterated to Gandhi's concept of self-supporting education: "Teachers may become slave-drivers and exploit the labour of poor boys".[59] All the expenses in education could be thought of as borne by the nation. It was pointed out that manual work was alright upto an extent, but the fact that this was an age of machines had to be remembered in that connection. A boycott of all the foreign-made goods and an embargo on all machine-made things would be an impossibility. Many thought that it was idle and improper to make education self-supporting.

The conference was entrusted with the task of reviewing the proposals made in Gandhi's basic scheme. The proposals contained the following : 1. English, having been made the medium of instruction in universities, has created gap between the highly educated few and the uneducated many. It has prevented from knowledge from percolating to the masses. The absence of vocational training has made the educated class unfit for productive work and has harmed them physically. 2. The course of primary education would be extended at to seven years and should include the general knowledge gained upto the matriculation standard except English, and a vocation. 3. All the training should as far as possible be centered around a craft for the all-round development of the boys and girls. This primary education should equip the boys and girls to earn their bread and the state should guarantee employment in the vocations they are trained in. 4. Higher education should be left to private enterprise, and for the meeting of national requirements. The state universities should be purely examining bodies, self-supporting through the fees charged for the examinations. Preparing and approving courses of studies in various departments will remain the business of the university. The state will cost nothing for the running of the university except looking after a central education department.

The committee drew its draft resolutions and passed them the following day: 1. Free and compulsory education be provided for seven years on a nation-wide scale. 2. The medium of instruction should be in the mother-tongue. 3.

The process of education throughout this period should be centered around some form of manual of productive work and all other abilities to be developed and be integrated to the craft. 4. This system of education expected in course time to cover the remuneration of teachers. These draft resolutions became central to what we know as the Wardha Scheme.

References

1. *Towards New Education*, p.85
2. Buck, Pearl, in *Profiles of Gandhi*, p.104
3. *An autobiography*, p.164
4. Thekkinedath, J., *Love of Neighbour*, p.68.
5. Diwakar, R.R., quoted in Thekkinedath, p.68.
6. *Young India*, 11 October 1928.
7. *Harijan*, 14 October 1939.
8. *An autobiography*, p.41
9. Holmes, J., in *Profiles of Gandhi*, p.126.
10. *Harijan*, 10 March 1946.
11. *An Autobiography*, p.255.
12. Tendulkar D.G., *Mahatma*. Vol. 4, p.218.
13. *An Autobiography*, p.224.
14. Ibid p.224.
15. Ibid p.226.
16. Tendulkar, D.G., *Mahatma*, Vol.1, p.68.
17. *An Autobiography*, p.228.
18. Tendulkar, D.G., *Mahatma*, Vol.1, p.68.
19. *An autobiography*, p. 247.
20 Ibid p.249.
21. *Mahatma*, Vol. 1, p.118.
22. *An Autobiography*, p.251.
23. *Mahatma*, Vol.1, p.119.
24. *An Autobiography*, p. 253.
25. *Harijan*. Sept. 1937.
26. *Mahatma*, Vol.1, p.119.
27. Ibid, p.119.
28. ,*An Autobiography*, p. 907.
29. Ibid p. 910.

30. Ibid p. 911
31. Ibid p. 316
32. Ibid p. 318
33. Ibid p. 318.
34. *Mahatma*, Vol.4, p.197.
35. *Towards New Education*, p.7.
36. *Basic Education* p.79.
37. Ibid p.11
38. Ibid p.12.
39. *Harijan*. July 1937.
40. *Mahatma*, Vol. 4, p.225.
41. Ibid p.246
42. Ibid p.246.
43. Ibid Vol.3, p.3.
44. *To The Students* p. 204.
45. *Mahatma*, Vol.3, p. 229.
46. Ibid Vol.3. p.5.
47. *To the Students* p.203.
48. Rousseau, In Tendulkar Vol.4.p.186.
49. Dewey , In Bhatia p.109.
50. Ibid p.99.
51. *Mahatma*, Vol. 4. p.189.
52. Ibid p.190
53. Ibid p.191
54. Ibid p.191
55. Ibid p.191
56. Ibid p.192
57. Ibid p.192
58. Ibid p.193
59. Ibid p.194

5

EDUCATIONAL IDEALISM AND PRAGMATISM IN GANDHI

1. Aspects of Educational Idealism

Idealism as a school of philosophical thinking can be traced back to as early as Plato whose classical thinking in absolute idealism is still considered the remote foundations of the idealist school. The very term 'idealism' goes back to Plato who proposed a world of 'absolute ideas' as the basis of his philosophical trends. This very absolutism that Plato once held has upto this day remained one of the most fundamental doctrines of idealism: "The conception of absolute or intrinsic values forms a fundamental principle of the idealist school".[1] Idealism leans heavily on the spiritual nature of the universe and holds that the mental or the spiritual is more real than the material. The material universe for them is only a reflection of the spiritual substantiality behind everything. In other words the material or the physical universe is only an incomplete and partial representation of what they called reality in existence.

Since reality is spiritual in essence some idealists do not even consider the material world in any way real. The ancient Indian schools of thinking covered under the Vedas and reinterpreted under the 'six systems of thought' often come to the conclusion that the material world is unreal or *maya*. These school may be called idealistic from these viewpoints. Since reality thus is spiritual "it is to be found in man's mind than in nature".[2] This idea is often carried to the extreme by several idealists who held that "man creates the spiritual and cultural environment and values as represented by morality, art knowledge and culture by controlling and changing the physical environment".[3] All idealists do not stress man's role as the creator of values related to art, morality and religion. Instead God as the Supreme Source of all that is spiritual whose reflection the material is, controls everything that part of reality. All values originate from this source and are therefore absolute in nature. This absolute characteristic of values is most fundamental to idealism.

While Plato, Descartes, Hegal, Kant and Spinoza were some of the leading exponents of idealism the West Plato, Socrates, and those of the traditional schools of education are considered the classical educational idealists. The spiritual nature of idealism and directions from that basis lead to the ultimate values of Truth, Goodness and Beauty. These concepts which are absolute in themselves constitute the three bulwarks of educational idealism. These values form the Supreme Good and are realised in God in all their absoluteness : God is Truth, God is Goodness and God is Beauty. The same is the supreme concepts of 'Satyam, Sivam, Sundaram' in the Indian philosophical thoughts : the highest good for man to achieve, the content of self-realisation. Coming down to the very bottom of these values, they are relatively realised in individual things and experience within the framework of this world.

The idealist curriculum is an embodiment of these supreme values of truth, goodness and beauty. The supreme value of truth is aimed at for realisation and apprehension in intellectual education which includes languages, literature, science, mathematical history, geography etc. In classical idealistic education one of the primary aims of teaching these is to provide 'mental discipline'. These are supposed to discipline the mind of the student in the rigorous process of learning. The values of goodness is aimed at for realisation in moral education which includes ethics and religion. These contribute primarily to the formation of the character. It is the value of beauty that is aimed at for realisation in aesthetic education which includes art, poetry, music, sculpture and handicrafts. Idealism conceives of a teacher-centered education as contrasted to the more modern child-centered, or life-centered education. In ancient Indian system of education too we have found that a heavily teacher-centered education prevailed. The teacher is not a passive onlooker but "he guides, directs, controls and suggests".[4] By organising himself this way the teacher idealises the the student's learning environment to expand the scope of the students' mental experiences. Curriculum consequently reflects the experience of the whole human race reduced systematically to classified knowledge which we know as subjects today.

2. Idealism, the Foundation of Gandhian Thoughts

Indian philosophy and religious thoughts constitute the background of the idealist framework of Gandhi in his attitudes towards education. In Gandhi we find an educational eclecticism of a characteristic type in which idealism, naturalism and pragmatism have found a place. Gandhi's aim was not to develop a professed school or tenet of philosophy. He was responding, in his own characteristic manner, to the educational needs of his time and he attempted at the same time to evolve a workable system to meet this need and to develop a rationale necessary for such a system. Idealism became the very foundation of the Gandhian system of education into which other tenets of thoughts have also found their way.

Will Durant says, "Gandhi is above all an idealist, not realist; he leaps far ahead in the moral consciousness of humanity"[5]. Gandhi's attempt was not merely to discover or propose passing and temporary solutions to problems of education; instead he tried to cross the limits of traditional thinking and to lead education to permanent and lasting values and principles through his idealistic thoughts. Bhatia says, "Gandhi was an idealist to the core. He has stressed the dignity of man and the significance of value in life like an idealistic thinker".[6] He possessed the pervasiveness, the depth of vision and the comprehensiveness of an idealist in his attitude towards education.

As an idealist Gandhi's depth of vision in education and in life takes him to ultimate values. No educationist in history dealing with practical problems of gigantic dimensions could so daringly fix his feet so well in God and spiritual values and permeate the entire scheme of education with these values. Luis Fischer says "Gandhi faced each mornings issues in the light of eternal and universal values".[7] He was not the least embarrassed to defend his moral and spiritual foundations in a more materialistic world of twentieth century which wanted education nothing to do with the world of religion and spirituality. For Gandhi the values related to the ultimate goals of education are absolute and unchanging. Man is expected to understand, accept and live these values to the best of his ability. Man's conscience is to be shaped accordingly, and not to shape the values to the satisfaction of the individual's relative conscience. Donald Harrington remarks,"All the questions that were asked he answered easily and spontaneously as from an inexhaustible wealth of spiritual assurance".[8] Gandhi wanted education to develop this spiritual assurance by shaping the individual's conscience in the practice of the values related to the ultimate goals of life and education.

Like that of any idealist Gandhi's was a search for truth, goodness and beauty. Of all these Gandhi found Truth to be the most adequate synonymn of God. If it is possible for the human tongue to give the fullest description of God, I have come to the conclusion that for myself, God is Truth".[9] It is in the description of truth that we find the idealist in Gandhi assuming fullest expression: "Truth is not......... only the relative truth of our conception, but the Absolute Truth, the Eternal principle, that God".[10] Gandhi's life and preoccupation with truth becomes a saga of life. Edgar P, Snow says, "He attained a genius with truth and became part of its immortality. He concentrated on eternal truths between men to the exclusion of everything else".[11] Gandhi's search for truth penetrated the barriers of human community. Bhatia says "Gandhiji envisaged a universal community of free persons without artificial barriers of caste, creed, wealth and power".[12] It was possible for him to bring down his universal values to their immediate applications. Gandhi did not wish to leave gap between his philosophy of life and his educational values. Every little educational practice springing from a practical individual, social or national problem he immediately related to the foundations of his ultimate system of values.

Like any idealist, again, Gandhi kept his eyes fixed on the ultimate goal of self-realisation, or attainment of God: "Gandhiji was a practical, socially determined idealist and that his greatest idealistic thought was that Truth which is God, has to be sought, has to be worked for in our daily life within a certain social order"[13]. The task of education in this sense is to keep this ideal constantly in the minds of the students, relate the personal, social and national dimensions of this principle and relate these immediate goals to the ultimate goal of self-realisation. Education thus for Gandhi becomes an enduring search for God in the idealist sense and the final self-realisation. Richard B.Gregg says. "The result of his incessant experiments was an unshakable belief and trust in God, and in the power of God acting in all men, and hence in the power of non-violence".[14] Gandhi himself was most outspoken, accurate and single-minded in this connection: "What I want to achieve is self-realisation, to see God face to face, to attain moksha".[15] The student as the brahmachari is an aspirant of moksha. Gandhi finds great depth in the word 'brahmachari' with reference to the student and reminds them of every aspect of this duty of being a 'brahmachari'. Gandhi says, "Brahmachari is a word better than student. Brahmachari means an intense seeker of Brahman".[16] Gandhi considers purity of life in thought and deed synonymous with the life of a brahmachari and this links education with self-realisation: "Purity in the life of an individual is the quintessence of an effective education".[17] Self-realisation as the movement of the self towards God in the attainment of His knowledge makes education the very central process in the life of an individual. Self-realisation thus becomes an experience conditioned also by the process of adequate education.

Together with the concepts of absolute values and truth, and self-realisation goes what we may call the concept of universality. All the while the modern pragmatists and materialists tend to speak about individuality, particularity and concreteness, idealist educationists are full of awe for the concept of universality in everything that they touch: "Gandhi faced each morning's issues in the light of eternal and universal values".[18] As Ved Metha says, "Gandhi held that his ideas were universally true".[19] On the basis of the spiritual principles governing reality, concepts are held to be universal entities that represent the real. For the realist the material world is the real and these concepts are universal varities of the real objects in the world and the concepts exist in the minds of man. For the idealist the spiritual is the only real and the material is *maya* or unreal that has no substantiality of its own. Gandhi's sense of universality crossed the bounds of values and concepts, and reached the heights of human brotherhood: "Gandhi envisaged a universal community of free persons without the artificial barriers of caste, creed, wealth and power".[20] All Gandhian efforts and directions for world peace stem from this universal sense of brotherhood and the love of neighbour: "To see the universal and all pervading spirit of Truth face to face one must be able to love the meanest of creation as oneself".[21] Chester Bowler writes"Gandhi held while in South Africa that members of the Indian minority must respect their white neighbours·as fellow human beings even while opposing their unjust discriminatory laws".[22] Gandhi's sense of universal love and brotherhood crossec the bounds of all forms rivalries : Personal, social or na tional. The idealistic basis provided Gandhi the firmest reli gious convictions that no exponent of more modern phi losophies is capable of. This universal brotherhood enable

Gandhi to radiate his influence to the far ends of a disunited country and to every corner of a divided world.

Within the idealistic framework Gandhi envisaged a spiritual society based on the concept of the unity and oneness of God: "Gandhiji was a practical, socially determined idealist for whom Truth, which is God, has to be sought ...... within a certain social order".[23] This social order Gandhi conceived of was a "spiritual society based on the supreme principles of truth, love, non-violence and justice".[24] Gandhian education cannot think of a social order which does not accept and live for God. An education which alienates society from God and the way of Truth, love and ahimsa is not worthy of its name. Right from the decision of the goals of education upto the success of the system depends on the spiritual basis which education is capable of providing to society. Gandhi writes, "I do not recoginse any God other than the one who dwells in the hearts of dumb millions. I worship God who is Truth, or Truth which is God through the service of these millions".[25] It is the power of this divinity or truth that links the millions of individuals into the formation of such a society.

Gandhi's spiritual society functions on the strength drawn from what he calls soul-force. This is a great Gandhian Principle Soul-force is the power of the divinity working in the spirits of the individuals. It is truth and love that binds this spiritual society under the one Divinity. The soul-force for Gandhi was capable of generating immense strength. This is the dynamism that functions in Satyagraha as the unifying and enduring force. Edmond Taylor speaks of "soul-force as the central energy of Satyagraha".[26] Education through its varied processes and learning experiences awakens the souls of individuals and thereby enlivens the soul-force working as the dynamism behind this Spiritual Society. The inner voice of truth and ahimsa enlivens this Soul-force further and strengthens the spiritual society. Concrete religious experiences arising from adequate educational background "should radiate from the individual the attitudes of love and service".[27] According to Gandhi the principal factor that functions behind the existence of such billions of people on earth is the spiritual strength based on the spiritual nature of human society: "The fundamental principle of existence is not the power of weapons, but the force of love and truth".[28] It is this force and not the power of weapons that Gandhi wants to rule his swaraj. For Gandhi one and the same principle governs very existence of mankind as well as the unity of humanity. That is the principle of love.

Idealism in education lays heavy emphasis on the development of the faculties of the mind more than anything else. Keeping intellectual development in focus they organised education on the basis of classified knowledge both for the content and the experience of education. This knowledge represented the total experience of the human race presented to the individual in the form of systematic subjects. The same mental development was the aim in the teaching of mathematics or languages, especially classical languages such as Latin or Greek in the West.

Gandhian idealism took up a different direction. Mental development was the Gandhian ideal too but with a major difference. Mental development, especially the disciplining of the mind aimed more at pure intellectual orientation and for its own sake and only in the case of highly God-centered idealists this training was immediately directed and channelled to the training of the spirit and the formation of the spiritual personality. For Gandhi the kind of mental development education was expected to cater for, directly and solely aimed at the formation of the individual's spiritual personality and the formation of the general character. In other words Gandhi made even knowledge and emotions subservient to his more ultimate goal: "Our creed was devotion to truth; and our business was the search for and insistence on truth".[29] He further says, "To develop the spirit is to build the character and to enable one to work towards a knowledge of God and self-realisation".[30] This mode of thinking makes Gandhi an idealist to the very core and we find the fullest meaning of the Gandhian position that the ultimate goal of life and education need to be one and the same.

Gandhian idealism penetrates the very core of Gandhian education. The very first aspect that required consideration in the present chapter has been thus, the spiritual basis of education and the spiritual orientations of Gandhian thoughts. Gandhi cannot think of any aspect of life in any way separated from life's ultimate goal : self-realisation and attainment, vision, of God. The greatest achievement of Gandhi in this regard was the closeness between his idealism and thoughts and the down-to-earth life that he recommended for his millions. There were absolutely no compromises for anybody so far as the Gandhian spiritual and moral orientation were concerned. Gandhi's idealism did not stop half-way through on and unrealistic platform of material reality such as the human mind being the sole seat of spiritual experiences; instead he leads us right up to the supreme values of truth, goodness and beauty, and to the vision of God Himself.

3. Gandhian Idealism and Educational Practices

It is fundamental to idealism that the human mind is educated to generate experiences in the process of leading the mind to greater maturity and perfection. Perfection is an important term in the context of educational idealism. The human mind is created to arrive at a level of perfection envisaged or planned by its creator. The duty of education is to explore the possibilities of enhancing the individual's perfection and provide the conditions necessary for the realisation of it. When Gandhi introduced the craft system it was designed to educate "the whole man : mind, body and soul". The craft he thought would enable the highest form of education of the mind and the soul. Gandhi says, "Man is not sheer intellect, animal body, heart or soul. To create a whole and integral man a suitable and perfect integration of these is required. This exactly is the essence of education".[31] He calls craft-centered education as "the education of the brain by the use of the hands".[32] The craft puts the individual's mind into productive work and sets a movement in the line of the idealistic perfection.

Gandhi saw the craft as the very centre of early education around which other subjects and experiences were to be provided. For Gandhi craft was "the meeting point of both physical and social environment represented by such subjects as general sciences, social sciences, and creative and expressional arts".[33] Like a true idealist Gandhi attaches the greatest spiritual significance to craft. The craft is seen as the starting point, again, of experience that would lead to the contemplation of truth and beauty. Dealing with the practical situations and problems that would arise from the handicraft the individual raises his mind in a variety of ways to the contemplation of the divine values permeating life's activities. Gandhian education provides opportunities of physical and intellectual nature for developing experiences of this kind that would in turn lead to mind in steps to the idealistic perfection in truth, love and beauty. The whole education becomes a chain of such experiences beauty. The whole education becomes a chain of such experiences towards the perfection of the individual's character.

Idealistic education puts increasing stress on the dignity of the human personality with reference to the educational experiences that are provided. Gandhi writes, "If teachers aim at developing the descriminative powers of the boys and girls under them, they will continually foster their reasoning capacity and enable them to think for themselves".[34] the dignity of personality in the Gandhian sense consists primarily in being able to think for oneself and become physically, emotionally and spiritually independent. Chester Bowles writes, "He conceived of Sevagram as a place where peace is natural and human dignity is fully recognised. Above all human labour has become dignified and creative".[35] Gandhi was throughout conscious of this dignity of the human individual. He believed as he professed that the logical finale of this dignity of human being lies in his communion with society through service and love of neighbour, and in his communion with God in prayer.

Gandhi exhorts students to be independent in their thinking, and enhance the powers of the human soul. This is thought of as the foundation of the freedom that Gandhi envisages. Education should do everything at its disposal to secure this freedom for the individual by providing, again, the necessary experiences. Gandhi writes, "Experience of the Soul is the richest and the only one that helps our development".[36] Gandhi proposes fearlessness to be the corner-stone of the freedom of mind that the student should secure for himself. Gandhi said to students, "We live in constant fear. We fear spiritual dependency just as we fear the worldly power and authority .... We fear worldly forces. By doing that we are causing harm to ourselves and to them .... ".[37] Gandhi made it very clear that we should have absolutely no fear other than the fear of God. This fearlessness he proposes to be the foundation of the freedom of spirit, dignity of human personality and the integrity of the mind that education should nurture in the individual.

Gandhi constantly referred back to the ancient Vedic education and the ashram type of education that prevailed in the *gurukula*. The *gurukula* education was highly teacher-centered in theory and practice. The dignity, the honour, the respect and the authority that the teacher or the *guru* commanded contributed to the success of the great spiritual basis that Vedic education established and the character formation that was achieved by the students. That was exactly the western idealistic position too. Traditional western idealism was highly teacher-centered rather than child or life-centered. Just as the idealist wants "fine roses" from the garden of education Gandhi is not content with anything less than the finest roses of truth, love and ahimsa. Like any true idealist Gandhi is not satisfied with anything less than God himself as Supreme Perfection in Truth and love. The teacher's authority becomes a means , a powerful means in the realisation of this supreme perfection in students.

Genuine freedom for Gandhi came from self-discipline. John Holmes remarks, "Gandhi had a disciplined process of putting his soul to work, with results that were patent to all, but none the less hard to understand".[38] This self-discipline that he exercised in every detail of his life has everything to do with his spiritual orientations and proved to be one of his most powerful weapons in the practice of truth and ahimsa. Albert Einstein wrote, "Gandhi's work on behalf of India's liberation is the living testimony to the fact that man's will, sustained by an indomintable conviction, is more powerful than material forces that seem unsurmountable"[39] Gandhi's idealistic vision of life and education enabled him to present to education a world of "high thinking and simple living" adequate for a country like India.

4. Aspects of Educational Pragmatism

Pragmatism is a twentieth century way of thinking by those who developed an aversion for everything that is supposed to be eternal, universal, absolute or permanent. These conceptions most characteristic of idealists were looked upon with contempt by a group of thinkers especially in the United States. The American way of life, their most practical and life problems against the red Indians and those problems that arose from the multiracial background resulted from the colonial settlements, contributed to a characteristic American way of thinking. To think practically and to care for only practical problems became their moto. That become a matter of survival for the Americans. The only concern naturally became success in practical life against soaring problems of modern life. This gave way to a new mode of thinking known as pragmatism.

In order to achieve practical success in life, pragmatic thinkers had to say good-bye to everything that was supposed to be absolute and unchanging. Life for them meant 'life-experiences': "Consequently, they built up a philosophy of life through experiences instead of being guided by established theories".[40] They believed that no form of fixed, established theories and attitudes to life could solve the constantly noval problems that they faced in life. Pragmatism is coexistent with utilitarian philosophy that was the heritage of the Victorian England. For the utilitarians whom Charles Dickens attempted to depict in his famous novels, the only value in life was utility or practical usefulness. Every aspect of life that included even religion and education, not to speak of social and business affairs, was judged from the utility viewpoint.

The pragmatists with this background developed their fundamental principle in life : truth is pragmatic and useful i.e. only whatever value or experience is pragmatic and useful in life, that alone is true. The validity of even truth is judged by the criterion of usefulness by the pragmatist. It is not any abstract truth or any other value that guides the pragmatist but the experiences of life as they are created and re-created by man himself. Pragmatism has dedicated itself to the progress of humanity as whole and of the individual in particular. Because of this it has become humanistic. In this humanistic development man creates his own values rather than following any ready-made values. In this process everything becomes relative. "All systems of ideas are relative to the situation in which they arise and the personalities they satisfy, and are subject to continuous verification by consequences".[41] All these amount to the power of man to shape his environment.

Pragmatism became the most outstanding philosophy of education in twentieth century. The exponents of this theory, William James, Schiller and John Dewey became most well-read educationists of the day. While William James is known for his pragmatic philosophy, Dewey is the most acclaimed educationist whose theory of education borne out of the remarkable experiments he conducted, has been followed world over. Pragmatic philosophy is considered 'life-centered' as against Naturalism which is child-centered and idealism that is teacher-centered. Pragmatism is closer to one tenet idealism in that it considers values as man-created and are the result of man's experimentation with life through life-experiences. Pragmatism is closer to naturalism where it stresses the role of the child whose potentials for creative and productive thinking and work are the bases of education.

Education does not begin with any a priori, traditional theory or values. The principles and goals of education are developed and shaped in the light of experiences. In other words education should evolve no fixed system to be applied for all ages. William James says, "philosophy is the theory of education in its most general phases".[42] As experiences are evolved so are the philosophies and the theories generated. Life-experiences are therefore central to pragmatic education, most decisive in the goals, methods and content of education. The starting point of all education are the instincts and innate powers of the child which constitute the material for the development of educational experiences. Dewey himself stresses "the development of all those capacities in the individual which will enable him to control his environment and fulfil his possibilities".[43] The child lives in society; he lives also for the community in which he lives. Hence the potentials of the child are to be developed for the sake of and with reference to this society. This process of preparing the child for a life in society through the provision of adequate life-experiences is what he calls education.

The pragmatists lay great emphasis on life-experiences that are generated on the basis of concrete involvements, manipulatory situations and practical work experiences. According to Dewey, "the best and the deepest moral training is precisely that which one gets through having to enter into proper relations with others in a unity of work and thought".[44] Dewey envisages concrete problem solving situations in which not only the training of the intellect takes place but also deep moral education. Moral education for Dewey is only an application of more integral social attitudes. Work experiences are so important in Dewey's conception. Gandhi read and appreciated Dewey for his great practical orientations in education. Dewey developed his 'Project Method' as a scientific way of providing work experiences to the learner and employing the mind of the individual in contact with the world of objective reality to generate self-activity and interest in problem-solving.

5. Pragmatism in Gandhian Education -1

The idealist in Gandhi ceases to be when it comes to a whole range of problems related to the practice of education and the provision of life-experiences, and the pragmatist in him begins taking shape. In Gandhi we find a very rare synthesis of idealism and pragmatism with reference to his educational thinking. Pragmatism attempted to exploit the potentials of human action to the Maximum extent and Gandhi viewed human action as a field of experimentation for the discovery of his spiritual energy on the one hand, and humanitarian benefits on the other: "He discovered a new dimension of action; he split the social atom and found a new source of energy".[45] Gandhi realised the great potentials they lay hidden in the human mind and he recognised education as the number one field for the tapping of these resources. Pragmatic education is known for its life-orientations and life-centredness. Gandhi too was not willing to begin from any apriori foundations. He constantly put every thing to experimentation like a pragmatist. Erikson recognises this great aspect of life in him when he says, "Gandhi's personality is one of minute and concrete interplay, perfect in every step of the long life of a craftsman like a series of 'experiments' with historical actuality in all political and existential aspects".[46] Gandhi's concentration on the minute details of life became the basis for the analysis he undertook of life and its experiences in order to use every bit of energy for the purposes he had in mind. He wanted education to scrutinise everything at its disposal to provide these detailed life-experiences. The major difference was that Gandhi wanted education to do this also keeping in mind more ultimate ideals, while the pragmatists stopped with purely humanitarian considerations. Luis Fischer writes that Gandhi wanted everyone "to share the experiences of life freely and fully".[47] Unless education was capable of providing scope for sharing these experiences in everything that it does instead of "presenting students with facts", education was not bound to succeed in its mission.

Gandhi wanted education to centre these experiences around the child and see things from his point of view. For this reason Gandhi is also called an educational naturalist, for, Naturalists advocate child-centred education. Gandhi's concept in this regard was a departure from his idealistic tradition. He always felt closer to children as his Autobiography proves. With the most austere and serious sentiments of a rishi as his basic demeanour, Gandhi often felt light-hearted in the company of others: "The ashram was not a dull community; he made eyes at the little children, provoked adults to laughter and joked with all and sundry visitors".[48] Everyone who visited him felt most at home. This homeliness and feeling at ease in his presence was noted by Indians and foreigners alike who had the privilege to be in his presence constantly: "Gandhi retained their (the British) respect, often their love through his softness, tenderness and patience".[49] This basic Gandhian attitude was complementary to all that strict and penitential personality that Gandhi was. Jo Davidson remarked on one occasion with Gandhi, "what a homely man this is;".[50] Gandhi regarded personal relationships as a most precious component of life-experiences : "He was interested in exchange of views, but much more in establishment of personal relationships".[51] Gandhi's personality radiated on attitude that became an experience itself for those who came in contact with him. John Holmes writes "To see and talk with Gandhi, even for a few hurried moments, was to be overwhelmingly impressed by the gentleness of the man, together with his dignity and authority".[52] Gandhi taught these very simple principle of human relationships and wanted these to become part of the system he wished to develop.

In his speeches to students and educationists Gandhi never spared energy to stress the need for deep and harmonious experiences from his pragmatic attitudes. Gandhi says, "I request teachers to train their hearts and deep close contact with their students. Unless teachers are willing to spend their extra hours with students, they will not be able to do much".[53] Education should go a long way in helping students derive great benefits from their social environment. They are to be taught to develop their personal relation ships to learn to go out of themselves in an attitude of love and service. Education keeping aside its tough-core theory and philosophies, should lead students to develop their humanistic attitudes in an attempt to exploit their dynamism for the greater good of themselves and society: "If your education is solid, then it should permeate to the neighbourhood and exercise its influence".[54] The Gandhian stress on the provision of life-experiences includes a whole rages of attitudes that education can take care of.

Against the abstractions of idealism, pragmatism wanted education to provide experiences through concrete involvement and work. This came to be known as work-experience or project method of learning. Work-experience became the foundation of Gandhian education at all levels, especially at the early phases. Gandhi developed what was called Basic Education with work-experience at the core: "We believe that one of the most valuable legacies that he has left to posterity is his educational teachings crystallised in the basic scheme of education and his diverse addresses".[55] Gandhi kept work-experience in focus wherever he imparted training, especially in the Phoenix Settlement, at the Tolstoy Farm and at the Sabarmati Ashram. Gandhi chose a craft of one kind or other to provide experiences of the concrete type around which everything else could be taught: "Craft is a meeting point of both physical and social environment represented by such subjects as general science, social sciences, and creative and experimental arts".[56] Gandhi envisages the teaching of all subjects through the medium of and starting from the craft. Like a pragmatist Gandhi believed that craft enables the cultivation of a dynamic and adaptable mind which will be in a position to face the problems of practical life, in the case of India the problems especially of life in villages. Gandhi writes, "There is no end to the amount of knowledge that can be communicated through the medium of the spinning wheal".[57] Again he says, "The teacher should teach all these using his own mental ability and power of vision through the medium of the craft and through oral instructions".[58]

The craft will help the creation of new life-situations since the craft is closely related to the individual and social environment in which the student lives. The craft becomes "purposeful learning" in the pragmatic sense because there in takes place a combination of knowledge, skill and experiences of different kinds that education can intelligently attach to the craft and the curriculum. Gandhi says, "We will introduce the complete man in the student through the scientific teaching of a skill in the school".[59] Learning would thus become an integrated affair, it takes place through a process of integration between the various facts of life-experiences emanating from the teaching of the craft. This integration of experiences in a purposeful manner becomes possible only if there takes place a correlation between the knowledge and the activity undertaken. While at the lower level this activity can be exclusively a craft, at the higher levels of education, especially in higher education this amounts to any correlated work-experience or socially useful and productive activity that students concerned will be directed to undertake.

Another important perspective that shows the pragmatism in Gandhi is the concept of usefulness. Utility of goals, methods, curriculum and content of education constitutes an important principle for the pragmatist. Gandhi was powerful advocate of this utility criterion. He deplored the uselessness and the failure of British education in India : "Todays primary education was planned absolutely not taking into consideration the economic development of the country".[60] Gandhi writes,"Only a tiny percentage of our students reach higher levels of education, as it is today, this education touches only a tiny part of our vast Indian villages".[61] In all his speeches to the student community on various occasions Gandhi deplored the futility of present-day education introduced by the British. Gandhi exclusively emphasises the usefulness of education, for him its usefulness for the vast Indian masses: "Whenever the state finds higher education of a particular type clearly useful, the state must bear the expenses for it".[62] Gandhi's concern for the welfare of the vast masses of population in India compelled him for a moment to forget a whole range of abstract principles, theories and recommendations for education that usually justify an education policy. Gandhi never cared what theoretical foundation his educational proposals may have. The only thing Gandhi worried about at its core was how useful the policy was for the people for whom it was conceived of. Gandhi recommended craft-centered education like a down-to-the core pramgatist because he found that India urgently needed an education that could help Indians to earn their daily bread and find themselves economically independent.

The criterion of utility was applied most to the curriculum of education. That was an area where much useless concepts and materials could creep into. Gandhi throughout stood deadly against English education in general and the teaching of English in particular at the high school level or at lower levels based on this criteria. He attempted to drive home that English served no purpose for Indians : "If we spend for learning the Indian languages half of the energy that we are spending for learning English, that would have created a new atmosphere in the country and would make considerable progress possible".[63] Gandhi constantly cautioned Indians not to neglect the regional languages: "We have made our own languages poor for love of English. We lower our own dignity by looking down upon our mother-tongue".[64] It is the futility of learning English and spending such a time and energy for learning this language, as he believed, that compelled Gandhi create an air of antagonism for Endlish language. Like English Gandhi did not want any element into the school or college curriculum in our country that may have no immediate application to the student's practical life. Gandhi defines national education from this sole viewpoint: "An education that does not take into consideration the starving millions of our country and device the ways for bringing them adequate relief, can in no way be a national education".[65] He was not willing to accept as valid any criterion other than the practical usefulness of education in solving the urgent problems the nation was facing. Gandhi wanted a national policy of education to be evolved solely on the basis of this criterion. Such a national policy on education should be based on resources and needs of the country, to cater to the needs of the masses in the villages. He wanted no efforts to go waste only because some theory recommends that.

6. Pragmatism in Gandhian Education - 2

Gandhi's total commitment to the welfare of his fellowmen in everything that he did theoretically put him with the pragmatist philosopher. The idealist got himself preoccupied with the divine and the spiritual. He was more other worldly than any other thinker and very often forgot the practical problems and difficulties of his fellowmen. This other worldliness of the idealist was counteracted his fellowmen. This other worldliness of the idealist was counteracted by the total commitment to materialism and to humanitarian concerns by the modern philosopher. Pragmatism in education too came in the form of reactions to far too much preoccupation with abstractions, theories and subjects. In spite of all the other worldliness and spiritual orientations of Gandhi, he developed a perfect commitment to the welfare of his fellowmen like the pragmatist educationist: Gandhi says, "If your education is substantial, then it should permeate to the neighbourhood and exercise its influence".[66] This orientation to the fellowmen takes the form of concrete service : "Gandhi wanted to convert every school into a community where individuality is not damped out but developed through social contacts and varied opportunities of service".[67]

Education of the most useful kind cared for the development of optimum social attitudes. The school is a Social institution in which the child's consciousness of social values are developed and where he is helped to develop his "inherited social resources" in such a way as to be useful to the society. "The school is to be a reflection of the larger society outside its walls in which life can be learnt by living. But it is to be a purified, simplified and better-balanced society".[68] John Dewey's conception of a school aimed at providing the conditions necessary for learning co-operation and mutual useful living. Gandhi writes, "If the education that we get separates us from God or if it does not help us to serve our fellow men, then such an education is not worthy of its name".[69] These social attitudes include the urgent removal of untouchability from the hearts of the younger generation: "The disease of untouchability and caste differences should be uprooted from the hearts of the Hindus".[70] Further he says, "Young men and women and in large numbers should come forward to dedicate themselves to the service of the people".[71] Gandhi makes service as a basic condition for the development of the right educational attitudes. This he drove home in his numerous speeches and writings and exhorted students to get right into the midst of the community where they hail from. He writes, "You should daily utilise a portion of your time in the practical service of the people around you. Thus you should be ready to take up the spade the broom and the basket. You should transform yourselves into cleaners most willing to tidy-up this sacred place. That will be the richest portion of your education, and not the mugging up of literary lessons".[72] Gandhi recommends social service as the panacea for all the social diseases that we are facing in our countries and exhorts students to use this weapon to fight social problems.

Gandhi like a pragmatist is not willing to speak of social service in the air. The pragmatist links the training of social attitudes to their project method and work-experience of one kind or other. Gandhi links the development of social attitudes to a craft or skill. He says, "The charka is the best link to bind the villagers with us in service".[73] He makes it clear that those who do not understand this basic principle of the relationship between the charka and the Indian villager will have no place in our schools. Gandhi was willing to sacrifice any theoretical principle of education traditionally well-established for the sake of this single orientation in education i.e. service and humanitarian considerations keeping the Indian villages in mind. No principle and policy of education is bound to succeed which does not take into consideration the future and the welfare of the starving masses of Indian rural population.

Like a pragmatist, again Gandhi believed in unfailing experiments with life. It was most remarkable that, for Gandhi, life consisted in a chain of experiments to discover the extent in which truth was embodied in human life: "I simply want to tell the story of my experiments with Truth, and my life consists of nothing but those experiments".[74] Gandhi's Autobiography unfolds the living story of this unfailing chain of committed experiments. We read about the Gandhian experiments in diet keeping. "As I searched myself deeper, the necessity for changes both internal and external began to grow on me. As soon as, or even before, I made alterations in my expenses and my way of living, I began to make changes in my diet".[75] Gandhi's experiments with diet keeping is well-known. It was a step by step process of becoming more rigorous and austere in food, eating just to maintain one's health and life rather than deriving any pleasure out of eating. Gandhi writes, "It is necessary for one to keep one's spiritual energy while at the same time deriving physical strength even when living on little food and without doing anything to external to preserve health".[76] Fasting and strict abstinence became a matter of routine for Gandhi as part of his experiments with diets.

Yet another attempt of Gandhi in the same direction was his experiment in earth and water treatment. He says, "With growing simplicity of my life, my dislike for medicines steadily increased..... I argued that, if I also dropped the morning breakfast, I might become free from headaches. So I tried the experiment".[77] Instead of depending on the usual allelopathic medicines Gandhi planned to resort to earth and water treatment what has come to be known today as naturopathy. "The treatment (in this particular case) consisted in applying to the abdomen a bandage of clean earth moistened with cold water and spread like a poultice on fine linen".[78] This was the treatment Gandhi used to relieve himself of constipation. The treatment, Gandhi says, proved a radical cure. Gandhi's further experiments in self-restraint and renunciation. were borne out of his immense love for the starving millions of India. On numerous occasions we find Gandhi saying to students, "Students should learn to sacrifice the things that the poor in India cannot afford for themselves". Gandhi's entire life was to prove to the world how important these identifications with the realities of our life were. Gandhi's was life of constant experimentation in living the simplest life possible reducing one's necessities to the bare minimum.

Like a pragmatist Gandhi saw his development as a continuous process of experiments. Gandhi carefully watched and judged the results and developed his perspectives of life in accordance to that. Gandhi did not blindly follow the dictates of any one for that matter. Life for him was a continuous chain of experiences that need to be linked by the spiritual and personal convictions regarding life. Education is not different from that. Like a pragmatist Gandhi stressed the role of these life-experiences. Abstract syllabuses and textbooks had only a partial role to play. For Gandhi, "character building was the aim of even knowledge".[80] The abstract knowledge needs to be presented through and transformed into concrete life-experiences that will in turn transform the students' personalities. "If I was to be their real teacher and guardian I must touch their hearts. I must share their joys and sorrows"[81]. Any education that does not help this transformation is deemed futile.

References

1. Bhatia, B.D., *Philosophy*, p.83
2. Ibid p.85
3. Ibid p.85
4. Ibid p.87
5. Durant, W., in *Profiles*, p.11

6. Bhatia,B.D.,*Philosophy*, p.138
7. Fischer, Louis, in *Profiles*, p.60
8. Harrington, D., in *Profiles*, p.156
9. *Young India*, 31 December 1931
10. *An Autobiography*, Intr.
11. Snow, E.P., in *Profiles*, p.106
12. Bhaita,B.D., *Philosophy*, p.122.
13. Ibid p.124
14. Gregg,R.B., in Profiles, p,168
15. An *Autobiography*, Intr.
16. *Towards New Education*, p.31
17. Ibid p.31
18. Fisher, Louis, in *Profiles*, p.60
19. Mehta, Ved, in *Profiles*, p.203
20. Bhatia, B.D., *Philosophy*, p.122.
21. *An Autobiography*, p.101
22. Bowler, Chester, in *Profiles*, p.124.
23. Bhatia, B.D., Philosophy, p.124.
24. Ibid p.123.
25. Harijan, 11 March 1939
26. Taylor, Edmond, in Profiles,p.22.
27. *Harijan* 13 April 1940
28. Gandhi, M.K., *Hind Swaraj*, Ahmedabad 1958 p.78.
29. *An Autobiography*, p.298
30. Ibid p.255
31. *Basic Education*, p.12.
32. Ibid p.72
33. Bhatia, B.D., philosophy, p.131.
34. *To the students*, p.71'
35. Bowles, Chester, in *Profiles*, p.162.
36. *Towards New Education*, p.85
37. To the Students, p.5.
38. Holmes, J., in *Profiles*, p.126.
39. Einstein, A., in *Profiles*, p.100
40. Bhatia, B.D., *Philosophy*, p.93.
41. Ibid p.94.
42. Ibid p.95.
43. Dewey, John quoted in Bhatia, *Philosophy*, p.106.
44. Ibid p.110.
45. Fischer, Louis, in *Profiles*, p.61.

46. Erivkson, in *Profiles*, p.187.
47. Fisher, Louis, in *Profiles* p.138.
48. Ibid p.59
49. Ibid p.61.
50. Davidson, J., in *profiles*, p.17
51. Fisher, E., in Profiles, p.60
52. Holmes, J., in Ibid p. 125.
53. *To the Students*, p.163.
54. Ibid p.173.
55. Bhatia, B.D., *Philosophy*, p.121.
56. Ibid p.131.
57. *Basic Education*, p.75.
58. Ibid p.75
59. Ibid p.51
60. Ibid p.79
61. Ibid p.79
62. Pillai, N.P., *Education*, p.46.
63. *Thoughts on National Language*, p.190.
64. Ibid p.191
65. *To the Students*, p.67
66. Ibid p.173.
67. Bhatia, B.D., Philosophy; p.130
68. Ibid p.109
69. Pillai, N.P., *Education*, p.22
70. *Harijan*, 18 March 1939
71. Ibid 18 March 1939.
72. *To the Students*, p.173.
73. Ibid p.67
74. *An Autobiography*. Intr.
75. Ibid p.41
76. *Harijan* 13 October 1940
77. *An Autobiography*, 201
78. Ibid p.201
79. *To the Students*, p.71
80. *Towards New Education*, p.31.

    An Autobiography, p.258.

6

SATYAGRAHA IN INDIAN EDUCATION

1. Foundations of Gandhian Satyagraha

Of all that Gandhi's teachings contain, there is nothing more powerful, potent and attractive than the concept of Satyagraha. It will be inadequate to call satyagraha a mere concept of an abstract nature, because for Gandhi this had been the very pulse of his thinking and life and no Gandhian attitude or principle had been developed except with close reference to satyagraha. Satyagraha as representing, as the embodiment of Gandhian concept of Truth, could sum up everything that he spoke or did: "Satyagraha is Gandhi's uncompromising insistance on truth".[1] According to Gandhi himself: "My religion is based on Truth and Non-violence. Truth is my God, and Non-violence is the means to reach Him".[2] Gandhi attaches an encompassing sense to Satyagraha that this becomes the vehicle of Truth that is God Himself.

The two Sanskrit words Satya (truth) and Agraha (Firmness) go into the making of the Gandhian term, 'Satyagraha'. Satyagraha would therefore mean 'adherence to Truth'. R.R.Diwakar says, "Satyagraha is a total and integral way of life based on truth and non-violence".[3] Satyagraha thus becomes an orientation to truth as the goal and non-violence or ahimsa as the means. Compared to Truth as Gandhi defines it, Satyagraha becomes a means, and comapred to ahimsa satyagraha becomes an end or a goal. But for Gandhi satyagraha is everything : the whole and soul of the Gandhian thought and movement.

The most concrete application of the principle of satyagraha is 'passive resistance'. The original application of this term was for any form of civil disobedience which Gandhi called passive resistance in South Africa. Passive resistance and civil disobedience are "methods of remedying injustice and bringing about social and political changes...... "[4] After developing the concept behind the term 'satayagraha' Gandhi made a distinction between mere passive resistance and satyagraha. For him, "Passive resistence is the weapon of the weak, while satyagraha could be practiced only by the bravest who have the courage of dying if necessary, without killing".[5]

Satyagraha contained the application of what Gandhi called the soul-force. The soul-force is the central energy of satyagraha. Satyagraha is a dynamic and positive virtue: "It means resistence to evil through love .... through suffering and sacrifice".[6] It is a confrontation with problems with truth as the witness and for the victory and realisation of truth. In satyagraha one wants truth to win. Gandhi says, "our creed was devotion to truth, and our business was the search for insistence on truth".[7] This insistence on truth in all details and aspects of human life is satyagraha. Everything in life is seen from the viewpoint of truth and everything is evaluated from the criteria of truth. That attitude is satyagraha. Satyagraha thus becomes our orientation to ourselves, to the neighbour and to God. It encompasses all reality from the viewpoint of truth alone. Satyagraha embraces even the enemy: "Satyagraha is gentle, it never wounds, never impatient, never vociferous. It is the direct opposite of compulsion. It was conceived as a complete substitute of violence".[8]

In short satyagraha becomes the saga of truth and love. The Gandhian concept of truth is so comprehensive and encompassing that for Gandhi truth is everything. As pearl Buck says, "Truth is more fundamental than the atom itself".[9] For Gandhi Truth became a personal discovery like the edge of a huge ice-berg whose tiny edge alone is manifest in life and the gigantic part is yet to be discovered through the Gandhian "experiment with Truth" and life. Truth is like the cream in milk that is absolutely hidden but can be gradually discovered and extracted through a lingering and constant process of living through satyagraha. Gandhi writes: "Seeing that the human mind works through innumerable media and the evolution of the human mind is not the same for all, it follows that what may be truth for one may be untruth for another, ... Just as for conducting a scientific course of instruction in the same way, strict preliminary discipline is necessary for a person to make experiments in the spiritual realm (i.e. Experiments with Truth)".[10]

Truth is thus to be discovered from the vast reservoir of human life. Hence a great mystery of life shrouds the Gandhian concept of truth. Truth for Gandhi was not an abstract philosophical concept, a metaphysical notion, but a principal of thought and life, that penetrates every detailed action and enterprise of the individual as well as society. To the question 'What is truth?' Gandhi answers, "It is what the voice within tells you".[11] This renders truth in a sense subjective rather than philosophically objective : It is faithfulness to the voice within, the voice of conscience, the voice of God. But truth or the adherence to truth i.e. satyagraha, is not everybody's cup of tea; satyagraha becomes thus possible through "a long training in singlemindedness and detachment through the discipline of the Ashram vows .... only one who has been through this discipline can safely rely on the ulterances of his inner voice".[12] With regard to this inner voice Gandhi cautions and says, "Everyone should, therefore, realise his limitations before he speaks of his inner voice".[13] This was Gandhi's encounter with God.

Truth essentially becomes the synonym of God: "My religion is based on Truth and non-violence. Truth is my God, and Non-violence is the means to reach Him".[14] Gandhi makes it clear in his Autobiography that he prefers to know, and worship God principally as Truth, a synonym that Gandhi liked most. He says, "There are innumerable definitions of God, because His manifestations are innumerable. They overwhelm me with wonder and owe and for a moment stun me. But I worship God as Truth only".[15] Satya, a derivative of 'sat' is a fundamental metaphysical notion in Indian philosophy. This was often referred as identical to Brahma : "Brahman is 'sat' (Being, Reality), 'chit' (Awareness, intelligence, and 'Ananda' (Bliss)".[16] Gandhi was overwhelmed by the Divine Identity of Truth as he felt that he was proximate to the reality of truth than to God Himself. To think of a God who could be away from or different from Truth would be a futile exercise for Gandhi as the life of ordinary people has proved it. God for most people became an alienated, isolated and abstract entity, if not concept. Gandhi believed that truth was as concrete as life itself and having a vision of God as Truth would be most concrete, encompassing and fruitful for personal encounter than seeing God in any other image.

If God as Truth or Truth as God is the Supreme End, non-violence or ahimsa becomes the supreme means, for Gandhi, for the realisation of Truth or self-realisation. In all Gandhian principles of thought and life non-violence takes the second place, the first being truth itself. In otherwords satyagraha as the adherence to truth in all details of life and thought has at its core non-violence truth in all details of life and thought has at its core non-violence embodied as a great Gandhian principle : "Non-violence is the first article of my faith. It is also the last article of my creed".[17] Gandhi attached great significance to the principle of ahimsa. It is the crucial constituent of satyagraha : as the end is inherently and unfoldingly realised in the means, so is satyagraha constantly and ever progressively realised in and through ahimsa. If for Gandhi "Satyagraha is a sovereign remedy"[18], then "Ahimsa is the only means to the realisation of Truth".[19] The two are so inherently merged that they can be distinguished only at the level of principles and concepts.

Edmond Taylor makes it clear "that non-violence applies to mental as well as physical violence, that it means avoiding hate and uncharitable thoughts about others, that it was not merely a political technique or ethical doctrine but a way of life".[20]

The word ahimsa connotes two levels of meaning : positive and negative. Etymologically the word means "renunciation of the will to kill or harm".[21] It means in the words of Gandhi himself, "avoiding injury to anything on earth, in thought word or deed".[22] The negative connotation of ahimsa comes from this basic meaning. Ahimsa thus avoids all forms of killing, injuring, violence in thought, word or action of any kind : "You may not harbour on uncharitable thought even in connection with one who may consider himself to be your enemy".[23] But the Gandhian ahimsa is not a mere negative principle. Ahimsa for him has positive, dynamic, all-encompassing directions; it is love in the most comprehensive sense as it is understood. According to Gandhi himself, "it is a positive state of love, of doing good even to the evil-doer.[24]

Thus satyagraha leads to the principle of love: "A successful search for Truth means complete deliverance from the dual throng such as love and hate, happiness and misery".[25] That is how Gandhi saw the relationship. Truth embodied in satyagraha orients the individual to love God and his neighbour. Gandhi identifies ahimsa and love. Love becomes an orientation to oneself in truthful thought, love becomes an orientation to the neighbour in truthful relationships, and love becomes an encounter with God in truthful worship. Love thus becomes encompassing and pervasive as truth itself. God becomes for Gandhi an embodiment of love : Hence I gather that God is life, Truth, Light. He is Love".[26] Gandhi articulated the identity between God and Love in ways more than one. He says, "To me God is Truth and Love ....For in His boundless love God permits the atheists to live".[27] As a result of this satyagraha would primarily mean seeing God and worshipping Him as Love.

Satyagraha, on the other hand leads to the love of man, one's neighbour in an encounter of humble service. Satyagraha, as we have seen in an orientations to the neighbour. Here Gandhi brings in self-denial, self-sacrifice and dedicated service of the needy and the poor. As E.Stanley Jones points out Gandhi became "the voice of the dumb millions",[28] In India and around the world. Gandhi wants the satyagrahi to suffer for the sake of truth and love. Ahimsa as love of the neighbour wants us to forget ourselves and be concerned only with the wants of others. He says, "Ahimsa consists in allowing others the maximum of convenience at the maximum of inconvenience to us, even at the risk of life".[29] Ahimsa does not permit the use of any form of violence on others, the evil-doer, the enemy. All the same there is the commitment of the satyagrahi to direct the evil-doer to truth, to the discovery of truth. This leaves with no option other than causing suffering to oneself. That is how love and suffering, ahimsa and suffering are related in satyagraha. Satyagraha without ahimsa and suffering are related in satyagraha. Satyagraha without some form of suffering is an illusion. Suffering is so great a reality for him that he says, "I must reduce myself to zero. So long as a man does not of his own free will put himself last among his fellow creatures, there is no salvation for him".[30] Satyagraha thus means emptying oneself through self-denial and positive suffering and filling the rest of humanity with love, care and service. By this Gandhi makes satyagraha a potent and great principle.

2. Satyagraha and Educational Goals

Gandhian thoughts on education are an integral constituent of satyagraha. Gandhian thoughts in any form do not render themselves to water-tight compartments. Different aspects therein are paths that lead to and lead out of the central principle of satyagraha. Such a great importance is given to this notion in the present work that satyagraha can be brought to bear upon every aspect of education. As we have seen throughout, education and life for Gandhi do not render themselves to distinct final goals, both explicitly and implicitly, and Gandhi wants educationists and teachers not to sacrifice these goals of education at the cost of proximate and practical aims, Gandhi constantly warned us of the danger of modern education, specially of the system of education that aims at westernising India as a nation and Indians as individuals for the sake of greater materialist sophistication. It is from this viewpoint that we need to see how satyagraha as a comprehensive principle penetrates all aspects of education.

Gandhian education or more precisely education in the Gandhian sense aims at the achievement of truth content of satyagraha. Education in any sense of the term enables man to know, achieve and apply truth in all things and experiences in life. Truth is existential. It pervades reality. For those who believe in the human intellect, there is no choice but to acknowledge the truth-validity of truth itself. If the human mind is not oriented to the grasping of truth, our life and actions are absolutely senseless. Whether truth lies fully outside the human mind (the position of empiricists), whether it is fully within the human mind (idealists) or whether it is corresponding to the reality outside the human mind (realists), is a deeper metaphysical question. But it needs no philosopher's support for us to know that our minds are capable of grasping not only the finite truths of our day-to-day experience, but also grasping and realising the Infinite Truth, the Summon Bonum of the human mind. It is on this supreme conviction that the life of the common man and what we know as his 'Common-sense experience' depend.

Truth and the realisation of Truth, are therefore the very foundation on which the principles and practices of education are ultimately based. It would therefore become the ultimate concern of education to search for truth, discover truth and bring truth to bear upon the life and thinking of the student community. That is what satyagraha embodies and reminds us. Gandhi conceives of truth as including "the relative truth of our conception and the Absolute Truth, the Eternal Principle, that is God".[31] Gandhi does not put his principles in the syllogistic language of the philosopher, instead he expresses himself and his faith in truth in concrete /language.

Gandhian satyagraha puts education on a different path with regard to its relation to truth. Inspite of the closeness of education with the principle of truth hardly any one is today aware of the concern of education with truth. If for Gandhi the beginning, the middle and the end of life is truth, then for education it should be no less than that. The path of truth should be the determined aim of education. Truth is the beginning because that alone validates the principles of education. Truth is the middle : the values and practices of education will imbibe truth only. Truth is the end because all education has discovery of truth as the final end. As "satyagraha is Gandhi's uncompromising insistence on truth"[32] educational aims have to search for an identity with the Gandhian satyagraha. Gandhi tells students, "The plant of truth will not grow and bear fruit, unless its roots are watered by ahimsa".[33] Truth has to be achieved through the process of education in which non-violence becomes the practice. Educational goals are to be tested on the anvil of truth as the supreme principle. What we are concerned today are with the proximate utility of educational practices and principles. Instead our eyes should be set on more ultimate, fundamental and permanent applications of truth. Gandhi tells students, "Truth will make you courageous"[34] and he has always made it clear that "Non-violence demands greater courage and sacrifice".[35] If education aims at making the individual more civilised, that can be achieved only through a training in experiencing truth. Gandhi says, "Experience has taught me that civility is the most difficult part of satyagraha".[36] It requires the greatest courage to be gentle on the face of adversities and Gandhi considers this true education. With this civility the individual would become capable of actively confronting and standing against injustices of any kind. He tells students, "No progress has been gained by any one other than those who have opposed the human laws and customs".[37] Education aims at giving shape to such a generation as Gandhi envisaged.

Gandhian education, again aims at the inculcation of ahimsa in the transmission of knowledge and culture. Like truth ahimsa is another major constituent of satyagraha most relevant to modern education. An education oriented to the realisation of satyagraha transmits human knowledge, culture and civilization in such a way as to develop in the individual and in society the genuine training in ahimsa. This training presuppose a gradual and thoroughly built knowledge of ahimsa in every component of education provided. Christian education is imparted through a kind of education in which Christian values and principles will predominate. Similarly, Marxist education is imparted using the kind of knowledge in which elements, theories, principles and practices of Marxism predominates. That may be done without giving any direct information regarding the details of Marxism.

In the same manner, an education geared to satyagraha through non-violence can be developed by presenting the educational aims with direct or indirect bearing on ahimsa. When educational aims are decided, specified and formulated, ahimsa should take the central place with the aim of helping the individuals emerge from the educational institutions well-grounded in practical knowledge of all the constituent elements of ahimsa as a principle. Gandhi says, "In education ahimsa should have a definite relation to the interrelationship among students".[38] If that is to be attained the starting point would always be defining the educational aims accordingly. By enunciating the principle of ahimsa, we shall be in a position to introduce satyagraha into the very heart of education. About the experimental schools in champaran (Bihar), Gandhi writes, "We have to make this training school a school for winning freedom and for the solution of all our ills, of which the primary one is our communal troubles. And for this purpose we shall have to concentrate on non-violence......... All problems are, therefore, to be solved non-violently".[39] Ahimsa is thus to be closely integrated to the goals of education to find adequate solution to the problems of life, because satyagraha is Gandhi's unique remedy.

Gandhian education, further aims at the development of love as an integral constituent of satyagraha. Within the Gandhian context ahimsa and love are identical principles. Yet I am treating love as a separate notion in the present context for the sake of the elaboration of it. Education 'aims at the formation' of the individual's character. For Gandhi education as we have seen throughout, is identical with the formation of the spiritual character or rather the spiritual personality. Love is at the very centre of all values. Gandhi says, "Satyagraha is a dynamic and positive virtue. It means resistence to evil through love ..... through suffering and sacrifice".[40] In other words love in satyagraha is co-extensive with truth, as God is both Truth and Love. Modern education has been made so abstract and information-centred that dynamic principles like love finds no place as part of its very system. Satyagraha defines education only with reference to truth and Love. Gandhi is not in two minds in this regard when he says, "Your education should be built on the foundation of truth and love. Unless this is done, your education will be rendered useless".[41] Gandhi could not think of providing an education leaving these principles aside.

When educational aims are specified and developed in Gandhian lines ahimsa becomes strong principle and love become the expression of it: the sides of the same coin. Where violence divides, love unites; where violence hates, love forgives. Violence is the weapon of a coward; love is the weapon of the courageous in the true sense of the word. Education by gearing all its energies to a passive development of the intellect and by not orienting the individual to the dynamic side of human nature is in fact encouraging this cowardice and thereby causing greater violence. Gandhi tells students, "In the hands of an educationist it (ahimsa) should assume the form of sacred and ever new love".[42] The educationist in order to develop education in Gandhian lines looks for ways and means for integrating the principle of love among the other principles of education in such a way as to help students discover it easily and lucidly in the process of education. It should enable the school in course of time to present to the children in concrete ways these principles and find out practical applications of these in real life situations.

Gandhian education aims, further, at the development of social attitudes as a constituent of the principle of satyagraha. Gandhi says, "A satyagrahi obeys the laws of society intelligently and of his own free will".[43] It is a basic goal of education to enable individuals to adjust themselves to society and grow up as useful members of society. Education defines its principles, organises its curriculum and learning experiences with this goal in mind. Education is out to harmonise individual and social development in such a way as to develop social attitudes in the individual. Satyagraha is not an eccentric or self-centered principle. On the otherhand satyagraha, using love as its major instrument draws people into itself and shows the willingness to give itself to others.

Education is made inherently socio-centric by satyagraha. Gandhi's own total dedication to the cause of individuals, society and the nation exemplifies this idea. Service became the climatic and logical conclusion of Gandhian satyagraha. No satyagraha is made genuine except by practicing the virtue of self-denial : giving up everything in the service of, for the good of others. Gandhi says, "Satyagraha served both the goal and method of service".[44] We have numerous constituents of the social attitudes that satyagraha can contribute to education. Apart from love, service and self-denial we have to help children develop the social values of civility which Gandhi was so found of, tolerance which is the very foundation of our existence as a nation, and social justice which guarantees the exercise of our fundamental rights in the Constitution. Social attitudes presented within the context of Satyagraha gathers greater strength and significance. Howard Thurman says, "Non-violence is an instrument of social change".[45] This social change presupposes the medium of education. Educational goals have thus to be purified in the light of satyagraha. This will help individuals, society and the nation to stop drifting away from those values which alone can provide development in the right direction. Only then can the final aims of life and education coincide the way Gandhi envisaged it.

3. Satyagraha as the Method of Education

The method of education, as a general notion, determines and specifies the activity and experiences through which the educational content and learning experiences are provided. It is a means to the realisation of the goals of education. It is the how of education in which socio-cultural and pedagogical elements have their roles to play. As the central process of education, the goals are gradually realised through the method which results in achievement of different levels. Satyagraha constitutes the method of Gandhian education. Educational goals are ideological and will consistently remain on the plain of ideology or ideals to a great extent. But educational method brings down this ideology to the plain of practice. Satyagraha is fundamentally ideological, but education will bring down this ideology to concrete methodology and help individuals attain or realise the principles of satyagraha.

Gandhian Education employs the principles of satyagraha as a method centered on truth. For Gandhi truth is a way of life. As a way of life truth becomes life-centered, and intrinsic to all activities and involvements of the individual. Truth is the central component of the Hindu sanatana dharma as the recommended way of life. It is here that truth comes down from the domain of the intellect to the level of morality on the one hand, and ordinary actions on the other. Truth was absolutely concrete for Gandhi that was why he subjected that principle to experiments : Gandhi says, "My object is to show that he who would go for noval experiments must begin with himself. That leads to a quicker discovery of truth, and God always protects on honest experimenter".[46] Gandhi was deeply convinced of the experimental potential of truth as a principle in satyagraha. This concrete nature of truth makes it amenable to become a method in education.

The educationist in the Gandhian context remains on the look out for truth in all the classroom learning experiences with reference to the individuals mode of involvement, response to situations and reception of the content of education. Truth would thus become a reality in education.

Education employs the principles of satyagraha as a method centered on ahimsa. Just as ahimsa determines and guides the goals of education, it can form an integral part of educational method. Gandhi says, "A perfect vision of Truth can only follow a complete realisation of ahimsa".[47] Just as truth becomes a concrete reality in education, ahimsa becomes a method of the most realisable nature. Ahimsa as a concept becomes applicable to all elements in education. Gandhi writes, "The boys and girls who grow up together in an atmosphere filled with the sacred odour of ahimsa will live a life of freedom and self-control like brothers and sisters. Students will treat their teachers with the love, mutual respect and faith that they deserve. That sacred atmosphere will itself be a living lesson in ahimsa".[48] Just as we have a methodology and a set of techniques for providing learning experiences in academic matters, so can we develop close relationships between the constituent elements of ahimsa that will become the method and techniques of education at home and in schools. Ahimsa will be concertised and practiced the manifold relationships in the school : between students themselves in all aspects of their mutual relations brought down to every detail, between students and teachers, teachers among themselves, between superiors and subordinates at all levels. What we are aiming at is the new focus in these relationships rather than the application of a new principle. Ahimsa has always been there on the anals of our history, but the ahimsa that satyagraha recommends is a total, integrated and holistic ahimsa that penetrates all the relations between the self, the other and God Himself. Ahimsa is so holistic in the Gandhian sense that in an ideal world-order ahimsa can substitute education itself.

Education further employs the principles of satyagraha

as a method centered on live. Gandhi says, "when my friend goes astray, if I undergo suffering in order to raise his noble attitudes, the whole thing will be motivated only by love".[49] Love becomes the roots and the flowering of satyagraha. Education has all the potentials to integrate this concept to the methods of work in all these details and bring it closer to the principles of satyagraha. Love can and should function as the motivating factor, as Gandhi said, in all activities and love will be the fruits that we shall be reaping. Education in the classroom can work on the principle of love as method of work when students will concern themselves with the total welfare of those others sitting there. Education can ensure that noble feelings are entertained by the individuals in the class even in moments of adversity. Numerous opportunities arise when the application of love can be practiced in the classroom. Love as Gandhi saw it was not a mere passive attitude of forebearance but a most active and dynamic attitude of concern for the welfare of others. Education outside the classroom offers much greater prospects for the practice of love as a method of education. Once everything is seen from the point of view of love as a uniting factor much can be done to ensure its relation to all forms of involvements.

Education employs the principles of satyagraha as a method centered, further, on humility. Gandhi recommends humility as a condition or prerequisite for the genuine practice of satyagraha. Gandhi proved himself to be a type with regard to the practice of humility and the consequent attitude of simplicity. Devdas Gandhi said of his father, "Gandhi was one of the most refined persons in the world, refined in his scanty dress, in his speech and in his manners".[50] The greatest expression of Gandhi's concept of humility came when he said, "The seeker of truth should be humbler than the dust".[51] Gandhi saw education as a process in helping the individual realise that he is nothing more than a speek of dust in the universe. For him "service without humility is selfishness and egotism".[52] Gandhi expressed his desire to train students in these lines in several ways. He admonished students to be always conscious of these fundamental qualities and put them into practice in their lines. Gandhi tells students, "you should learn to wash your clothes, cook your food, and do you work".[53] Right from the student days we are most unwilling to do our own work and help ourselves chiefly because we do not possess the qualities of humility and simplicity that were the quite essential qualities of the brahmachari of the Gurukula days.

Education, again, employs the principles of satyagraha as a method centered on tolerance. India is a multi-religious, multi-social and multi-lingual nation. The Constitution has accepted tolerance as a Constitutional virtue to be upheld and taught at all cost for the very survival of the nation. Tolerance is a basic quality that Gandhi insisted students to develop if they wished to make any significant contribution to the nation. Edgar P.Snow writes, "Gandhi never ceased to try to unite his countrymen and indeed the whole world under the homely injunctions common to all faith : tolerance, individual perfection, humility, love of nature (God), equality, brotherhood and cooperation".[54] George C. Marshall writes, "In his devotion to peace and tolerance of the brotherhood of man, the Mahatma was one of those rare spokesman for the conscience of all mankind".[55] Gandhi evidently projected tolerance to be a basic constituent of satyagraha.

Indian education is always to be understood as an education of tolerance. As part of Gandhian education, satyagraha would use the quality of tolerance as a method of training. The student comes across hundreds of opportunities for the practice and development of this virtue or value. Tolerance cannot be separated from ahimsa and love. They are all mutually bound together in a cause-effect relationship. All forms of education not only organises the goals for the integration of tolerance, but brings it down to the level of practice as a method. Educational experiences can be worked out for the students to develop their consciousness and practice tolerance. Education becomes a practice of satyagraha when it is brought down to its constituent qualities and aspects.

Education, lastly employs the principles of satyagraha as a method centered on social justice. Dwight Macdonuld writes about Gandhi, "He practiced tolerance and love to such an extent that he seems to have regarded the capitalist as well as the garbage man as his social equal".[56] The Gandhian concept of an ideal society was spiritual society: "The individual can reach his highest development in and through a spiritual society".[57] Satyagraha contains social justice as a constituent element. Gandhi loved to fight for social justice as part of his commitment for the realisation of the swaraj. Gandhi's most significant work : 'Hind Swaraj' in ways more than one brings out the ideal of social justice brought down to the most concrete form in the swaraj: "That the good of the individual is contained in the good of all ....That the lawyer's work has the same value as the barber's in as much as all have the same right to earn their livelihood from their work".[58]

Education, for Gandhi, is the arena of social activities based on social justice. This related to the kind of attitude we have towards lower-grade work. Gandhi writes, "You do not regard as students whose who work on plantations. Their labour is not part of education".[59] We have narrowed down the definition of education in such a way as to include only the teaching of literacy and bookish knowledge. According to Gandhi that had been the starting point of all our problems, especially that of unemployment. Because of the social unequality that education entertains, there has arisen the belief and feeling that certain kind of work is more noble and desirable than others. The feeling of superiority of the educated to such a detestable extent is the result of the kind of education that we are imparting. Gandhi always cautions us about the role of justice in life; he says, "My experience has shown me that we win justice quickest by rendering justice to the other party".[60] Education in all forms can oneway or other ensure the practice of social justice and equality as a major component in the educational process.

Satyagraha, for Gandhi, is a "sovereign remedy".[61] Gandhian education or education conceived of and developed in Gandhian lines employs satyagraha as centered on a large number of constituent principles such as truth, ahimsa, love, social justice, humility, self-denial, service of mankind, civility etc. The Gandhian satyagraha is a comprehensive and encompassing principle and can embrace all aspects of educational theory and practices into its fold. Satyagraha as we have seen is so great a principle and so great a practice that it can simply substitute education and still lose nothing. If education can mean all that Gandhi wanted it to be in the personal, social and spiritual sense, the system of education will indeed assume a shape quite different from today's. Satyagraha as we have been seeing becomes the effective method of education through the delineation of the constituent principles developed in the present section. Educational method is a process and involves activities and experiences. Therefore the goals and concepts satyagraha enunciated will be brought down to concrete learning experiences in and outside the classroom when satyagraha is employed as an educational method.

4. Satyagraha as the Content of Education

Goals or aims of education determine the directions which education should take as well as the end that needs to be achieved. The method of education determines the process through which education is imparted. The content of education is what the individual receives i.e. the what of education. The content may be knowledge of one kind or other, formation of one type or other, or training in the concrete sense of the term in a skill or an occupation. Satyagraha in its pervasive and comprehensive nature functions as the content of Gandhian education. Satyagraha can be presented in the most adequate manner as the content of education. There are greater practical limitations in the presentation of satyagraha or its realisation as the goals or method of education.

Gandhian education develops as its content satyagraha

based on truth. Gandhi says, "Our creed was devotion to truth and our business was the search for and devotion to truth".[62] Truth becomes the content of Gandhian education as the first constituent of satyagraha. A trainee or aspirant of satyagraha "considers truth and ahimsa as his religion; thus he tries to develop that goodness through his own truthfulness and suffering".[63] He exhorted students constantly saying, "Truth will make you courageous".[64]

We can do justice to the educational ideals of Gandhi only by making truth the content of education. The content of education would first of all mean the knowledge or information that we are imparting with a view to satisfying the individual's intellect or providing a basis for the inculcation of a particular habit. In either case truth is introduced as knowledge or information. At the school or college level the elaboration of the constituents or elements of truth can be developed into a system of truth. Just as history or geography at the subject level is developed into systematic knowledge for a given level, truth and the constituent elements of truth are developed into the subject matter for learning at different levels of education. In otherwords truth becomes a subject matter on its own right presented in the text or in the classroom using different modalities such as stories, narratives and discourse formats of various kinds. When education arrives at an integrated synthesis of truth as goal, truth as method and truth as the content of education, there can be fascinating results in developing in students a conviction regarding the value of truth as the towering principle in their lives. Then students can be proud of following Gandhi's advice, "My powerful exhortation to you is that you should sustain truth in all circumstances and under any sort of adverse pressures".[65]

Education develops as its content satyagraha based on ahimsa. Education would thus become the chief vehicle for the practice of ahimsa. Gandhi writes, "Identification of everything that lives is impossible without self-purification; without self-purification the observance of the law of ahimsa must remain an empty dream".[66] A perfect vision of Truth can only follow a complete realisation of ahimsa. Gandhian education has ahimsa as a principal content that needs to be communicated to students in a variety of ways. Education in its knowledge, formation and training aspects as its contents can safely transmit the elements of ahimsa. Since present day education puts a heavy premium of the aspect of knowledge, ahimsa should be translated into a modality of knowledge through whatever means possible. Teaching materials in the classroom can embody the details of ahimsa in ways more than one. It is not possible to transform the whole spectrum of present-day education into a process of mere character formation or development of the spiritual personality of the student as Gandhian had desired. But keeping the overall texture of education as it is ways can be found out to incorporate the elements of ahimsa as a constituent of satyagraha.

Similarly, ahimsa forms the content of the formation of the Gandhian character of the satyagrahi. Gandhi tells students, "The sun of ahimsa keeps away all the dark realities of hatred, envy and dislike. Ahimsa shines light up in the realm of education. No one can hide it like the sun".[67] Gandhi envisaged ahimsa to be a bulwark of education. It is capable of hiding and protecting education from all sorts of waywardness. In the formation of character undertaken by education at all levels, ahimsa constitutes the content of the process of formation. The student at a given level should have a tangible experience of ahimsa in thought, word and action. Wherever we can envisage, chalkout and discriminate character formation in education in a concrete manner, ahimsa should find a place as a shining principle. Since knowledge is more relevant at a higher level or at the level of higher education, and character formation is more relevant at lower levels as we practice it today, ahimsa as the content of formation becomes a matter of greater concern at lower levels of education.

In the same manner ahimsa becomes the content of training of one kind of skill or other. All skills or occupations enable the individual to develop his tactile and manipulatory aptitudes based on the muscular system. A breach of ahimsa is not merely a matter of the intellect or of the pure emotions but of the whole personality involving all these faculties of the individual. Hence even in the kind of education in which the skill predominates we have great opportunities for the inculcation and practice of the elements of ahimsa as the content of education. In all the three aspects of knowledge, formation and training (the three aspects forming the content of education) we have great scope for introducing ahimsa as a constituent of satyagraha in Gandhian education.

Education, further, develops as its content satyagraha based on love. Gandhi was at a loss for words when he spoke of love as the sustaining principle of the whole creation. He says,"To see the universal and all-pervading spirit of Truth face to face one must be able to love the meanest of creation oneself".[68] Gandhi tells students, "Students growing up in such an atmosphere (of ahimsa) can be distinguished by this kind-heartedness, generosity and their capability to serve. Social evils are not a problem for them. Their power of love itself will destroy these evils".[69] Like ahimsa, love a most concrete form of ahimsa for Gandhi, becomes the content of Gandhian education. Attempts have always been made to include universal love as part of the content of education all round the world. Education in its knowledge, formation and training aspects can subsume love as a constituent of satyagraha. The knowledge aspect of the content would require that love be developed into a system of knowledge or information to be conveniently presented to children. It is true that the sciences and the humanities are important. But for Gandhi the most significant knowledge that forms the core of education should be that knowledge which brings us closer to God and to our neighbour in love and service. Gandhi writes to students, "Modern education has the tendency to turn its eyes away from the soul. Hence we are not excited by the powers of the human soul".[70] For Gandhi all education should serve to inculcate in the individual the real religion. He says, "Real religion should radiate from the individual the attitudes of love and service".[71] The knowledge aspect of education should closely reflect this aspect of love so that all knowledge however varied it is boils down to the principle of love.

The formation aspect of the content of education subsumes love as a constituent of satyagrahs. Love radiates among the individuals under the aura of Gandhian education when the formation of character is aimed at under a given scheme of education. Gandhi reminds us, "True education is that which draws out and stimulates the spiritual, the intellectual and physical faculties of the children".[72] Keeping this in mind the formation aspect of education provides opportunities for the experience and practice of mutual love and concern as individuals who are adequately oriented to development of a spiritual personality as envisaged by Gandhi.

The training aspect of the content of Gandhian education is based on the principle of love as part of the training given in a skill or occupation. This is the sort of education that has the least component of knowledge attached to it as practiced today. But that does not leave the possibility of love being incorporated into it. Gandhi writes, "Through the vocation in which the student receives training the personality hidden in him or her should receive full development".[73] This skill-centered education incorporates love as the content of the training as part of the development of the total personality Gandhi thought of. Love becomes manifest in the manipulation of every situation that the student is offered for the training. Right from the handling of the tools upto dealing with the community in which he receives the training love can be reflected in its one element or other. What is required basically is a constant awareness of this great principle, and the feeling that all the training is geared to the end of satyagraha.

Gandhian education lastly develops as its content satyagraha based on self-denial. Gandhi's life was a saga of self-denial. His experiments with truth was nothing but a story of ever unfailing self-denial: "I must reduce myself to zero. So long as a man does not of his own free will put himself last among his fellow creatures, there is no salvation for him".[74] That was, perhaps, a very fundamental message Gandhi passed on to us. It was a central message Gandhi gave to students in a clear voice : the message of sacrifice. He writes, "A student is like a rishi; he should be an embodiment of simple life and high thinking".[75] Gandhi further says, "students should learn to sacrifice the things that the poor in India cannot afford for themselves".[76] Every aspect of Gandhi's life and teaching testifies the message of self-denial. E.Stanley Jones writes, "And there was Mahatma Gandhi..... he gripped the soul of modern India by relating renunciation to the needs around".[77] Gandhian education is in fact an education for self-denial to be incorporated into the content of education for satyagraha. Gandhian education delineates all the constituents of satyagraha as seen above in the content of education. Knowledge that is prepared to be presented to children permeates with the principles of satyagraha. Formation of all types which children undergo is stimulated by satyagraha. And training as the content of education embodies satyagraha in all the aspects seen above.

5. Satyagraha as Providing Directions in Education

Gandhian education subsumes satyagraha as a principle and a force that has an encompassing potential to penetrate every minute detail of education and bring in a powerful transformation. Satyagraha in the present context is thought of as a great principle of powerful potentials to generate the spiritual personality in the individual and the spiritual and moral transformation in society. Satyagraha becomes an instrument thus of change in the individual and society. What is required is the discovery of the techniques to effect this transformation. This is what satyagraha in education has the capacity to do, because education is the major instrument of transformation in the individual and society. Education helps us recognise our right task in the context of satyagraha. Gandhi was clear in his views: "Swaraj does not depend on jail-going. It depends on everyone doing his or her own task. And that task has been shown to you. Go to the villages, identify with villagers, befriend the untouchables, make Hindu-muslim unity a concrete fact".[78] The scope of satyagraha is thus broadened to include every aspect of welfare in the swaraj.

Satyagraha provides the necessary directions in Gandhian education. It provides directions in the development of curriculum in education. Education is a time-consuming process. The formation of the personality of the learner, acquisition and internalisation of knowledge, acquisition of mastery over skills, all these would mean the development of a suitable curriculum in the school or in the college. Curriculum contains everything that is organised for the provision of education. Curriculum includes everything that the student does from the moment he enters school upto the time he leaves it on a day. Satyagraha shows what these details should be. A systems analysis of satyagraha yields the detailed constituent elements a few of which we have analysed in the present chapter. Curriculum includes knowledge, and activities of various kinds. Chiefly it is a holistic affair through which education is imparted. Constituent elements of satyagraha like the values find suitable place in the curriculum. Curriculum development takes thus directions from satyagraha.

Satyagraha provides directions in organising learning experiences that are central to education. Gandhi writes, "If teachers aim at developing the discriminative powers of the boys and girls under them, they will continually foster their reasoning capacity and enable them to think for themselves".[79] Every educational institution depends, for its success, on the learning experiences that the institution is capable of organising and providing. By learning experiences in the narrow sense we mean the activities in the classroom for communicating some knowledge or skill, and in the broadest sense we mean all the systematic and educationally definable activities that we organise in the school as a whole. Satyagraha provides directions necessary for these learning experiences. In most cases in schools these learning experiences are purely of an academic nature, consisting of academic activities or literary involvements. Instead, Gandhian education attempts to transform these learning experiences into an experience of satyagraha, perhaps in simulated situations, together with an awareness of the concreteness of satyagraha in such experiences. These learning experiences differ in different types of education, with focus on knowledge, formation and training as the content of education. Determined by these directions provided by satyagraha education will be in a position to organise its learning experiences to develop the constituent principles that satyagraha includes.

Satyagraha, further, provides directions for developing self-dependency in students. Gandhi considered this component as quite basic to satyagraha. Not only with reference to the training in a vocation (see ch.7), but also independent of it self-dependency was regarded by Gandhi as a pre-requisite for a life committed to truth and ahimsa. This is considered fundamental to his swaraj: "Swaraj does not depend on jail-going. It depends on every one doing his or her own task".[80] Gandhi tells students, "You should learn to wash your clothes, cook your food, and do your work".[81] This aspect was a fundamental message of Gandhi to students. Satyagraha embodies the dynamism for every individual to practice self-dependency, exercising one's energy to manage one's own affairs without exploiting the services of others. This aspect is part of education. Education basically prepares individuals to become independent. This is not an independence of not from doing one's own work, but of doing it. Satyagraha ensures the least emphasis of one's own self and most emphasis of others' selves. Education has directions from satyagraha to develop the individual's potential to depend on himself under all possible circumstances by organising learning experiences accordingly.

Satyagraha provides directions in materials preparation

in education. Learning experiences in education are provided on the basis of a large variety of materials such as reading materials and audio-visual aids. The goals of education are closely reflected in the nature and preparation of those materials on whose basis educational process takes place. All types of education make use of one kind of material or other. The principles of satyagraha are brought to bear upon the preparation of materials. If curriculum offers a more general scope for the application of satyagraha, materials narrow it down to a considerable extent. Materials are those things with which the students come into contact. The principles of satyagraha and its constituents are presented to them in auditory, visual and audio-visual modalities. Right from the blackboard upto the latest technological device like the VCR fall under the scope of materials and can become the medium for the experience of satyagraha. A very strong awareness of this great principle can be developed in them through these materials.

Satyagraha provides directions in life-orientation in education. Gandhi was convinced that "we shall share the experiences of life freely and fully".[82] For this he made his own life a process of discovery through constant experiments. Gandhi developed a proper life-orientation in all its dimensions. He writes, "I very much liked the company of children, and the habit of playing and joking with them has stayed with me till today. I have ever since thought that I should make a good teacher of children".[83] Education aims at providing to children adequate life-orientation. This is to guarantee that they are not lost in the world of abstractions and knowledge of an unreal type. All education is imparted to help individuals to adjust themselves to society. Life - orientation, a process of knowing, loving and looking towards those aspects which make human life worthwhile, is an important goal of education. Satyagraha is life-itself experienced in its raw-reality. The principles of satyagraha make this life-orientation of education real and down-to-earth. It becomes for the individual a training in life.

Satyagraha, further, provides directions in co-curricular experiences. We make a distinction in present-day education between curriculum and co-curriculum. Curriculum includes all direct learning experiences with reference to an academic course. While co-curriculum includes all related, indirect experiences that can be provided. Community experiences are for that matter co-curricular activities. Similarly literary activities in the school are also co-curricular. In the Gandhian context this distinction is hardly possible. He thinks of education in a holistic manner, and gives much importance to varied activities. He says, "The teacher should not be a slave to textbooks. He should have opportunities to give his own experience to students".[84] Again, he writes, "students should participate in all sorts of creative activities".[85] Co-curricular experiences can easily relate students to Indian villages, their own community, to the occupations, interests and material of the community. Satyagraha has great potential to enhance this experience, render co-curriculum greatly valuable and achieve the Gandhian targets in education. Satyagraha has a extensive applications to the co-curriculum.

Satyagraha provides directions for discipline in education. Discipline has been subject to great controversy in education down the Ages under different schools of thinking. We have had variations in the attitude to discipline from 'the task-master attitude' of idealism to the 'observer-attitude' of naturalism in education. For the idealist of the middle ages discipline was everything, while for the naturalist of modern period the teacher is a mere observer to the natural growing-up of the child. All the same discipline is as well as will be a factor of great significance in education. Gandhi was conscious of this role of discipline. But he was against physical punishment: "The training of the spirit was possible only through the exercise of the spirit....... The exercise of the spirit entirely depended on the life and character of the teacher".[86] Gandhiji further says, "I have always been opposed to corporal punishment. That exhibits not the spirit but the brute in us".[87] Discipline here becomes a matter of conviction rather than enforcement, and depends on the model that the teacher provides. Satyagraha is centered on discipline : self-discipline enlivened by self-denial. Satyagraha is capable of laying deep roots of self-discipline in the individual through the process of education. Inculcation of the spirit Gandhi has in mind becomes a reality in education.

Satyagraha, again, provided directions in educational planning. Educational planning has become the focus of the attention of educationists and administrators as well. We have come to the realisation that adequate and comprehensive planning with a telescopic vision of the future of the country has become the necessity of the day. Educational planning in India is right on the cross-roads due to the overwhelming problems that we are facing. Satyagraha presents itself for our rescue. Gandhi was single-minded in the conviction that Indian education cannot afford to have drastic departures from the traditions on the path of modernisation. Gandhi had clear and fundamental directives in this regard. Educational planners have to discover how rural India can secure the right share of the national income for developmental purposes on the basis of the Constitutional guarantee of equalization of educational opportunities. Satyagraha can highlight through its constituent principles how the right planning can be developed, without explaining away the evidence of backwardness of staggering dimensions that we still find in rural India.

Gandhian education subsumes satyagraha as its bulwark. Satyagraha as we have seen determines the goals of education because the encompassing nature of satyagraha is potent with the principles necessary for the right kind of education. The "universal hope of social redemption"[88] that Gandhi proclaimed through satyagraha is to be achieved through education. Education is the right arena for the development and realisation of the Gandhian principles. Just as Gandhi's principle of ahimsa made a spiritual revolution practicable, so too ahimsa can make modern education redeem the lost values. Satyagraha is the beginning and the end of this revolution. Just as Gandhi "enriched polities with ethics"[89], so too the whole field of education is enlivened by satyagraha whose constituent principles are capable of penetrating and enlivening every detail of education. Gandhian education becomes a process of discovering the greatest truth in the context becomes a process of discovering the greatest truth in the context of satyagraha by living the truth in one's day-to-day life. The student is out to discover this truth from the vast reservoir of life in which it is hidden, and this very process makes education worthwhile in itself.

References

1. Mehta, Ved, in *Profiles*, p.203
2. Jesult Scholars, *Hinduism*, p.295.
3. Thekkinedath, J., *Love of Neighbour*, p.68.
4. Ibid p.69.
5. Ibid p.69
6. Bhatia, B.D., *Philosophy* p.123.
7. *An Autobiograhphy*, p.298.
8. *Harijan*, 15 April 1933.
9. Buch, Pearl, in *Profiles*, p.104.
10. *Young India*, 31 December 1931
11. Jesuit Scholars, *Hinduism*,. p.296.
12. Ibid .296.
13. *Young India*, 31 December 1931
14. Jesuit Scholars, *Hinduism*, p.295.
15. *An Autobiography*, Intr.
16. Jesuit Scholars, *Hinduism*, p.77.
17. *Young India*, 23 March 1922.
18. *An Autobiography*, p.285.
19. Ibid P.382.
20. Taylor, Edmond, in *Profiles*, p.71.
21. Thekkinedath, J., *Love of Neighbour*, p.97.
22. *Harijan*, 7 September 1935.
23. Jesuit Scholars, *Hinduism*, p.298.
24. *Young India* 25 August 1920.
25. *An Autobiograhpy*, p.261
26. Thekkinedath, J., *Love of Neighbour*, p.42.
27. *Mahatma*, Vol.4, p,308.

28. Jones, Stanley, in *profiles*, p.132.
29. *Young India*, 2 December 1926.
30. *An Autobiography*, p.383.
31. Ibid Intro.
32. Mehta, Ved, in Profiles, p.203.
33. *To the Students*, p.213.
34. Ibid p.113.
35. *Mahatma*, Vol.7, p.55.
36. *An Autobiography*, p.330.
37. *To the Students*, p.222.
38. Ibid p.145.
39. *Mahatma*, Vol.4, p.246.
40. Bhatia, B.D., *Philosophy*, p.123.
41. *To the Students*, p.113.
42. Ibid p.145.
43. *An Autobiography*, p.357.
44. Ibid p.298.
45. Thurman, Howard, in Profiles, p.44
46. *An Autobiography*, p.231.
47. Ibid p.382.
48. *To the Students*, p.145.
49. *Harijan*, 15 September 1940.
50. Gandhi, Devdas, in *profiles*, p.132.
51. *An Autobiography*, Intr.
52. Ibid p.298.
53. *To the Students*, p.91.
54. Snow, Edgar, in *Profiles*, p.106.
55. Marshall, G., in *Profiles*,p.96.
56. Macdonald D., in Ibid, p.110.
57. Bhatia, B.D., *Philosophy*, p.130.
58. *An Autobiography*, p.224.
59. *Better Education*, p.42.
60. *An Autobiography*, p.136.
61. Ibid p.285.
62. Ibid p.298.
63. *Harijan*, 25 March 1939
64. *To the Students*, p.113
65. Ibid p.11.
66. *An Autobiography*, p.383.
67. *To the Students*, p.146.

68. *An Autobiography*, p.383.
69. *To the Students*, p.145.
70. Ibid p.172.
71. *Harijan*, 13 April 1940.
72. *Mahatma*, Vol.4, p.187.
73. *Basic Education*, p.19.
74. *An Autobiography*, p.383.
75. *To the Students*, p.266.
76. Ibid p.71.
77. Jones, Stanley, in *Profiles*, p.134.
78. *Mahatma*, Vol.4, 29.
79. *To the Students*, p.71.
80. *Mahatma*, Vol.4, 29.
81. *To the Students*, p.91.
82. Gandhi, M.K., in *profiles*, p.138.
83. *An Autobiography*, p.66.
84. *Harijan*, 9 September 1939.
85. Ibid 10 March 1946.
86. *Mahatma*, Vol.1, p.119.
87. *An Autobiography*, p.256.
88. Gandhi, M.K., in *Profiles*, p.44
89. Cousins, Norman, *Profiles*, p.61.

7

VOCATIONAL EDUCATION

1. Gandhi's Basic Education - 1

One of the most well thought out schemes that emerged out of the Gandhian thoughts was basic education. Gandhi consistently spoke about the need for a drastic modification of the system of education introduced by the British. He bewailed the failure of that system in this country which had a great culture and traditions of its own. Gandhi wrote, "I firmly believe that Government schools have made us incapable, lacking individuality, as well as atheists".[1] According to him education introduced by the British lacked all the nobility, purposefulness and vigour of the ancient gurukula system: "The kind of English education imparted now-a-days makes the English educated individual impotent".[2]

Present-day Indian education, according to Gandhi revealed only a story of short comings. Education did not in any way cater to the needs of the largest chunk of the population. Education at all levels did not touch the vast villages in the country. The entire thing was a sheer drive for literacy and for the acquisition of irrelevant knowledge that did not help the student in later life. Gandhi says, "I could never blindly worship literary education".[3] Education, again, was a one-sided affair, that did not provide for earning one's daily bread : "India has become poorer than fifty years ago ..... the system of education is its worst part".[4] The most outstanding drawback of Indian education according to

Gandhi was that it made students totally dependent, instead of liberating them. Consequently, "Today, the youth, educated in Indian universities either ran after government jobs or fell into devious ways and sought an outlet for their frustrations by fermenting unrest".[5]

Gandhi regarded education as the most urgent need of the day because of these problems. His writings in 'Young India' and 'Harijan' reveal that he remained fully conscious of the need for a drastic revolution in the sphere of education. Gandhi promulgated his basic education as the only solution to the problems India was facing. Gandhi did not develop his concepts of basic education just in a day or two. It was the sum total and the result of experiments and thinking for several decades right from his days in South Africa upto the days of Independence. It took such a long period for him to synthesise an approach that aimed at the total development of the child in the school. Gandhi says, "By education I mean an all-round drawing of the best in child and man-mind, body and spirit".[6] This is what Gandhi found sadly absent in the education in his contemporary India. This is what Gandhi wanted Indian education to imbibe in order to evolve a system of education that would revive the ancient religious and social spirit.

While inaugurating Gujarat Vidyapeeth in November, 1920 Gandhi said, "Every home in this country is a school; and parents teachers".[7] Gandhi's basic education is broad-based. He wanted education to be free from the narrow limitations of the formal classroom. By this he brought home the basic fact that parents and the community have great responsibility in education. It is against this background that Gandhi builds his concept of basic education. Gandhi envisaged universal and compulsory education for all boys and girls in the country: "If education had to be made compulsory and accessible to all boys and girls in the country, schools and colleges should become self-sufficient".[8] This self-sufficiency on the economic front can be obtained only if literary education and craft-centered education can go hand-in-hand. Gandhi says, "Apart from recognising that along with literary education students should have craft education, there is apparently the necessity of continuing craft education in this country for making education self-sufficient".[9]

The Gandhian concept of basic education consists primarily in a synthesis between literary education and craft education. Gandhi firmly believed that "for the all-round development of boys and girls, all training should as far as possible be given through a profit-yielding vocation".[10] The absence of an education of this kind was the principal cause for the fact that education rendered itself useless. Education, for Gandhi, should cater to the needs of whole personality : head, heart and hand. Gandhian education is built on these foundations.

Education aims at the development of the individual's mind in its intellectual and spiritual dimensions : the mind and the spirit. Provision of knowledge on the one hand and formation of the spiritual personality on the other are central to any form of education that we may attempt. Gandhian education as we have seen in the present work attaches great importance to this aspect of the development of the individual's personality. But this development is not isolated from the craft which Gandhi envisaged. He says, "The fundamental aim of basic education is to provide mental and moral development through any handicraft".[11] Education, again aims at the development of the individual's heart, the seat of human emotions conventionally speaking. Gandhian education puts high premium on emotional development of the individual from a variety of view points. Gandhi says, "But I had always given the first place to the culture of the heart or the building of the character, and as I felt confident that moral training could be given to all alike, no matter how different this ages and upbringing, I decided to life among them all the twenty-four hours of they day as their father".[12] On the Tolstoy farm, again, Gandhi gave the highest importance to the education of the heart : "No text-book was used in the school. In education he (Gandhi) gave the first place to the culture of the heart or the building of the character".[13] Character development thus constitutes a central principle in basic education.

Education, lastly, means the training of the hand. This is where basic education bears a mark of distinction. Gandhian education puts a heavy premium on craft education or what we today call, vocational education. Gandhi was convinced that in order to train the whole man education need to be made craft-centered: "The craft chosen should be manual and productive".[14] Education in the present Gandhian context is conceived of as an integral phenomenon with a thoroughly holistic foundation for its success. Ultimately Gandhi is not willing to compromise or rather Gandhi is not willing to compromise on ultimate issues. Every moment he makes us aware that we should not lose sight of the ultimate concerns of education however forceful the more proximate and material values may seem to be. This emphasis on the ultimate spiritual, moral and humanistic values underlie Gandhi's concentration on vocational education also. We shall go fully wrong if we divert our attention from this point even for a moment. Basic education is centered on a number of fundamental values that Gandhi wanted children to develop as well as education to posses. The most attractive of these values is that of self-reliance or self-dependency. Ralph Templin says, "The Gandhian way is an alternate revolution, based on the soul-force and swadesism, the economics of group self-help".[15] It is this Gandhian spirit that has received expression in basic education. Gandhi developed a powerful passion for self-help : "My passion for self-help and simplicity ultimately expressed itself in extreme forms".[16] In this connection Gandhi exhorts students: "You should learn to wash your clothes, cook your food and do your work".[17] Basic education aims primarily at helping the individual develop this ability of self-reliance in all respects. For Gandhi this would mean economic self-reliance: "I can not find anything wrong with students meeting the cost of their education by means of some occupation even in the initial phases of their education".[18] This self-reliance also means physical self-help as found expression in Gandhi's own personal life where he learned to carry out most of his personal work himself. Lastly this would amount to emotional self-reliance in Basic education. Gandhi says, "Through the vocation in which the student receives training the personality hidden in him or her should receive full development". [19] Basic education aims at emotional integration and development centered on the craft.

Respect for manual work is yet another important value that basic education develops in the individual: "Manual training must be given side by side with intellectual training, and that it should have a principal place in national education. The principal means of stimulating the intellect should be manual training".[20] The Gandhian concept of human dignity is centered not on false assumptions on manual labour but on penetrating into the very depth of human life from whatever avenues available to man. Gandhi quotes Ruskin saying, "A life of labour, the life of the tiller of the soil and handicraftsman, is the life worth living".[21] This became a fundamental principle for Gandhi's later pursuits, especially in his Ashram life. Basic education is an education in which the dignity of manual labour is upheld. This is a training that would help the child to organise his own life: "It is to be emphasised that every minute of man's life is to be used in a productive manner".[22]

Basic education is a composite of numerous principles and values that render itself a unique place in Gandhian thought on the one side, and education on the other. Basic education is in essence on obedience to the law of bread labour in order to bring about a revolution in society. Man has to be shown his proper place in the whole economy of life on this earth. Only then will, as Gandhi envisages it,"the law of the brute be replaced by the law of man".[23] Basic education embodies this spirit.

2. Basic Education - 2

Basic education is primarily centered on the concept of craft as the focus of education. Education within this framework begins from the craft, moves around the craft and receives directions with reference to the craft. Gandhi says, "The fundamental aim of basic education is to provide mental and moral development through any handicraft".[24] Gandhi further envisages that "we will introduce the complete man in the student through the scientific teaching of a skill in the school".[25] Craft education is not a new thing in the context of education in India. Ancient and medieval education had numerous forms of craft included as part of it. The Buddhists concentrated on and introduced craft for vocational purposes. For Buddhist monks craft education was a means of strengthening their active presence in a community.

But Gandhi's concept of craft-centered education is quite different from the way followed in ancient India. For the Buddhist craft was proximate end itself. It was taught for its own sake i.e. to train individuals in order to make a living. Gandhi does not concentrate on the craft for its own sake. The craft, whatever be its nature, is a proximate means for the co-ordination of a vast repertoire of educational experiences. It is the centre for the radiation of everything that we want the individual to learn in the school. According to Gandhi, "craft is a meeting point of both physical and social environment represented by such subjects as general science, Social sciences and creative and expressional arts".[26] It is in and through the craft that education is thought of. Gandhi wanted the potentials of the craft to be fully exploited.

Gandhian craft education has a sound philosophical basis. He at once links craft with the most fundamental concerns of Gandhian thought : Truth and love. Gandhi envisaged a thoroughly integrated approach to the problem of craft-centered education: "The notion of Truth and Love penetrating life's activities".[27] The student is helped in several ways to experience truth in day-to-day life. Gandhi does not want education to be converted into an abstract and wholly intellectual affair. This he drives home on numerous occasions. The craft enables the student to exercise his mind on tangible materials and keep himself on the realm of concrete experiences. Every aspect of education is thus made relevant to the experience of truth in the personal life of the student. In other words, in this context, Gandhi sees craft as the principal means for the student to experience and realise truth and love in day-to-day life.

Gandhi envisages craft as the principal means for the stimulation of the intellect: "Manual training must be given side by side with intellectual training, and it should have a principal place in national education. The principal means of stimulating the intellect should be manual training".[28] Gandhi was often accused of holding an anti-intellectualist attitude. Writings as quoted above clearly show that Gandhi was not an anti-intellectualist. Gandhi did not advocate vocational or craft-education for its own sake. He clearly recognizes the role of intellectual preoccupations in student life and the need for knowledge-centered training. But the fact is that Gandhi does not worship knowledge for its own sake. For him all these are the means for the development of the moral, social and spiritual personality. Education caters to all these needs of the individual. Gandhian basic education uses the craft as the principal means for the stimulation of the intellectual powers in the individual. Gandhi says, "Thus, we give importance to physical and vocational training. Do not misunderstand that this training would in any way adversely affect your intellect .... An intellectual approach to vocational training would prove more useful to the intellect than doing leisurely reading of literature".[29]

Literary education, according to Gandhi should come after the introduction to the craft: I will not teach them the alphabet before they acquire basic information in history, geography, arithmetics and spinning".[30] Gandhi does not wish basic education to start with education in literacy instead the craft should be the beginning. Gandhi stresses this point: "I would therefore begin the child's education by teaching it a useful handicraft and by enabling it to produce from the moment it begins its training".[31] Other knowledge-oriented subjects should emanate from the basic knowledge of craft at the elementary level.

Gandhi was confident that development of the intellect was possible through the charka: "Such a thing was miraculously possible if teaching is not done in a mechanical way".[32] It is possible when the details and the reasons for every mechanical activity involved in spinning or any craft is explained to children. The child is introduced to a lot of information when the history of cotton and the intricate relation of this history to civilisation is explained to them. All these processes and the information that these processes can generate will hold his attention and provide training to his eyes and mind.

Craft education in the Gandhian sense is not mere provision of opportunities for manual labour as it is often accused of. Several important factors and principles are involved in the learning of the craft: "Stress should be laid on principles of co-operative activity planning, accuracy, initiative and individual responsibility in learning".[33] A whole set of such attitudes and aptitudes develop in course of the craft-centered education. The craft enables cooperative interaction among students at the level of activity centered on the craft. This cooperative interaction becomes necessary for the social development of the individual. As Gandhi says, "craft is the meeting place of both physical and social environment".[34] It will not be possible to generate such a high degree of cooperative interaction in education by any means other than working on a craft. Similarly, craft enables the individual to develop his aptitude of accuracy and clear-headedness. Acute and accurate observation is intended as an object of education which cannot be ordinarily developed in theoretical education. Craft provides opportunities for this and helps the student to develop this sense of accuracy.

Craft-centered education is a chief means, according to Gandhi, to develop a problem-solving ability in the individual. The craft is a complex phenomenon so far as the child is concerned. The processes of the machine, the handling of the machine, the production of the commodity, organising the materials etc. constantly pose problems that the student will have to face. These problems are very different from those that arise in purely academic education. The student is called on to apply his mind on every such problem, see the problem from a number of viewpoints and try out various solutions. This is the kind of training that Gandhi wanted education to provide at all levels. All education should have an ultimate impact on the individual, in the formation of his personality and character.

In regard to basic education Gandhi attaches the highest possible importance to the income of a poor rural family. Gandhi writes, "something is basically wrong, especially in such a poor country like ours, when parents are compelled to take care of such grown up children and at the same time bear such a heavy expenses of their education".[35] Gandhi was throughout conscious of this important factor. For him the charka was the only solution to this problem of economy. The charka was for him a redemptive factor as far as the Indian rural population was concerned. Gandhi envisages a time when all the members of the rural family resorted to spinning and weaving and earned their decent lively income: "Such families will achieve the kind of fame in self-confidence and independence hitherto not thought of". [36] Under these circumstances children's education will not become a burden on the parents.

According to Gandhi knowledge and mental development should come from life-experiences, and not merely from the pages of books or from the classrooms. He says, "Mental development should come from hard experiences; it need not come from the school or college classroom".[37] Basic education centered on the craft makes these experiences available to the child to a great extent. These life-experiences include all the efforts on the part of the individual for a decent survival of himself and the family of which he is a part. Gandhi does not want any individual to desire a level of life that most others are not privileged to have: "First of all, we should develop an attitude that we do not want to enjoy any property or facility that millions of others like us are deprived of ".[38] This becomes possible at least to some extent only by facing the hard reality of life where one can. Basic education through the craft puts the student down-to-earth, confront a set of problems related at least to the successful handling of the craft, and organise learning experiences not as unrelated to life but as totally related to the life in the community. Then the whole process will have its impact on the personality of the individual.

3. Need-based Education in India

The British gave us a system of education that has since then constituted the infrastructure of Indian education. All the attempts during the post-Independence era to depart from the deepest British system have only affected things at the surface, superficial level. The British system did not leave room for the development of a national policy on Indian education that would effectively cater to the manifold socio-economic needs of this country. A development of this concept of a national policy on education was possible only after Independence. After two decades of fluctuating experiments we had the first National Policy promulgated in 1968 which was a significant step in the history of education in Post-Independence India. The policy "aimed to promote national progress, a sense of common citizenship and culture, and to strengthen national integration. It laid stress on the need for a radical reconstruction of the education system ....., the cultivation of moral values and a closer relation between education and the life of the people".[39] The major effort lay in trying to recognise and define the problems and provide directions to those solutions.

Education in India as envisaged by Gandhi as well to fall in line with the Gandhian thoughts should be need-based. India has vast human and material resources. India is like a home which has a treasure in safe-keeping while at the same time starvation prevails there. We are over-whelmed with problems while we have tremendous resources in safe-keeping. Hence the most urgent constituent of our national policy on education is to bridge the gap between our problems and our resources. In other words the country requires a full utilisation of its human and material resources to meet the challenge of unfailing national development. Education itself is the principal step to the utilisation of human resources. Recognising this we have come to use the term 'Human resources development' for education. A Need-based pattern of education would primarily cater to the full use of the available resources rather than carry on with an abstract pattern of work unrelated to the problems a country is facing. The material resources available in plenty in this country should be converted into the material on which education should make the students apply their minds. Gandhi is clear on this issue: "That requires that we must utilise all available human labour before we entertain the idea of employing mechanical power".[40] Gandhi upholds the dignity of human labour and proposes a system in which every body should bear in mind the dignity of labour. Education should help individuals in course of time to employ oneself to the utilisation of material resources available in this country and contribute to national production.

Need-based education, again, should be problem-oriented. Education in the rightsense as well as in a way Gandhi visualises it, deals with problems. The pragmatic education proposed and developed by John Dewey is a problem-oriented education. Gandhi too thought in these lines. In this relation Gandhi wanted "to convert every school into a community where individuality is not damped out but developed through social contacts and varied opportunities of service".[41] A problem-oriented pattern of education brings the child right into the midst of the community to put him in touch with the concrete problems of real life. Education in India should enable the student to develop a complete sensitivity to the problems the country is facing. No aspect of the training should help him to shut his eyes on the face of problems.

This would mean application of the student's mind to problems. This is an essential element of Gandhian thoughts on education. Gandhi saw life as a chain of experiments. His entire life was a continuous history of these experiments. Gandhi wrote, "I simply want to tell the story of my experiments with truth, and my life consists of nothing but those experiments".[42] Gandhi's own life is a testimony of experiments in living a simple life. He wants students to know and develop this habit as closely related to one's personal life and character formation. Gandhi's convictions in this regard find expression in the following when he says, "I have tested the truth by experience that the primary virtues of mankind are possible for cultivation by the meanest of human creation".[43] Education should thus be problem-oriented. It would mean developing an ability to perceive the problem, define the problem and subject various alternative solutions to clear test and experiment so that truth will finally reign in one's life.

Need-based education in Gandhian lines amounts to mass education. Gandhi thought, worked and lined for the masses in rural India. He wanted all educational efforts to be geared to the benefit and development of the population in the vast rural India. He says, "I am firm in my conviction that India should have free and compulsory elementary education. In my opinion this objective can be realised only by providing training in a useful craft and by developing their physical, intellectual and spiritual potentials".[44] Vocational education at once becomes relevant much more to the rural India at large and to mass education in particular. Gandhi always had the masses in mind when he spoke of national policies. Education of the masses can be achieved through a variety of educational techniques that we have begun employing : non-formal education, adult education programmes, open university education and so on. Mass education is the need of the day and all educational efforts are to be oriented to provide educational and literacy experiences to the masses in this country if we have to do justice to the Gandhian ideals.

Need-based education further, focuses on the eradication or illiteracy. Mass education and the eradication of illiteracy are fundamentally the same at the conceptual level. All the same illiteracy is something to which attention can be paid on its own right. Gandhi viewed this problem in a peculiar way: "Let the readers remember that India has more illiterates today than fifty years ago, and the reason for it is not the unwillingness of parents, but a scheme of education that is totally foreign and unnatural with respect to this country".[45] The post-Independence India set a ten year target in 1949 and wanted to achieve universalisation of elementary education by 1959. But even during the third five year plan in the sixties we had not achieved the target of universalisation in accordance to the demands of the Constitution. Even in the 80's we are still to achieve this target and India is left with a sizeable illiterate population. A Need-based education aims at directing all possible energies to the total eradication of illiteracy from this country in accordance with the Gandhian ideals.

Need-based education calls for a continuous revision of educational policies and for the re-definition of the aims of education. Major efforts in this direction are made in the 1986 Policy on National Education initiated by Rajiv Gandhi. The educational infrastructure laid by the British in India makes things difficult for drastic alterations on the one hand, while India has been able easily to develop a system on the other because of that. Education in this country cannot neglect the overwhelming problem of unemployment. Periodical review of educational programmes and an evaluation of the success of these programmes will enable the country to partly meet these demands. A Need-based education will think twice before importing to this country merely for the sake of change educational innovations initiated in other countries.

4. Rural Reconstruction

Vocational education is concerned of by Gandhi as the principal means of his most ambitious village reconstruction. It is not an exaggeration if we say that Gandhi thought and lived for the rural India. The upliftment of the rural population was Gandhi's primary concern. Every aspect of education he thought only with reference to the welfare of the rural masses. He says, "If our education should become compulsory, considering from the viewpoint for the needs of Indian villages, we should begin from the belief that education will become self-supporing".[46] Vocationalisation of education is a comprehensive phenomenon which enables Gandhi to provide solutions for most of the evils and pitfalls found in Indian villages. Gandhi invents the charka as the unique solution for all these problems which the rural India faced.

By rural reconstruction Gandhi means several specific things. For him it becomes a process of enlivening village life in this country. The villages are the nerve-centre of India. He says, "My mind is living in the villages. They are calling me to bury myself in them".[47] In spite of his most busy political schedules later Gandhi found time to 'bury himself' in villages to experience their life and to feel one with them. Village reconstruction for him meant leading them to a healthy and hygienic life. He tells students, "Visit the dwelling place of harijans and clean up these places. If the harijans are willing to help you in the process, gladly accept their help".[48] The dangers of unhygienic environment are often the focus of Gandhi's discussions with villagers wherever he went. Gandhi's efforts in village reconstruction in this regard in Champaran was a memorable episode. Leaving his active political involvement for a while Gandhi travels to Champaran in Bihar to help the planation labourers there.

Village reconstruction for him meant economic liberation. Gandhi reminds us of the past glory of the Indian villages when villages were economically self-sufficient and independent. Gandhi alleges that the introduction of British economic system and consequent industrialisation destroyed the Indian village economy: "The village economy of the time was based not on the rights of the people, but on doing their duties. Those who were involved in such occupations earned their livelihood ...... There was more light in the eyes of the people than now; their hands were much more lively. Life at that time was based on a well-accepted law of ahimsa".[49] Today people in the villages are deserting their village life for lucrative jobs in towns destroying the structure of Indian villages. Gandhi's village reconstruction plans aims at the economic liberation of the villagers so that their overall life-pattern will be safe and sound within the framework of a simple life that Gandhi envisaged.

Rural reconstruction for Gandhi means all forms of self-employment for the village population. All plans for vocationalisation for villages concretely aim at ultimately providing jobs for every individual;. Gandhi says, "I would therefore begin the child's education by teaching it a useful handicraft and by enabling it to produce from the moment it begins it training".[50] Gandhian education is liberal or rather liberating. It liberates the individual from the bondage of economic dependency. Education has no sense unless it gains this independence. Rural India is what it is today only because of the economic backwardness, exorbitantly low per-capital income and manifold dependence and evils arising from this economic backwardness. Rural reconstruction through self-employment is the unique ways of helping the villages to become independent and partly manage their own affairs.

Gandhi attaches great significance to manual labour with reference to rural reconstruction. Manual labour is significant for Gandhi not because it is related to poverty. Gandhi discovered in manual labour a dimension of self-expression within the frame work of the simplicity that is precious to him. Manual labour is an expression of the individual's social attachment. It is the best means of associating oneself with the day-to-day survival and progress of a community. It is the most concrete way an individual can contribute to the welfare of other persons in particular and of society at large. It is an expression of the ultimate service Gandhi envisages: "So a man can only exercise perfect love and be completely dispossessed, if he is prepared to embrace death and renounces his body for the sake of human service".[51]

The dignity of manual labour is to be understood in this wider and nobler sense. Gandhi wants education to uphold this dignity of labour: "Obedience to the law of bread labour will bring about a revolution in the structure of society ...... the law of the brute will be replace by the law of man".[52] All this is based on Gandhi's perfect conviction regarding the value of life. He says, "It is to be emphasised that every minute of a man's life is to be used in a productive manner".[53] Everything is ultimately traced back to the ultimate values of life: truth and love.

It is this dimension called manual labour that Gandhi sees as a perfect means for village reconstruction. Education should enable individuals in the village to fall back on manual labour as the principal means of participation in the rural development programmes. Gandhi says, "Manual training should be given side by side with intellectual training, and that it should have a principal place in national education. The principal means of stimulating the intellect should be manual training".[54] Education not only provides a background for the proper development of these attitudes but also pave way for a systematic application of these principles in village reconstruction. A number of attitudes require development in regard to the exercise of manual work. Gandhi considers all these attitudes as essential elements of the individual's personality development: "Through the vocation in which the student receives training the personality hidden in him or her should receive full development".[55] On completion of education Gandhi wants a perfect man to emerge, a man perfect in the social, psychological and spiritual sense.

Gandhi admonishes students to take active participation in rural reconstruction and feel for themselves the dignity of labour. Gandhi bewails, "It is a pity that our students look upon physical labour with dislike if not with contempt".[56] He was convinced that a nation could never march towards progress without committing themselves to physical labour : "There is nothing more unworthy of a nation than to dislike physical labour".[57] Villages are the nerve-centres of the nation. A reinvigoration of the village through plans of rural reconstruction cannot be brushed aside for anything apparently more important. Vocational education accepts rural reconstruction, as a principal objective and a perennial urgency for which no efforts can be spared. Gandhi's thoughts on the villages are far-reaching. He says. "The problem is whether this basic scheme of education fulfills the genuine needs of the people living in villages. I do not hope that India will never be industrialised so fully as to leave no village. The village therefore will always be the most important unit of India".[58] Vocationalisation will be the chief means of the reconstruction of Indian villages.

5. Vocational Education in the 1986 National Policy

The National Education Policy of 1986 is a far-reaching and significant step in coordinating education in India within the framework of the fundamental constitutional demands regarding education in this country. The Policy says, "It aimed to promote national progress, a sense of common citizenship and culture and to strengthen national integration. It laid stress on the need for a radical reconstruction of the education system, to improve its quality at all stages, and gave much greater attention to science and technology, the cultivation of moral values and a closer relation between education and the life of the people".[59] It was a policy of this kind that British education did not care to develop and one that Gandhi so badly wanted to guide education in India. The New Policy recognises the Gandhian overtones in regard to the direction the policy would take: "The new pattern of the Rural University will be consolidated and developed on the lines of Mahatma Gandhi's revolutionary ideas on education so as to take up the challenges of micro-planning at grassroot levels for the transformation of rural areas. Institutions and programmes of Gandhian basic education will be supported".[60] Not only have Gandhian basic thoughts but also aspects of vocational education in particular have become focus of attention in the 1986 policy.

The Policy on Education primarily aims at providing a national orientation in the details of educational programmes. Education has been recognised more fully as 'human resources development' more than anything else. Attention of the nation has been called on to focus education more than ever and education is projected as a major issue with its most urgent needs and vast untapped resources. A national debate on the issue of educational problems is called for with a view to creating an increased conscientisation of the nation's responsibility in this regard. A national orientation to reforms in education would affect all stages of education and all the educational institutions as well as agencies that are at work.

The 1986 Policy on Education attempts to redefine educational objectives. The necessary directives for the formulation of a National Policy of this kind were given by the Kothari Commission (1966) in a very detailed manner. According to those directives and recommendations a National Policy on Education in India was formulated in 1968: The first National Policy after Independence. In spite of all the efforts made to renew the Nation's approach to education problems of massive dimensions still remained unsolved: "The rural areas, with poor infrastructure and social services, will not get the profit of trained and educated youth, unless rural-urban disparities are reduced and determined measures are taken to promote diversification and dispersal of employment opportunities".[61] Hence the 1986 Policy undertakes a redefinition of the educational objectives in this country in the light of the most urgent problems so that stringent measures can be taken to promote the expected national development. Equalisation of educational opportunities will receive the highest priority. Education for women's equality, education of scheduled castes, education of scheduled tribes, all sorts of minority communities, education of the handicapped, illiterate adults and early childhood care and education come under the priority-based policy decisions. Educational objectives in India are thus seen from a new and dynamic perspective in the National

Policy.

The National Policy recognises with care that "the intro-duction of systematic, well-planned and rigorously imple-mented programmes of vocational education is crucial in the proposed reorganisation".[62] Vocational education aims at the development and supply of skilled manpower. Education has come to be aptly called 'human resources development' in recognition of the role education plays in the development of manpower for the nation. Manpower will mean several things in different contexts. The nation can march towards progress within the framework of the constitutional provisions only through the availability of educated, skilled manpower. Academic provisions of higher education at the university level provides for the national manpower of professional and semiprofessional kind. As we are well aware today every educated man and woman in the country looks for a white-collared job. Nobody is willing to recognise the dignity of skilled and manual labour which constitute the backbone of the country's development. The flight for professional and white-collared jobs by everyone who passes out of schools and colleges poses for the country a serious problem.

Vocational education is the sole means to provide for the nation the necessary skilled manpower. The National Policy endeavours to concentrate on vocational education to enable the country to have people capable of handling a large variety of occupational and skilled production situations. The country already has a distinct vocational stream meant for concentrated vocational education. The multipurpose high schools, technical higher secondary schools, technical high schools, Industrial Training Institutes and Polytechnics are part of the institutional network that are today endeavouring to train skilled manpower as part of the larger vocational pattern of education.

The National Policy of 1986, the policy of 1968 as well as the Kothari Commission of 1966 paved way for a clear bifurcation of education after the secondary level. The ten year school education with its primary and secondary segments as envisaged as the universal and compulsory foundation for the building of an educated population, with a knowledge of the traditions and culture of the country. As much as possible no bifurcation or specialisation is permitted upto this level except in the technical high schools where the students is allowed to opt for a technical subject for training along with the regular school subjects. On completion of the ten year schooling a major bifurcation is allowed to take place. Students who pass out the ten year secondary phase can opt for a clear-cut vocational stream of education provided in the vocational institutions mentioned above or pursue higher education at the university level. The +2 stage of the higher secondary is provided all over India today as the foundation for university education for academic pursuits. Today's vocational higher secondary schools can be regarded as a vocational parallel for the usual non-vocational +2 level. This bifurcation has been a major step in the vocationalisation of education in India.

The National Policy envisages health services as an important area for the promotion of vocational courses: "Health planning and health service management should optimally interlock with the education and training of appropriate categories of health manpower through health-related vocational courses".[63] Health education has been considered an integral component of school education for the last one decade. Physical education and health education are made integral part of the teacher education programmes in our country. Health education has a central place in Gandhian education: "Along with the vocational courses for which they spend most of their time, lessons will be given in geography, history and arithmetic. They will learn good manners and will have lessons on practical hygiene and health science".[64] Health education in schools, and health services in the community provide considerable scope for vocational education. The employment opportunities national health services offer will be able to yield a variety of health service courses and subsequently provide employment for the trainees in lines with their training. The National Policy aims at making provisions for this.

Another important area for the promotion of vocational education is agriculture and marketing. India is an agrarian society where the large majority subsist by agricultural income and products. Agriculture has been recognised as a most potential area for the generation even of vocational courses. The Mudaliar Commission of 1953 as well as the Kothari Commission of 1966 gave high priority to education based on agriculture leading to active participation in agricultural development. As a result the recent five year plans have included several measures to link agriculture and education. The establishment of agricultural universities in all the states has been a major step ahead in this direction. Similarly marketing is recognised as dynamic area for vocational courses. Marketing Federations such as Milk and fish Marketing Federations have sprung up in different States in India. The National Policy on Education envisages on increased number of vocational courses based on agriculture and marketing in such a way as to provide employment and increase agricultural and marketing efficiency as part of national development.

Efforts will also be made as part of the National Policy to generate vocational courses based on Social Service. For Gandhi social services constituted an important area for students to keep themselves in touch with the community for their own development. Gandhi says, "Swaraj does not depend on jail-going.... It depends on everyone doing his own task. And that task has been shown to you. Go to the villages, identify with villagers, befriend the untouchables make Hindu-Muslim unity a concrete fact".[65] Social services in this country offers numerous opportunities for the employment of full-time or part-time hands with a view to carrying the message of development to the rural India. Rural and urban based social service schemes will open up vocational courses that can be significant contribution to vocational education on the one hand and development programmes on the other.

Catering to the needs of women and rural students is another area that offers prospects for vocational education. The National policy gives special consideration to women's education and that of students from backward areas. Volunteers of several kinds may be educated to reach women and rural students in a very special way. These orientations offer prospects for vocational courses that can be provided in vocational institutions together with that of other social services. Gandhi is unconditional in his insistence on students reaching out to the rural regions: "Students should spend every day of their vocation in the villages around their schools and colleges".[66] Vocational courses can bridge the widening gap between university and school students and the rural India.

Vocational courses can also meet the increasing need for equalisation of educational opportunities. As in the case of rural students, the deprived and the handicapped sections of our society offer opportunities for vocational education. We require special training to reach out and provide educational and welfare facilities for the handicapped and socially deprived sections of society. The National Policy makes special mention of this area of vocational courses in which a major Gandhian objective will be fulfilled.

All these and others amount to a need-based vocational programme for national development. The New Policy also envisages vocational courses for those who pass out the higher secondary stage. Vocational education as part of the wider Gandhian education is envisaged as the unique solution for meeting present-day problem of unemployment. Vocational education either incorporated as part of academic education or as bifurcated from higher education is the unique Gandhian solution for bridging the gap between the problems and the resources of our country. The National Policy aims at developing the scope of vocational education to its fullest extent and provide employment opportunities that constitute the most urgent problem of the country.

References

1. *Towards New Education*, p.5.
2. Ibid p.8
3. Ibid p.5
4. Ibid p.8
5. *Mahatma*, Vol 7, p.176
6. *Harijan*, 14 July 1937
7. *To the Students*, p.48
8. Ibid p.142
9. Ibid p.142
10. *Mahatma*, Vol 4., p.198
11. *Harijan*, 6 April 1940.
12. *An Autobiography*. 251.
13. *Mahatma*, Vol.1, p.119
14. Bhatia. B.D., *Philosophy*, p.130.
15. Templin, Ralph, in *Profiles*, p.116.
16. *An autobiography*, p.186.
17. *To the Students*, p.91.
18. Ibid p.54
19. *Basic Education*, p.19.
20. *Mahatma*, Vol.4, p.187.
21. *An Autobiography*,, p.224.
22. *Harijan*, 6 April 1940.
23. *Mahatma*, Vol.4, p.36.
24. *Harijan*, 6 April 1940.
25. *Basic Education*, p.51.
26. Bhatia, B.D., *Philosophy*, p.131.
27. Ibid p.131.
28. *Mahatma*, Vol.4, p.187.
29. *To the Students*, p.139.
30. *Basic Education*, p.13.
31. *Harijan*, 14 July 1937.
32. *Basic Education*, p.13.
33. Bhatia, B.D., *Philosophy*, p.131.
34. Ibid p.131.
35. *To the Students*, p.54.
36. Ibid p.54.
37. Ibid p.70

38. Ibid p.70
39. *National Policy on Education* (1986) 1:4. MHRSD, Government of India, New Delhi, 1986.
40. *Mahatma*, Vol.7, p.180.
41. Bhatia B.D., *Philosophy*, p.130.
42. *An Autobiography*, Intr.
43. *Mahatma*, Vol.4, p.40.
44. *Basic Education*, p.47.
45. *Towards New Education*, p.68.
46. *Basic Education*, p.36.
47. *Mahatma*, Vol.4, p.40.
48. *To the students*, p.197.
49. *Harijan*, 1 September 1940.
50. Ibid 14 July 1937.
51. *Mahatma*, Vol.4, p.11.
52. *Mahatma*, Vol.4, p.36.
53. *Harijan*, 6 April 1940.
54. *Mahatma*, Vol.4, p.187.
55. *Basic Education* , p.19.
56. *Towards New Education*, p.37.
57. Ibid p.41.
58. *Harijan*, 14 February 1939
59. National Policy on Education (1986). 1 : 4.
60. Ibid 5 : 42.
61. Ibid 1 : 12
62. Ibid 5 : 16
63. Ibid 5 : 18
64. *Towards New Education*, 29.
65. *Mahatma*, Vol.4, p.29.
66. *To the Students*, p.169.

8

HOLISTIC EDUCATION IN GANDHISM

1. Aspects of Holistic Education

Gandhism stands for the total and integral approach to all life's problems. This was the approach Gandhi had towards economic, educational, social and moral problems, not to mention his political and religious approaches. Gandhi always remained convinced that a partial and one-sided approach to personal, social or national problem could only lead one to a greater difficulty. Gandhi is in other words holistic in his attitudes towards problems. Spirituality and religion for him mean something so total and encompassing that even a morning dew is not exempted from it. Every aspect of his day-to-day life had everything to do with religion. John Gunther testifies that "His approach to everything is religious".[1] In the same manner, economics does not mean for him merely something to do with money and production, but again so total and encompassing as to include questions of religion and spirituality. Gandhian economics has everything to do with Gandhian spirituality: "When a man looks upon himself as a servant of society, earn his wealth for society and spend it for the good of society, then his wealth becomes sacred; there is non-violence in his attempts".[2] Here economics does not become an isolated phenomenon.

Similarly education does not merely mean, for Gandhi,

something to do with teaching in the classroom or passing on knowledge to children. Education is so total and encompassing that the goals of education are identified with the goals of life itself: "The Summum Bonum of life and education is self-realisation".[3] Again, "If the education we get separates us from God and if it does not help us to serve our fellowmen then such an education is not worthy of its name".[4] This encompassing and comprehensive approach to education that enables education to subsume the highest ideals of human life makes Gandhian education holistic by nature. Every aspect of man's life is so integrally knit together into a harmonious whole which is called education within Gandhian thoughts. It is therefore most difficult with the Gandhian system to develop a concept, a theory or a discipline in isolation without close reference to the rest of the Gandhian system.

The notion of holistic education is applied to Gandhian education also in very specific and concrete sense. Gandhian education as a holistic system incorporates every aspect of the individual's personality : spiritual, moral, mental, social, psychological and physical. Most reformers who study the human personality have the tendency to neglect, overlook or deny the importance of one aspect of the individual's personality to emphasise another aspect. It is unique of Gandhi to bring together into focus every conceivable aspect of the individual's personality to develop the fundamental concept of education. The Gandhian definition of education testifies this : "By education I mean the all round drawing of the best in child and man-body, mind and spirit".[5] Education by this becomes a holistic phenomenon in theory and in practice. Any one who wishes to confine the scope of education to mere academic achievement finds himself in serious error because thereby the process of education becomes unrelated to its ultimate goals.

Holistic education assumes an integrated approach to learning. Modern education lacks this quality : "Modern education has the tendency to turn our eyes away from the soul. Therefore the potentials of the soul-force do not excite us".[6] Knowledge today is compartmentalised. By this process of specialisation our attention becomes more and more concentrated on absolutely peripheral information wholly unrelated to and too much segregated from the source about which the knowledge is developed. Study of the life of man on this earth has become so specialised that as the specialisation progresses the source or the object, man, is fully forgotten. This gives rise to a very funny state of affairs. The human being for Gandhi is a wholly integral person and what modern science does is to disintegrate his personality. Gandhi says, "Man is not a sheer intellect, animal body, heart or soul. To create a whole and integral man a suitable and perfect integration of these three is required. This exactly is the essence of education".[7] Efforts in education cannot therefore drift away from its centre i.e. the personality of the learner.

Holistic education means that all the knowledge aims at ultimate values. Just as a non-integral approach has the tendency to drift away from the person of the student, a non-holistic education has the tendency to restrict and limit knowledge to the levels of merely immediate objectives. The student's vision is led only to an immediate and limited horizon with regard to human values. A holistic education as envisaged by Gandhi cannot keep things in a proximate range but leads the student directly to those values related to the ultimate aims of education i.e. God himself and truth and love, His expressions. Gandhi says, "To develop the spirit is to build the character and to enable one to work towards a knowledge of God and self-realisation".[8] Again for Gandhi "True education is that which draws out and stimulates the spiritual, the intellectual and physical faculties of the children".[9] Education should keep the ultimate values close at hand in everything that is imparted. Losing sight of this vision endangers the objectives of education.

Holistic education develops a whole range of values that constitute an integral part of the kind of personality that Gandhi wants the student to develop. This amounts to the modern concept of value education. Gandhi's own life was an exemplification and a living testimony of a whole range of personal values that radiated the greatness that Gandhi was. Holistic education keeps value education at its very centre and organises everything else from this perspective. Gandhi was conscious of the significance of this when he said, "The teacher should not be a slave to textbooks. He should have his opportunities to give his own to the students".[10] The teacher's personal perfection is the aim of holistic education. Louis Fischer writes, "One of the greatest news pictures ever made of Gandhi was with Lady Mountabatten walking together with his hands on the shoulders of the Viceroy's wife and let her support him as he walked".[11] Louis Fischer makes a special mention of this in proof of Gandhi's immense personal perfection. It was this personal perfection that made Gandhi great in the eyes of the world : "Gandhi retained their (the British) respect, often their love through his softness, tenderness and patience".[12] Gandhi wanted education to develop personal qualities in such a way as to produce persons in whom the most refined human qualities find realisation.

Holistic education is made vocational to include aspects of education that only a vocation can provide. Aspects of integral development mentioned above can be better realised in the framework of vocational education: "The notion of education through handicrafts rose from the contemplation of Truth and Love penetrating life's activities".[13] Vocational education, for Gandhi, is the embodiment of the basic principles of life that children will be given to practice. The skill, the occupation, or the craft on which vocational education is based becomes the centre of a spectrum of principles and values that Gandhi wants education to develop in the individual. Gandhi's vision takes a concrete form in vocational education: "We will introduce the complete man in the student through the scientific teaching of a skill in the school".[14] This is the true scope of education in the holistic sense. The student is not lost in world of abstractions and information unrelated to a life for which he is prepared in society. The vocation renders education concrete and links knowledge with experiences and a system of values. Thus occasional education if conducted in proper lines becomes holistic education.

Holistic education, lastly, includes training in social attitudes. Dwight Macdonald writes about Gandhi. "It is true that Gandhi 'compromised' with the rich, those untouchables of the class struggle, living at their villas. But he also compromised with the poor spending as much time with them".[15] Education itself is socially oriented with scope of developing social attitudes. Holistic education is organised to enable students to life for the community as a whole and other individuals in particular. The great social attitudes of Gandhi merged intensely with his religious concerns and it is difficult to distinguish between both. Holistic education thus includes ways and means of developing in the individual attitudes that will help him feel one with society.

Modern education has an increasing tendency for disintegration through specialisation. Attempts brought about to integrate different discipline often only worsen the situation. Gandhi foresaw this danger and wanted all education to keep the person on the focus. This is exactly the function of holistic education. All sorts of value-orientations are developed in the student's personality within the framework of the curriculum and the syllabus. The total personality of the learner becomes the object of holistic education.

2. Tradition Vs Modernism in Gandhi

E.Stanley Jones wrote, "And there was Mahatma Gandhi, the leader of the New India, an ascetic. It gripped the soul of ancient India. But he gripped the soul of modern India by relating renunciation to the needs around".[16] Gandhi is the symbol of the unity between the ancient and the modern, between tradition and modernity in India. Gandhi is the symbol of an essential integration between the two dimensions of life. This attitude is all the more important in an age ultramodernism of a meaningless kind where we have the tendency to stampede whatever is traditional and old.

Gandhi kept his eyes firmly on the Indian tradition: "Your only desire should be to reinstate everything that is great and lasting in our ancient culture".[17] But this is done not for the sake of traditions or merely to prepetuate these traditions. Gandhi wants traditional values to be perpetuated as a principal direction in our attempts to modernise ourselves. Traditions, as they are great in our country, are the chief guidelines in our religious, social and cultural life. Gandhi moved and worked on the basis of this conviction. Gandhi employed the values of Indian tradition as parameters to measure modern trends, values and idealism. Traditional values and beliefs have undergone the great test of time as against the often whimsical trends that become easily established for the sake of modernity.

This integration between tradition and modernity and values relating to these deeply characterised Gandhi. He was a personification of this integration. In Gandhi we find "an ascetic and a servant",[18] an ascetic of ancient India who sought God in total isolation, and a servant of modern India who seeks God in the service of others. Gandhi was both and he excelled in both and arrived at a perfect integration of prayer and service. He never allowed any one to predominate the other and this integration was perhaps the greatest success in his personal life. This integration governed every aspect of his life and gave him immense courage to face problems. K.L.Gauba says, "The essence of Gandhi's teaching was fearlessness and truth and action allied to these, always keeping the welfare of the masses and the down-trodden and the helpless in view".[19] This courage made him one of the greatest champions of humanity the world has ever seen.

Traditionalism in Gandhi means educational traditionalism. Gandhi most often goes back to the Vedic days of education recalling the efficacies of the gurukula system : "As a lover of the gurukula system allow me to make a couple of proposals for the committee and the parents. If the children of the gurukula are to develop self-dependence and self-sufficiency, they should be given a complete training in a craft".[20] Gandhi is overwhelmed by the value specifications of education in the Vedic India whose benefits he is not tired of recalling. Traditional education in India never overemphasised the role of knowledge. The principal focus was character formation : "I regard character building as the proper foundation for the education of the young people".[21] Gandhi goes to the extent of even saying that "character formation is the aim of even knowledge".[22] In other words, for Gandhi, "The principal aim of all education is character formation".[23]

The student, for Gandhi, is a brahmachari, a concept most central to traditional Indian education: "Equivalent to the term 'student' we have the beautiful term 'brahmachari' in our languages. 'Student' is an artificially coined word. This cannot substitute the word 'brahmachari'".[24] The word and the value of purity is synonymous to brahmachari and Gandhi projects this value as central to education: "purity in the life of an individual is the quintessence of effective education".[25] Traditional Indian values intensely grip Gandhi's soul and his thoughts on education permeate with these concepts and values. Gandhi says. "A student is like a rishi; he should be an embodiment of simple life and high thinking".[26] Gandhian education aims at the development of a moral and spiritual personality according to the dictates of traditional Indian values that we still hold as precious.

Traditionalism in Gandhi would mean religious traditionalism. Gandhi always held fast to the most basic religious values of Hinduism as practiced in ancient India. In spite of his intense research into world religions and attempts to study religions in depth, he says that he found no other religion greater than Hinduism which is an embodiment of all that traditional India was. Gandhi tells students, "I do not hold that everything old is good just because it is ancient. I do not ask anybody to sacrifice his power of discrimination that is God-given before laws that are ancient. Gandhi obtained intense training in his traditional religion right from his early childhood. He recalls the role his mother played in that regard. Gandhi's education lead him to an ever greater depth of religious fever in later years. Self-realisation and dharma became the catch-words of his life: "What I want to achieve is self-realisation, to see God face to face, to attain moksha".[28] The religious values and beliefs of traditional Hinduism made such an appeal on Gandhi that it was on the foundation of these that he built his own spirituality and personal attitudes towards God and religion. No one can ever deny that Gandhi was a religious traditionalist at the very core and in a positive sense of the term.

Traditionalism in Gandhi would mean sociological traditionalism. Modernism in social attitudes in life as looked upon by Gandhi with considerable care and suspicion. The life of Gandhi always remained an example of great simplicity and humility with a constant readiness to sacrifice one's comforts for the sake of others in the community: "I must reduce myself to a zero, so long as a man does not of his own free will put himself last among his fellow creatures, there is no salvation for him".[29] Gandhi always took pains to warn us against the glamour of the West. He said, "We must not be overpowered by the glamour of the West, we must not mistake this glamour for true light".[30] Education in the Gandhian sense aims at the development of correct social attitudes. These attitudes as Gandhi visualises them must not depart from the well accepted and noble traditions of the country as based on truth and ahimsa.

But all the traditional beliefs, approaches and attitudes in Gandhi are not meant for the sake of tradition itself: "I do not hold that everything old is good just because it is ancient".[31] Gandhian traditionalism constitutes the concrete and solid foundation for the kind of revolutionary modern concepts and attitudes he developed and exercised: "There are very few people who have understood in the complete sense that Gandhi introduced and successfully experimented his dynamic programmes to stimulate the good in the individual and society and expand and organise it to defeat evil".[32] Traditionalism or modernity were only conditions for Gandhi in the realisation of the great principles in his life. Gandhi was one of the greatest ideologists and idealists the world has seen. He was not willing to compromise tradition for the sake of sheer change into western sophistications and ways of life and thinking. He was also not willing to sacrifice his great ideals of truth and ahimsa even if his great religion, Hinduism itself wanted it. Gandhi is powerful in his voice when he says, "If I ever happen to discover that the Vedas, the Upanishads, the Gita and the other texts of Hinduism support and provide divine sanction for untouchability, as I understand it, then nothing in this world will allow me to stand firm in Hindu Religion".[33] Gandhi's commitment to his convictions and ideals assumes great dimensions.

The world sees Gandhi as a great reformist. Martin Luther King writes, "Gandhi was probably the first person in history to lift the love ethic of Jesus above mere interaction between individuals to a powerful and social force on a large scale".[34] Arthur vandenbery says, "Gandhi was one of the deathless few across the centuries who have lifted human character to immortality".[35] Ralph Templin recognises that, "The Gandhian way is an alternate revolution based on the soul-force and swadesism, the economics of group self-help".[36] Gandhi is recognised world over as one of the greatest sociopolitical reformists. This made him as modern in his approaches as any world leader could have been. Gandhi was modern in the same sense as he was traditional. There was hardly any socio-economic and religious field where Gandhi did not advocate changes. Gandhism symbolised changes in his contemporary ways of life.

Modernity in Gandhism means changes for the better. The Gandhian principles of truth and ahimsa make changes inevitable. At the educational front changes meant the adoption of a novel way of teaching centered on a craft so that education is imparted touching all aspects of the human personality. This meant a shift in focus from knowledge to the formation of a holistic system of values. At the economic front changes meant a shift in focus from the concentration of urban economy to rural economy, to the upliftment of the rural population with the development of rural industries. At the religious front changes meant a total commitment to the principles of truth and love through service of humanity and the vision God in the poor and the needy. All these mean modernity of stupendous proportions which only a true revolutionary can envisage. Gandhian modernization is one of character and quality rather than quantity.

3. Character formation in Gandhism

Holistic education in Gandhian lines would amount to the formation of personal and spiritual character. Gandhian conception of personality is a holistic personality in which every aspect, attitude and aptitude is given a balanced development. Gandhian education puts the highest importance on the formation of the individual's personality which will be capable of subsuming the highest and ultimate ideals of human life. Not only had Gandhi a concrete conception of such a personality but also he possessed a personality of the kind he wanted others to develop. Norman Thomas writes, "He was a saint with a humility, a sense of humour and love of human beings which appealed to the West as to the East".[37]

A holistic personality of the Gandhian kind embodies a spectrum of numerous values, attitudes, and aptitudes. Gandhian considers it the duty of education to discriminate these attitudes and values, associate them with the right educational practices and help develop a holistic personality that will know and love and as the ultimate reality and man as our proximate reality. For Gandhi "life is an aspiration. Its mission is to strive after perfection which is self-realisation".[38] The Gandhian personality in the last analysis is a spiritual personality that constantly strives for perfection in everything that the individual is out to do and education is no exception to this.

Gandhian education in the holistic sense provided a sense of direction in the formation of character. Education itself aims at providing directions in the manifold aspects of human development. Education and development are the sides of the same coin. The one in the right sense is correlated to and feeds from the other. Since holistic education is the development of a comprehensive attitude to subsume all that is good, this development requires a proper sense of direction not to go astray. In the case of Gandhi this sense of direction is provided solely by religion. He says, "My life is guided by religion. I have said that even my polities has sprung from my religion".[39] This shows the depth in which religion provided an adequate sense of direction for Gandhi. Richard B.Gregg writes, "The result of his incessant experiments was an unshakable belief and trust in God, and the power of God acting in all men, and hence in the power of non-violence".[40] Gandhi had this unshakable sense of direction in everything that he said and did and he wants education to provide this sense of direction in the formation of the kind of character he envisaged.

Character formation in holistic education is altruistic or the other oriented. In fact it is the essence of Gandhian education. Gandhi lived and died for others. Other-centredness became the quintessence of his personality. Gandhi always felt the intense presence of others and made others feel his warmth in all details. Jo Davidson, an admirer of Gandhi while in London with him exclaimed: "What a homely man this is".[41] An expression of intense personal feelings. On the attitude of teachers Gandhi writes, "If I was to be their real teacher and guardian I must touch their hearts. I must share their joys and sorrows".[42] This becomes the total expression of holistic education concretised in the formation of character. Gandhi's other orientation assumes concrete expression when he tells students, "If your education is substantial, then it should permeate to the neighbourhood and exercise its influence".[43] Gandhi's concentration goes always in terms of the community, the neighbourhood, the poor and the needy. He says to students: "You are the hope of the future. As soon as you come out of the school you will be called on to enter into public life to lead the poor in this country".[44]

Holistic education provides directions for the formation of the attitude of love in the individual. The formation of the holistic personality in education amounts to the development of love in the sense Gandhi understood it. As it has been seen in detail in preceding chapters the principles of truth and love constitute the substratum of Gandhian thought and the foundation of the Gandhian personality. Love for Gandhian is synonyms with ahimsa which is a most positive attitude that encompasses only the welfare of others in society. Gandhi's own personality radiated with this attitude. Frederil Ficher exclaims, "Gandhi, the man, the living, breathing, loving, serving, repenting, triumphant Gandhi who is my friend".[45] It is this Gandhian personality that education endeavours to develop through holistic education. Gandhi exhorts students, "Your education should be built on the foundation of truth and love. Unless this is done your education will be rendered useless".[46] The component of love in the Gandhian personality radiates within the spectrum of the holistic concept of education.

Gandhi was essentially a man of peace. Holistic education provided direcitons for the development of the attitude of peace in the individual who is educated. The personality of Gandhi was built on the very foundation of peace as a condition for the exercise and realisation of truth and love. The national and world peace Gandhi achieved and all the efforts he had directed for the cause of peace were all the culmination of the inner peace that Gandhi developed and possessed within himself. Norman Thomas writes, "If ever men achieve a world peace, to no single man will it owe a greater debt than to Mohandas K. Gandhi".[47] Gandhi was one of the greatest messengers of peace the world has seen. Holistic education aims at inculcating the attitude of peace in the individual as a component of the Gandhian personality. Education and peace are, again, the sides of the same coin, both so integrally coordinated to each other. If we do not find it that way then the education imparted may not be education at all.

A passion for self-help is an attitude which holistic education aims at developing in the individual. Throughout in the speeches and writings of Gandhi we are constantly reminded of the significance of self-help. Gandhi's experiments with truth primarily contained experiments in the form of self-help. Gandhi resorted to all forms of self-help: "My passion for self-help and simplicity ultimately expressed itself in extreme forms".[48] Whenever and wherever possible Gandhi attempted to do his own work himself and set an example for others. Gandhi wanted students to be self-dependent and self-sufficient in ways possible to them: "You should learn to wash your clothes, cook your food and do your work".[49] All this is based on Gandhi's conviction as he says, "I have tested the truth by experience that the primary virtues of manking are possible of cultivation by the meanest of human species".[50] Holistic education aims at the development of this component of the Gandhian personality in the individual so that a passion for self-help can go a long way in the realisation of the ultimate aims of education.

Humour and cheerfulness are attitudes which holistic education helps develop in the individual as part of the educational process. Many cannot digest the idea that an ascetic and a strict disciplinarian like Gandhi could be humorous and cheerful. Edmond Taylor writes, "Gandhi spoke softely, casually, intimately like grandfather speaking to his children .....full of self-discipline and inner harmony".[51] Norman Thomas writes, "He was a saint with a humility, a sense of homour and love of human beings which appealed to the West as to the East".[52] The holistic nature of Gandhi's personality revealed itself several complementary attitudes that often surprised his close associates. Gandhi himself says, "I very much liked the company of children, and the habit of playing and joking with them has stayed with me till today. I have ever since thought that I should make a good teacher of Children".[53] Gandhi's autobiography gives numerous instances of Gandhi's sense of cheerfulness. Holistic education is expected to provide scope for the development of this attitude of humour, cheerfulness and optimism that has much to do with the development of a holistic personality. Education is not a mechanism for merely taking care of the useful and productive elements of the human personality. It requires holistic education to take into account the more sensitive aspects of the personality with the refinements necessary for their development.

Gandhian education in the holistic sense calls for the organisation of education to cater to the needs of the complete personality. However hard we are making our attempts to move out of the clutches of knowledge-centered education, no head-way is made in this direction. Gandhism offers the correct alternative and the directions necessary for this holistic alternative. Constant reference can be made to those attitudes and aspects of Gandhi's own personality as the basic directions for holistic education. In an age of ultramodernism and deviant personality formations, these directions to the formation of a holistic personality are most valuable. Education cannot afford to forget this and blindly concentrate on the more materialistic and emperistic values for the promotion of the modern technological and scientific values. Gandhi's directions of truth and love have most fundamental applications in education. Gandhi's attitude of humility and simplicity alone can save India from a materialistic and economic catastrophe. The rate of consumption and the avarice for the greater consumption of material goods leave a vicious circle which only the Gandhian norms of simplicity of life can break. Gandhi's essential community-orientation is the key-note of successful rural development which always remained a major Gandhian commitment. Holistic education in its attempts to develop the individual's character has a whole range of directions within Gandhism for help.

4. Education for Balanced Development

Holistic education means an education organised and provided for the balanced development of the individual. The term balanced connotes several very important Gandhian concepts related to education. All development should be balanced only a development taking place in a balanced manner can be properly called development in a positive sense. Other 'Developments' are mere changes from one state of affairs to another. The concept of development in the framework of education takes several directions. Development would necessarily mean the development of personality as understood in education. The directions this development should take in holistic education has already been discussed from a given perspective. Development would again mean that of a given set of attitudes organised into a balanced spectrum of values. Development in education would mean economic development and that of social and political attitudes. All these need to be balanced in order to keep the process holistic. Balanced development would mean balancing between knowledge and values. The goals of vocation and information need to be balanced. Again, the Gandhian bread and knowledge aims are to be balanced. Finally a balance is to be achieved in holistic education between spiritual and material development concerns. For education to be rendered holistic a balanced development of this kind need to be envisaged.

A balanced development of the individual's personality is the first concern of holistic education. As we have already seen the personality of Gandhi is available to the Indian as a model for this balanced development. We have a number of specifications attached to the term balanced with reference to the personality. Those who stress the psychological dimensions of the human personality thereby shut their eyes on any other dimensions of personality. In an urge to bring home any one aspect of man, say, psychological there has been a historical tendency to keep out other aspects, say the spiritual or anything abstract. Balanced development does not exclude most conspicuous elements of the personality from its preview. Whatever is understood to be the dimensions of personality i.e. spiritual, psychological, social, cultural and physical dimensions require emphasis in the purview of balanced development. Gandhi's emphasis of each of these aspects give holistic education a firm ground. Gandhi does not bear with the attitude of shutting one's eyes on reality just for the sake of fashion, modernity or because of inconvenience. It is convenient and easy for education to be solely concerned about the provision of knowledge and related experiences without touching the core of human existence on earth.

Balanced development in education within the holistic framework would include the right organization of attitudes. Gandhi writes, "If teachers aim at developing the discriminative powers of boys and girls under them, they will continually foster their reasoning capacity and enable them to think for themselves".[54] Such an ability for independent observation, thinking and reasoning becomes a prerequisite for the right organisation of attitudes for the achievement of balanced development. The whole life of Gandhi is projected to contain a series of experiments for the discovery of these attitudes within the framework of truth and ahimsa: "My purpose is to describe experiments in the science of satyagraha and not at all to describe how good I am. In judging myself I shall try to be as harsh as Truth, as I want others also to do likewise".[55] Every little attitude within the framework of satyagraha as the science of truth was put to test by Gandhi in his day-to-day life. The aim was thus to achieve a holistic organisation of these individual attitudes to have the most harmonious development towards truth and ahimsa.

Balanced economic development is a major objective of holistic education. Education for development includes economic considerations since economics and education are inseparable from a personal and national viewpoints. Gandhi wrote in Harijan (25 August 1940) : "when a man looks upon himself as a servant of society, earn his wealth for society and use it for the good of society, then his wealth becomes sacred; there is non-violence in his attempts".[56] This is the quintessence of a balanced Gandhian economy. The moment the individual and the nation stop looking upon many as an end itself and develop a degree of disinterestedness in regard to the love of money most of our problems will be solved. Or else we shall be at least at the right direction to the solution of our problems. Gandhi says to students, "students should learn to sacrifice the things that the poor in India afford for themselves"[57] This is a Gandhian message to students for a balanced perspective in economics which has great significance for education.

The balanced development of social attitudes is a constituent of education for balanced development. Social attitudes include everything that puts a student in touch with the members of his community at different levels. Unless the right social attitudes develop in individuals the very purpose of education will be defeated. Louis Fischer writes, "Gandhi is the symbol of unity between personal morality and public action".[58] The right social attitudes and the integration of these attitudes will be based on an ultimate personal morality which the individual develop without compromises. Modern society has the basic tendency to exploit social situations for the benefit of the vested interests of individuals and socio-political groups. D.Macdonald writes, "Gandhi practiced tolerance and love to such an extent that he seem to have regarded the capitalist as well as the garbage man as his social equal".[59] Balanced social development enables a man to focus all his energies for the welfare of a larger section of humanity while at the same time lead his own personal life in that spirit.

Holistic education helps balanced development in political attitudes. Education is again the foundation of all political thinking and the two are intimately related. The right political attitudes find development only in and through the right kind of democratic education. Education is the very foundation, again of democracy. In Gandhi we find one of the rarest world leaders who synthesised politics and religion and derived a new ethics of politics. Gandhi says, "politics divorced from religion is a corpse, fit only to be buried".[60] Recognising the importance of politics Gandhi says,"I felt compelled to come into the political field because I found I could not do even social work without touching politics".[61] Gandhi never viewed politics an end itself for personal gains of any kind. A balanced development of political attitudes so necessary for the formation of the leaders of a nation is based on the right kind of education. Holistic education in Gandhian lines develops this component of political attitudes in a balanced manner.

Balanced development in the holistic context means the correct and proportionate emphasis of knowledge and values. Gandhi had no two minds in this regard. He never wanted education to be solely preoccupied by the transmission of knowledge. Knowledge and values are two objects of education in any sense of the term. But values are, for Gandhi, never subordinate to knowledge. Values are the components of character formation in the personal or spiritual sense. Gandhi says, "Man is not sheer intellect, animal body, heart or soul. create a whole man an adequate and perfect integration of the three is required. This exactly is the essence of education".[62] Education has always professed its commitment for value education but the focus of education has nevertheless been always on knowledge. Holistic education attempts to remedy this by attempting to provide a balance between knowledge and character formation or education in values. Gandhi makes it clear that he is not against knowledge but wants knowledge to be subordinated to the right objectives in education. R.K. Mukherjee writes, "The mere intellectual development without the development of character, learning without piety, proficiency in the sacred love without its practices, will defeat the very end of studentship".[63] The proper balance between knowledge and character formation is most central to holistic education in its endeavour to promote balanced development.

Lastly balanced development in the holistic context means a correct and proportionate emphasis on vocation and information. The post-Independence India has been struggling under the burden of, perhaps, an unbalanced higher education which could not easily be tagged on to the solution of our problem of unemployment. Under the label of science and technology we have been making our higher education more and more alienated from the real problems of our own country. Gandhi's great humanitarian concern for the poor and the rural population in the country has made him perhaps overstress the role of vocationalisation of education which is examined in a preceding chapter. Gandhi says, "Through the vocation in which the student receives training the personality hidden in him or her should receive full development".[64] Gandhi envisaged a full integration of vocation and information. Knowledge in the form of information should be derived from the vocation in which the student receives training. Balanced development would thus include the right integration of vocation and information under the framework of holistic education. Education aims at development. Development assumes different dimensions. This includes the areas we have seen in detail above. Holistic education looks for the right integration of a large variety of constituent values and attitudes along with aspects such as knowledge and a variety of vocational and other skills. What is important is development of the individual, society and of the nation in the educationally defined and acceptable direction. This direction becomes holistic in the Gandhian context.

5. Liberal Education in Gandhism

The concept of liberal education was originally applied to the study of liberal arts such as grammar, rhetoric, arithmetic, music and astronomy. It was believed that these arts would introduce the pupil to human culture and consequently liberate him from mere bookish knowledge. Liberal education however has come to mean in modern times on education that liberates our minds from extrinsic bondage. "It is an education for freedom - freedom to use one's intellectual and emotional powers, freedom from slavery to one's natural and primitive tendencies, freedom from the exampling influence of ignorance, prejudices and wrong beliefs and freedom to think independently".[65] As such education aims at liberating the learner's mind and spirit from the bondage of ingnorance on the one hand and on other from dependence on all forms of slavish attitudes and tendencies. Everything that would enslave one's personality is against the very objective of education and students need to be liberated from that.

Liberal education makes men and women capable of understanding the world and adequately respond to it. Education is so organised as "to unlock the energies of the learner".[66] Education becomes a springboard for the individual for further release of his energies and realisation of his creative potentials. Liberal education assumes a new role in the Gandhian, holistic context. Against the background of India's dependence on the British rule, liberal education was conceived of by Gandhi as a powerful weapon for independence. Gandhi embarks on the ancient saying and reminds us that "Education is whatever liberates us".[67] According to Gandhi we were a slavish nation and our education was planned to serve the interests of our rulers. Over and above education is used by people as means for earning for themselves money and position". By education Gandhi does not means spiritual education or by liberation he does not mean spiritual liberation. Gandhi makes this point most clear: "By liberation I mean the liberation from all kinds of bondage including that of our day-to-day life".[68]

Liberal education becomes holistic in the Gandhian sense because this education enhances the scope of the personality from the viewpoint of basic freedom of the spirit. In spite of all forms of development the spirit can still remain slavish to the pulls and pushes of modern life. Hence the attainment of total freedom from bondage is fundamental to perfect Gandhian education: "It is high time that those who see the Gandhian way as a way of liberation based on truth and love should work for the spread and study of Gandhian thoughts with greater vigour".[69] Gandhi's way is a way of total and holistic liberation in which the human spirit is helped to shed its manifold dependence even in day-to-day life, and education functions as the principal means to the attainment of this freedom.

Liberal education for Gandhi consisted in an education for freedom from the bondage of a foreign rule. Gandhi's concept of Swaraj is based on total liberation from this, foreign bondage on the one hand and self-imposed bondage on the other. Gandhi says, "There are two kinds of bondages : the extrinsic slavery under the yoke of the foreign rule, and the slavery to one's own artificial needs. Real education consists in the knowledge acquired from the search for the realisation of these ideals".[70] Education in Independent India should from this viewpoint consist in reminding ourselves of the need for recognising the impact of this extrinsic bondage had on our minds and for making attempts to liberate ourselves from the consequences of such a bondage. This extrinsic bondage also continues as we have an attachment to things that are made abroad i.e. foreign-made goods. This love and craze for foreign goods also come under the extrinsic bondage which Gandhi wants Indians to avoid under the 'Swadeshi' principles that became so important to him.

Liberal education for Gandhi consisted in an education for freedom from our dependence on excess needs. This dependence amounts to a kind of self-bondage. Gandhi's life was a constant and lingering struggle against the power of this bondage within his own personality. Gandhi's experiments with truth consisted in gradually eradicating any thing excess found in his personality that did not suit the spiritual goal Gandhi strived for. All this require the strength of great personal conviction that only education can provide. Albert Einstein writes, "Gandhi's work on behalf of India's liberation is a living testimony to the fact that man's will, sustained by an indomitable conviction, is more powerful than material forces that seem unsurmountable".[71] Liberal education attempts to develop this strength of personal conviction so that the struggle against the bondage within the personality can always be made more vigorous.

Liberal education for Gandhi consisted, further, in an education for freedom from all sorts economic bondage. Gandhi was terribly conscious of the economic problems rural India faced. Gandhi developed his concept of the priority of manual labour as a unique solution to this: He says,

"Manual work prevents exploitation and slavery".[72] What is relevant for us in the present context is the spirit of the Gandhian position. He tells students, "It is a pity that students look upon physical labour with dislike if not with contempt".[73] The mastery of a profit-yielding vocation ina spirit of truth and the pursuit of this vocation in a spirit of truth and non-violence are the only means to the kind of economic liberation Gandhi envisaged for India. Economic liberation would primarily mean the absence of dependence on others for one's day-to-day and future needs. According to Gandhi "Education ought to be for them a kind of insurance against unemployment".[74] Liberal education helps the individual to find himself economically free through a profit-yielding vocation.

The role of the right kind of knowledge is central to the concept of liberal education. This is central, again, to the Gandhian concept of education. Gandhi does not in any way advocate knowledge for its own sake even within the framework of Gnana-marga (the path of knowledge). Knowledge has a basic liberating function in education. Gandhi says, "Character formation is the aim of even knowledge".[75] Gandhi further recognises, "I could never blindly worship literary education".[76] Gandhi could not recognise the role of knowledge for its own sake without any sort of ethical, social and spiritual implications. By the right kind of knowledge Gandhi means that knowledge which leads the individual to God through the principles of truth and non-violence. He says, "Modern education has the tendency to turn its eyes away from the soul. Hence we are not excited by the powers of the human soul".[77] Education can liberate the human spirit by the right kind of knowledge that leads it to the ultimate reality, God. This is the essence of liberation in the holistic context.

References

1. Gunther, John, in *Profiles of Gandhi*, p.47
2. *Harijan*, 25 August 1940.
3. Bhatia, B.D., *Philosophy and Education*, p.126.

4. Pillai, N.P., *Education*, p.22.
5. *Harijan*, 14 July 1937.
6. *To the Students*, p.108.
7. *Basic Education*, p.12.
8. *An Autobiography*, p.255.
9. *Mahatma*, Vol.4, p.187.
10. *Harijan*, 9 September 1939.
11. Fischer, Louis, in *Profiles*, p.67.
12. Ibid p.61.
13. Bhatia, B.D., *Philosophy*, p.131.
14. *Basic Education*, 51.
15. Dwight, M., in *Profiles*, p.110.
16. Jones, Stanley, in *Profiles*, p.134.
17. *To the Students*, p.121.
18. Jones, Stanley in *Profiles*, p.134.
19. Gauba, K.L., *The Assassination of Mahatma Gandhi*, New Delhi 1969, p.2.
20. *To the Students*, p.8.
21. *An Autobiography*, p.251.
22. *Towards New Education*, p.31.
23. Ibid p.46
24. Ibid p.31
25. Ibid p.31
26. *To the Students*, p.266.
27. *To the Students*, p.232.
28. *An Autobiography*, Intr.
29. Ibid p.383
30. Cousins, Norman, in *Profiles*, p.52.
31. *To the Students*, p.232.
32. Pillai N.P., *Education*, p.30.
33. *Harijan*, 26 Janjary 1934.
34. King, M.L., in *Profiles*, p.207.
35. Vandenberg, A., in *Profiles*, p.97.
36. R Templin, in *Profiles*, p.116.
37. Thomas, N., in Ibid p.166.
38. *Matatma*, Vol. 4, p.33.
39. *Harijan*, 17 November 1933.
40. Gregg, R.B., in *Profiles*, 168.
41. Davidson, Jo, in Ibid, p.17.
42. *An Autobiography*, p.258.
43. *To the Students*, p.173.
44. Ibid p.97.
45. Ficher, F., in *profiles*, p.21.
46. *To the Students*, p.113.
47. Thomas, N., in *Profiles*, p.166.
48. *An Autobiography*, p.186.
49. *To the Students*, p.91.
50. *Mahatma*, Vol.4, p.40.

51. Taylor, E., in *Profiles*, p.72.
52. Thomas, N., in Ibid, p.166.
53. *An Autobiography*, p.66.
54. *To the Students*, p.71.
55. *Mahatma*, Vol;.1, p.271.
56. *Harijan*, 25 August 1940.
57. *To the Students*, p.71
58. Fischer, Louis, in *Profiles*, p.61.
59. Macdonald, D., in Ibid, p.110.
60. Thekkinedath, J., *Love of Neighbour*, p.54.
61. *Harijan*, 6 October 1946.
62. *Basic Education*, p.12.
63. Bhatia, B.D., *Philosophy*, p.123.
64. *Basic Education*, p.19.
65. Bhatia, B.D., *Philosophy*, p.146.
66. *Harijan*, 19 March 1946.
67. Ibid 10 March 1946.
68. Ibid 10 March 1946.
69. Pillai, N.P., *Education* , p.30.
70. *Harijan*, 25 August 1940.
71. Einstein; A., in *Profiles*, p.100.
72. *Harijan*, 25 August 1940.
73. *Towards New Education*, p.37.
74. *Mahatma*, Vol.4, p.187.
75. *Towards New Education*, p.31.
76. Ibid p.5.
77. *To the Students*, p.172.

9

EDUCATION AND SPIRITUAL VALUES

1. Nature of Gandhian Morality

Gandhi's vision of morality is fundamental to all his religious considerations. Morality for him is the unquestionable foundation of all religious beliefs and practices. Gandhi writes, "where morality incarnates itself in a living man, it becomes religion; because it binds, it holds, it sustains him in the hour of trial".[1] Gandhi could not believe in a religion that is not founded on a set of moral principles that would easily appeal to the human reason: "I reject any religious doctrine that does not appeal to reason and is in conflict with morality".[2] Morality is the springboard from which religious considerations should arise. Morality for Gandhi is the essence of all socio-cultural and community life. Moral principles are the maxims of human life at all levels. If a man violates these maxims and yet claim to be a man of God, he becomes a hypocrite.

Morality and education are intimately associated. Education in its broad sense penetrates all aspects of our socio-communal life. Thus education of morality is a very basic duty of the community on the one hand and family in particular as both these are informal agencies of education. From time immemorial, especially in our vedic system of education, by education was meant primarily the inculcation of dharma, the principles of a righteous life.

Education is the principal vehicle for the training of moral values in the individual. It has been a traditional phenomenon that the parents and elders in the community manifest a moral responsibility to see that the young in the community grow up in the moral and righteous ways. Gandhi attaches this responsibility even to with formal education: "The education that you receive from this noble institution will be empty unless it is built on the foundations of a pure character".[3] Morality provides to the directions for the right kind of education while education becomes the most efficient vehicle for the inculcation of moral principles.

Gandhian morality is the basic of Gandhian economics. Moral values guide all economic transactions. Traditionally speaking economic dealings have the highest degree of moral considerations. The purushartha of wealth (artha) and the use of wealth have high level moral bindings as understood especially in traditional India. The righteous use of wealth is a prerequisite for the ultimate liberation of the human soul in self-realisation. Gandhian principles of truth and non-violence have intense application to matters pertaining to the righteous use of money. In economics Gandhian morality finds immediate relevance. Man is born to be a fundamental "seeker of truth".[4] And a seeker of truth cannot afford to be led astray by the lustre and attractions of wealth. For this reason Gandhi says, "students should be familiar with the poverty and problems of the common man".[5] In order to counteract and overcome the dangerous attractions of wealth and to identify oneself with the poor in India Gandhi says, "Our ambitions was (in Tolstoy Farm) to live the life of the poorest people".[6] Gandhi ensured himself that material goods should never stand on the way of his self-realisation: "The colony was as far as possible self-supporting and life's material requirements reduced to a minimum".[7] Gandhi developed a superconsciousness of this phenomenon of wealth in every detail of his moral and spiritual life. Gandhian morality of economics consists not merely in just and righteous dealings but in developing an attitude of disinterestedness in all matters pertaining to money.

Politics is a field of human involvement where moral principles have high level application. Gandhi's political thinking constitutes a major part of his view-points of human life. For Gandhi the intimate connection between morality and politics is most apparent. He can not think of any politics without morality and moral considerations. More conspicuously religion is closely associated to politics and Gandhi could not alienate religious considerations and norms of behaviour from politics. Gandhi says, "those who say that religion has nothing to do with politics do not know what religion means".[8] Gandhi further recognises, "My politics and all other activities of mine are derived from my religion".[9] Within the framework of religion Gandhian morality controls and determines political thinking and activities. Gandhi says, "If they (students) wish to avail themselves of the education which schools and colleges provide - it is clear that they desire it - they should obey all the rules and regulations of the institutions. Therefore if the Heads of those institutions do not consent they should not undertake any political strikes".[10] Gandhi had similar very clear stipulations as norms for political behaviour for leaders as well as students. Morality penetrates every segment of the individual's political involvements. Hence for Gandhi politics too becomes not an end itself as most people consider it but is subservient to moral and religious ends.

Moral values control the entire spectrum social life of the individual. Social life governed by social attitudes control interpersonal relations and dealings between individuals in a community. All this is controlled by the Gandhian concept of love : "Real love is to love them that hate you, to love your neighbour even though you distrust him".[11] The basic Gandhian morality that govern all social attitudes is love of which is for Gandhi another name for ahimsa. Basically this love consists in an obedience of the laws of human society. Gandhi says, "A satyagrahi obeys the laws of society intelligently and of his own free will because he considers it his sacred duty to do so".[12] Based on this socred obedience of social norms the individual builds his higher attitudes he moves towards a complete vision of truth. He achieves this through a complete realisation of the moral principles that govern the social norms.

Gandhi's conception of morality is founded on the principles of truth and non-violence. Gandhian morality is not a sterile set of moral principles just for the survival of society. Gandhian morality has supernatural and more ultimate ends to serve. Gandhian morality is the essence, the centre and the foundation of his spirituality. For Gandhi truth is the beginning and the end. It is God Himself. Morality is synonymous with non-violence in Gandhism. In the Gandhian context nothing in human life is left out as amoral which has nothing to do with morality. Morality as identified with non-violence provides all the direction for the individual's and society's path towards spiritual goals.

2. Spiritual Values in Gandhism

E.Stanley Jones writes, "And there was Mahatma Gandhi, the leader of the new India, an ascetic. It gripped the soul of ancient India. But he gripped the soul of modern India, by relating renunciation to the needs around".[13] Mahatma Gandhi emerged to the modern world not merely as political leader India during Independence but as the spiritual leader in whom were combined great statesmanship and intense spirituality. Will Durant writes, "Not since St. Francis of Assisi has any life known to history been marked by gentleness, simplicity of soul and forgiveness of enemies".[14] Any one who attempts to understand Gandhi in all his fullness can do so only in and through his spirituality. Gandhi's spirituality is the quintessence of all his religious beliefs and attitudes as well as the culmination of his religious sensitivity. Gandhian morality as we have understood above is an outer shell and a basic foundation that nurtures his intense religious and spiritual temperament. The word 'religion' is not very apt in the case of Gandhi as conventionally understood because we do not find him attached to any conventional formalism and institutional ritualism of established religions, even of Hinduism for that matter. John Gunther writes, "His approach to everything is religious, but aside from Hinduism it is difficult to tell what his religion is".[15] Gandhi did not advocate any institutionalised religion, not even his own Hinduism. The greatness of his religious attitudes, perhaps, consists in this.

Gandhi's experiments with truth central to his personal, social and political life was in face an experiment with spirituality. Spirituality became for him a close confrontation and a close communion with God. Richard B.Gregg says, "The result of his incessant experiments was an unshakable belief and trust in God, and in the power of God acting in all men, and hence in the power of non-violence".[16] Gandhi's belief and trust in God became the very foundation of all his religious attitudes and the essence of his spirituality.

The concept of God is the very foundation of Gandhian Spirituality. As John Holmer writes, "His whole life was an obedience to God. He had no personal ends to serve".[17] God for Gandhi became the quintessential and all-pervading reality that touched every detail of even his personal life. Gandhi consolidated his living faith in God by means of his experiments with truth. Gandhi says, "He who would in his own person test the fact of God's presence can do so by a living faith".[18] Gandhi provides all forms rational arguments to prove the existence of God. But he warns us that no amount of rational justification can consolidate the relationship between God and man. This relationship is a living communion founded on intense faith. Gandhi says, "He is no God who merely satisfies the intellect, if he ever does. God to be God must rule the heart and transform it. He must express Himself in every smallest act of His Votary".[19] This transformation of the human heart into the total commitment and communion is the essence of Gandhian spirituality founded on the intense faith in One living God.

Gandhian spirituality therefore transcends all institutionalisation and all spatio-time bound religious ritualism of even the most positive kind. Gandhi transformed his living faith into an intense, mystical communion with God : "Without an unreserved surrender to His Grace, complete mastery over thought is impossible".[20] E.Stanley Jones recognises, Gandhi was mystical and practical. He was an ascetic and a servant".[21] Gandhi explicated all the attributes of God to intensify this living faith and for the rest of humanity to see His Divine Light: "Hence I gather that God is Life, Truth, Light. He is Love".[22] Gandhi's intense preoccupation with this Reality, God, in all forms of thought and action resulted in an identification of God with Truth. He says, "There are innumerable definitions of God, because His manifestations are innumerable. They overwhelm me with wonder and awe and for a moment stun me. But I worship God as Truth only".[23] Gandhi takes the principle of truth to so supreme a level that he arrives at an ultimate identification of Truth and God and says that Truth is God. Since nothing exists other than Truth, according to Gandhi, "it is more correct to say that Truth is God than to say that God is Truth".[24] Identification of God with Truth, thus, provides for Gandhi the fullest possible description of God as the ultimate reality.

Self-realisation constitutes the goal of all Gandhian Spirituality. If God is the ultimate Reality, the Summum Bonum, then man is destined by creation to reach and realise this God. The Vedic Sages and the rishis down the Ages in the history of India during Vedic, Brahminic period considered self-realisation as the ultimate goal of man's life on earth. Self-realisation is the ultimate union with God which is considered moksha or liberation or salvation for every Hindu. Since self-realisation is such an intricate and comprehensive process that involves the entire life-period of the individual passing through the four ashramas (brahmacharya, grahasta, vanasprasta and sanyasa, respectively, the state of life of the student, house-holder, mendicant and sanyasin) Hinduism proposes and practices a variety of ways of self-realisation for the individual. Hinduism thus recommends the three paths of gnana (concentration and philosophical knowledge), bhakti (devotion) and karma (action).

In order to attain self-realisation Gandhi practised the three ways of Hinduism: the path of knowledge, the path of devotion and the path of action as mentioned above. Gandhi's experiments with truth contained a never-ending clarification of and enquiry into the intricacies of these three-fold ways. Gana or knowledge could never constitute for Gandhi the pure philosophical, metaphysical knowledge. R.R.Diwakar writes, He knew that God could not be recognised by the intellect, by reading or hearing about Him. Knowledge by identity, by communion, by meditation, by silence and silent prayer was the way he followed more than argument, discussion and logic".[25] In Gandhi we find a most sublime synthesis of the three traditional way to self-realisation. There is synthesis of knowledge and devotion, knowledge and action, of asceticism and service, of prayer and love of neighbour.

Gandhian spirituality was permeated with a constant thirst for and enquiry into an ever deeper knowledge of god and man considered so essential for the Gandhian perfection in truth and ahimsa, expressed in love. Gandhi says, "To see the universal and all-pervading spirit of Truth face-to-face one must be able to love the meanest of creation".[26] This knowledge is not a sterile but living knowledge expressed by itself in a living and lingering faith : "One who has faith in ahimsa believes in a living God".[27] Gandhi's constant interest and curiosity was behind his attempts to study all other religions whenever he could. Gandhi made an intense study of Christianity as contained in the New Testament and as practised by Christians: He writes, "the New Testament produced a different impression, especially the Sermon on the Mount which went straight to my heart".[28] Gandhi's search for knowledge was ever manifest in these attempts to know how other religions saw God, truth and love. Gandhi's concern for the path of knowledge for self-realisation made him cross the boundaries of Hinduism and enter into other religions as well.

Bhakti-marga or the path of devotion meant many things to Gandhi and became crucial to Gandhian spirituality. Gandhi did not believe that knowledge by its own right as an intellectual preoccupation had any salvific effect. He says, "Real religion should radiate from the individual the attitudes of love and service".[29] This love and service should spring from the individual's attachment to God through an intense attitude of devotion. Gandhi says, "Prayer is the heart and soul of religion. Therefore prayer should be the core of human life and no one can live without religion".[30] Gandhi developed a life of prayer and he had a deep faith in prayer. Gandhi's devotion to God expressed itself in a variety of forms. He worshipped God as Love : "God is light, not darkness; God is Love, not hate......."[31] Gandhi recognised love as the only means to the attainment of God as Truth. Love, in other words, is the essence of devotion. The devotee enters into a close communion with God and establishes an intense rapport reflected in every detail even of his daily life.

Gandhian sprituality reaches its culmination in Karma-marga or the path of action. Gandhi could not envisage a spirituality as separated from the concrete, living poor in India. This is where Gandhi emerges as unique in the realm of religion and spirituality. For the first time such immense energy was generated to promote cause of the poverty-stricken people in India by a synthesis of two extreme ends : religion and politics, asceticism and service. No spirituality could drive Gandhi to state of total ascetic isolation away from the suffering masses of humanity. Gandhi, therefore arrived at a high-level and sublime synthesis of spirituality and service, action and devotion, Gandhi's passion for the poor in India found expression in several ways. He says, "My mind is living in the villages. They are calling me to bury myself in them".[32] Gandhi make it clear that he could not have faith in a religion that had nothing to do with the poor in this country: "I do not recognise any God other than who dwells in the hearts of the dumb millions".[33] In other words, for Gandhi, religion means fundamentally service and the two could never be separated. Gandhi's path of action, thus found intense expression in service. Gandhi's religion became a religion of service : " I had made the religion of service my own, as I felt that God could be realised only through service".[34] This synthesis could be considered the secret behind the immense success behind the person and life of Mahatma Gandhi.

Gandhian spirituality reveals its refinements in Gandhi's concept of prayer. The bhakti-marga of Gandhi consisted not merely in a vague attachment to the divinity. Bhakti or devotion to the one true God takes concrete shape and clear form in the instrument of prayer. Prayer for Gandhi is the principal vehicle of communion with God. All of Gandhi's writings permeate with the importance prayer had in Gandhi's life. Gandhi says, "The meaning of prayer is that we desire to rouse the divine essence in us".[35] Gandhi attaches the greatest importance to prayer in the life of the individual. Gandhi writes, "Begin therefore your day with prayer, and make it so soulful that it may remain with you until the evening. Close the day with prayer so that you have a peaceful night free from dreams and nightmares. Do not worry about the form of prayer".[36] He wants the individual to organise and conduct his day in a spirit of prayer. Gandhi spared no occasion for talking about the role of prayer in personal and social life.

Prayer is not a ritualistic activity in the Gandhian concept of religion. It is not a mere lip-service or utterance of any formula: "Prayer does not mean the movement of the lips. Prayer should be that which is expressed in active. How shall we pray during the Sacred Week? We shall pray by washing away the stain of communal hatred and cunningness hidden in the mind. Achieving communal harmony thus becomes a kind of prayer".[37] Gandhi always envisaged prayer as a primary instrument for achieving peace of mind in the individual and communal harmony so necessary for a multi-social nation like India. For this Gandhi called on Hindus and Muslims to pray on a regular basis. Gandhi helped organising community prayers wherever he went so that people would develop a constant awareness of prayer as an instrument of peace and harmony. Gandhi advocated prayer also as a means of strengthening one's attitude of sacrifice. He says, "The answer is that prayer is the first and the last lesson in learning the noble and brave art of sacrificing oneself in the various walks of life, culminating in the defense of one's nation's liberty and honour".[38] Gandhi's spirituality is founded on prayer. Prayer is considered the light that should permeate and enliven every activity and thought of one's day-to-day life and raise everything to the plan of spirituality.

Gandhian spirituality assumes the most concrete form in Gandhian renunciation. The Gandhian principles of truth and ahimsa reaches a synthesis in renunciation. Renunciation functions as a vehicle for ahimsa realised as love. The greatest expression of Gandhi's sense of renunciation is found in his own words : "I must reduce myself to zero. So long as a man does not of his own free will put himself last wrong his fellow creatures, there is no salvation for him".[39] Gandhi throughout his public life attempted to identify himself with the poor. The vows Gandhi wanted the members of his Ashram to profess included the vow of Poverty. This vow he wanted the members to adhere strictly symbolised renunciation most fundamental to his spiritual life. This vow enabled one to realise that "civilization in the real sense of the term, consists not in multiplication but in voluntary and deliberate reduction of wants".[40] Gandhi's love of the poor took most concrete expression his acute renunciation which at the same time was the most concrete expression of his spiritual life. All these aspects of Gandhian spirituality point towards a powerful interior life that Gandhi developed in his consistent search for Truth. Self-realistion ever remained a concrete goal in Gandhi which he attempted to remember in every detail of his life. Spirituality did not mean for him an isolated thing consisting of a few rituals. It meant a total dedication to a whole set of spiritual values totally integrated into his ultimate principles of spirituality : truth and ahimsa.

3. Spiritual Values in Education

Gandhian education becomes essentially an education for spiritual values. Education provides the necessary climate, directions and orientation for the formation of the spiritual personality in the individual. In this context the goals of education becomes spiritual goals defined within the framework of Gandhian spirituality: "Gandhiji is an idealist who believes in ultimate values and view education as a process that leads men to these values".[41] Gandhi could not envisage the aims or the process of education as alienated from its spiritual dimensions. Gandhi most often sounds unearthly and unrealistic when he most naturally and easily links education with God and religion: "If the education that we get separates us from God or if it does not help us to serve our fellowmen, then such an education is not worthy of its name".[42] Gandhi clearly identifies the goals of education and the ultimate goals of life as one and the same: "Self-realisation is the Summum Bonum of life and education".[43] This ultimate goal of education is thus the possession of God. This ultimate goal is thus the one that specifies and determines the more proximate aims of education. Thus for Gandhi spiritual values become proximately attached to education not only as its final end but also in its day-to-day processes.

Gandhi does not want us to deviate from the thought of God even for a moment: "I live and move and have my being in pursuit of this goal. All that I do by way of speaking and writing, and all my ventures in the political field, are directed to the same end".[44] Educational goals of a proximate type which specify educational activities must thus be guided by this very end of possessing God. This causes confusion and often sarcasm in the minds of educationists as to how such a thing could be possible when we wish to make education a fully materialistic, behaviouristic and positively scientific enterprise. These attitudes have to be withstood by Gandhian education and enquire into the possiblilites of realising these goals in day-to-day education: "Every one of us is child of God. Therefore every one has the potential for perfection. It is because of this that education needs to be universalised".[45] Thereby every individual who undergoes education will become capable of discriminating good from evil and apply this discrimination in his or her personal search for truth.

An education for spiritual values become closely associated with and synthesised to the development of the intellect. Education stands for the development of the intellect. Mental development is usually understood on the sheer material, behaviouristic plain. Education, as if, is capable only of providing orientations in the development of a materialistic, behaviouristic mind which subsumes quantitative knowledge in the form of information. In the context of Gandhian spirituality there can be no separation between the development of the spirit and of the intellect. Materialists and behaviourists recognise the role of an intellect in the human being subject to the total control of the physical brain. They, on the otherhand, do not admit the existence of the spirit or soul in man and within these comes a total rejection of the entire world of spirituality. Hence in the true sense of the word Gandhism and materialism of any kind can never go hand-to-hand except in the sense of a materialistic humanism corresponding to the Gandhian humanism which is motivated by spiritual principles.

The development of the intellect and spirituality, for Gandhi are the sides of the same coin, wholly inseparable and intertwined: "Experience of the soul is the riches and the only one that helps our development".[46] The training of the mind through the accumulation of knowledge is only a means to the experiences of the spirit. Knowledge in this sense becomes subservient to the development of the human spirit. Gandhi says, "Character formation is the aim of even knowledge".[47] Knowledge as such was given a value in the traditional context especially in the West. Education was often considered by many as a means for knowledge for its own sake. This does not go smoothly in the context of religion. Knowledge separated from spiritual values does not have a significant function within the framework of any religion. As for Gandhian the two have become inseparable because both have one and the same fundamental goal.

The parallel development of the mind and the spirit is considered most essential in education: "Education is the integral development of the human soul. Man is not sheer intellect; development is not merely of the body, heart or soul. For the creation of the complete man the integral and harmonious union of all the three are require".[48] For a variety of reasons education tends to forget its most fundamental commitments. The over-emphasis of knowledge and provision of information shuts the door of education on spiritual development. Truth is, philosophically speaking, the object of the human intellect. The intellect is made for the reception and absorption of truth, just as the faculty of imagination is made for images corresponding to concepts in the human mind. Since the intellect is made for truth, it cannot fail short of anything other than truth. According to Gandhi, the intellect should absorb truth under all circumstances: "Truth is like a vast tree which yields more and more fruit as you nurture it".[49] The mind must be constantly in search of the truth which is its natural object.

It is the same truth that becomes the corner-stone of all spirituality. Gandhi's spirituality is founded on the principles of truth and ahimsa. If the intellect which is the object of education strives after the discovery of truth, on the plain of the same truth spirituality can meet education and realise a suitable integration of the two fields of preoccupation. There is absolutely no contradiction between the two and for the same reason Gandhi wants us to achieve the parallel and harmonious development of the mind and the spirit for the holistic development of the individual.

An education for spiritual values becomes closely associated with emotional development. Modern education has had no reservations in the generous emphasis on emotional development. The materialistic, behaviouristic schools of the education attaches unique importance to the development of the individual's psychological personality. These schools do not accept any personality other than the psycho-social personality. Emotional development in this context means the ability to adjust himself to the psycho-social environment in the process of development. Gandhian education cannot in any manner isolate emotional development from the development of the spirit. For Gandhi the two are so integrally unified that no such isolation becomes possible.

Education for spiritual values aim at an integration of the emotional and spiritual values and enabling a sublimation of these emotional aspects to the spiritual level. John Holmer writes, "Passion, not unknown, had been successfully subdued to the perfect discipline of the inner spirit".[50] Gandhi wants the disciplining of one's emotional life in line with the principles of spiritual life. The dictates of the spirit alone should govern the emotions of the individual life. Modern education in its concentration of knowledge centered teaching and training leaves out the whole dimension of the emotional life of the individual. Eventhough guidance and counselling has been introduced for this purpose, very little is achieved in helping students solve their emotional problems and secure a balanced emotional development. Gandhi tells students, "When your heart is not pure you will not be able to control your emotions and then the status that you are educated ceases to be".[51] Gandhian spirituality is a training for orienting the individual's emotional development not for any psycho-social adjustment as an end itself, but for obtaining the vision of God through the principles of truth and ahimsa in every aspect of one's emotional life.

Education for spiritual life would mean harmonisation of emotional life aimed at spiritual upliftment. Love and orientation to 'the other' is the central constituent of an individual's emotional development. Gandhi wants individuals to stop the incessant preoccupation with oneself. He writes, "I am endeavouring to see God through service of humanity, for I know that God is neither in heaven nor down below, but in every one..."[52] Gandhi's love assumes gigantic dimensions in his dedication to the service of humanity. Emotional education should enable the student to recognise the role love has in one's psychological, social and spiritual development. Self-control in all aspects of one's life is, again, central to emotional development. Control over oneself is a privilege that thousands wish to have for themselves when they analyse their own emotions. Gandhi says, "when you obtain self-control and control of emotions you will never have to utter a word in distress".[53] Emotional development intellectual development and spiritual attitudes require full harmonisation to produce the necessary holistic effect in the Gandhian lines. Gandhian spirituality is the right orientation towards God, communion with Him in a dedicated encounter. All aspects of Gandhian spirituality can have synthesis with the goals and components of education. The development of the spirit, mind and emotions need to be undertaken in the individual in an integral and harmonious manner.

4. Developing Spiritual values in Education-1

The dichotomy between modern education based on materialistic, behaviouristic tenets and spiritual education has been on the increase. The gap between the two has been ever widening with the result that no body had the courage to speak in the public about education of spiritual values. Christian education down the Ages as well as specific educational trends of other religions have done much in this regard under the label of 'Value Education'. All these efforts have become just a cry in the wilderness as compared to the immense scope modern education has at the national level in promoting spiritual education or education of spiritual values. Education and spirituality are not in loger-heads with each other. Modern trends have just brought it to this stage for the vested interests of certain schools of thinking.

Modern education has become a consistent response to the phenomenon of knowledge explosion. Educational achievement is measured wholly in terms of the content of knowledge acquired in the process of education. Because of this disciplines have found exorbitant development and students have become more preoccupied with responding to this greater knowledge explosion. For these reasons spiritual values have come to a stage where the name God or religion cannot be mentioned in our school or college classrooms.

It is not possible on the other hand to substitute the contentst modern education with spiritual or moral values. Education of any given period is the result of the great sociocultural and economic transformation mankind is undergoing. It is therefore possible only to find a harmonious coordination between modern trends in education and spiritual values. We need not sacrifice one for the other. We are able to arrive at this conviction based on Gandhi's life and teachings as examined in the present work. Consequently modern education should make attempts to develop ways and means of integrating education and spiritual values a part of one and the same process of education.

1. Conscientisation is a principal method of synthesising spiritual education with the stream of formal education. Ways and means should be developed to provide spiritual education as part of the streams of formal, informal and non-formal education. Of these three areas informal education is naturally out of the control of educational agencies. Education in the family and in the peer-group can be controlled by educational agencies only in a very indirect manner. Such a control can be exercised at the level of non-formal and continuing education still more directly. Efforts can be made to control and move the radio, the press or agencies like associations, clubs and libraries to imbibe the values of Gandhian spirituality. All the same formal education as taking place in the thousands of educational institutions like the schools, colleges and universities is the area which can be fully controlled and moved by the methods of providing education in spirituality and religion. Conscientisation is envisaged as a method of developing in the students of these institutions an intense awareness of the spiritual principles from the viewpoint of their religious and existential significance, the right attitudes to be developed with reference to these principles and the moral significance of these principles. This can be based on the right focus spiritual values should be given in education in general and the learning experiences in particular.

2. A value-centered syllabus is an effective method of promoting education for spiritual values. These spiritual values and principles can be made the objectives of several aspects of theoretical education. When such objectives are stated these values can be consciously incorporated into it. This can be done in the case of academic, professional and semi-professional courses at the collegiate level and of every course at the school level. Again, separate and specific syllabus can be framed for education in spiritual values. These syllabi should be given added importance in a value-oriented education and students will look upon this syllabus with much greater degree of seriousness. In other words it is a concrete method of providing spiritual education through incorporating such values right on the syllabus. Ways should be found out to achieve a proper integration of the academic course and the programme in spiritual principles.

3. Orientation programmes constitute another method of providing education in spiritual principles. Very often it becomes difficult to incorporate spiritual values into the syllabi of regular academic courses. In such cases the school or the institution can arrange orientation programmes on a regular basis. With the Gandhian ideals of spirituality right in focus these orientation programmes cannot be considered a secondary affair. By offering courses in spiritual values parallel to the regular academic course we are leading and directing students to the very ultimate goals of education and life, God Himself. If proximate aims become capable of clouding the remote or ultimate aims, then something will be fundamentally wrong with these proximate aims of education. These orientation programmes should be capable of communicating to students whole range of values relating to spirituality and religion that have everything to do with human life. These programmes will help the students remain constantly aware of these spiritual principles and imbibe them into their personal lives.

4. **Student Literature** is another method of inculcating in the student community values pertaining to spiritual life. Reading materials of a specific kind can be prepared that will embody the spiritual values that we wish to communicate to children. These materials can be in the form of regular text-books, phamphlets or booklets which students can handle in a convenient manner. Ways must be found to provide sufficient incentive for students to read these materials. This should be primarily by way of making them aware of the urgency for training in spiritual values. Religious institutions already use such materials for religious instruction. Plenty of models of these will be available for education to develop its own suitable materials for schools, colleges and other vocational institutions. The advantages of education through such literature are several. Students will be able to pursue these studies in their own way. These materials can become the basic of instructions provided at school. An awareness and acceptance of spiritual realities should be the outcome of such literature.

5. **Work Experiences** constitute another method for developing spiritual values in students. Work experiences have become an accepted mode of correlated activity and provision of related experiences to make education a concrete activity. Work experiences are attached to all educational institutions one way or other under every discipline taught at the institution. The same field of activities should be used for the provision of spiritual education. Students find themselves highly motivated in the participation of these activities even when they become disinterested in the academic work of the institution. We should find suitable techniques for developing work experiences with reference to the spiritual values under consideration. Care must be taken so that students do not become parochial and communal minded and lose the spirit of spiritual instruction by losing sight of the objectives. Work experiences should constitute the material or medium for the concrete communication of spiritual values.

6. Village Reconstruction Programmes offer ample opportunities for the development of spiritual values in students. Gandhi said, "My mind is living in the villages. They are calling me to bury myself in them".[54] Gandhi's love of the village took different directions. He came preoccupied with rural reconstruction not only to improve their material and psychological environment but also to show them the light of truth and ahimsa in the right perspective. The same rural life will provide Indian students the greatest possible opportunity for the realisation of spiritual values. Confronting the poor and the suffering masses of people with the toil they put up for survival help students have a spiritual vision in concrete. They will have the opportunity thereby to identify themselves with the suffering and the poor. This will be the starting point of their sincere search for spiritual values for the development of their spiritual personality. Village reconstruction would thus become the background of the student's spiritual development.

7. 'Self-help drives' can be thought of as a method through which the spiritual values can be developed in the student. Gandhi's life was a constant experiment in living a simple and sacrifice-oriented life: "In course of time I became an expert washer-man so far as my own work went..... my passion for self-help and simplicity ultimately expressed itself in extreme forms".[55] Gandhi confronted spiritual values in every moment of his own practical life. Students in ways more than one can be educated in voluntary self-help in their own private, home and school life. Orientations to this effect and training can be given at school so that they convert their school and day-to-day life into a field of experiments with self-help. Spiritual values of several kinds will be attached to these attempts to transform their personality into one founded on a God-centered spiritual life. These self-help drives need to be initiated at school and extended to the family.

5. Developing Spiritual Values in Education-2

8. Prayer Services have a big role to play in developing spiritual values in students. Gandhi says, "Prayer is the heart and soul of religion. Therefore prayer should be the soul of human life, and no one can live without religion".[56] Although fundamental work in regard to the development of a prayer life rests with home, academic institutions can present to students the significance of prayer life from several new and compelling perspectives. Schools and colleges should find time for regular prayer services to inculcate in students the habits of prayer. Ways must be found as much as possible not to attach these prayers to any one specific religion but to keep the prayers of a general kind while at the same time capable arousing the students' spiritual sentiments. Most students are bound to find prayer meetings very attractive, stimulating and meaningful. Prayer is the best link between life and spirituality.

9. Cultural Studies of a particular kind can be helpful in developing spiritual values in students. The culture and religion of a given community are the sides of the same coin. Cultural analysis and study can be undertaken as a medium precisely for the inculcation of spiritual values. Most often aspects of spirituality born out of any particular religion cannot of themselves attractive to students. These spiritual aspects can be attached to the cultural values and beliefs in a very concrete manner. Culture then becomes the material for the presentation of spirituality to students. In order to render spirituality concrete, sustaining and dynamic it is always safer to achieve an integration of culture and spiritual values as much as possible.

10. Health Services can be a method of developing spirituality in students. In these cases health services are carried out with the specific intention of deriving spiritual values out of them. Health services carried out in society will help students come in contact with the ordinary masses of humanity with their own unique problems. These contacts most systematically carried out will develop in them again several unique and desired spiritual sentiments and influence the development of their spiritual personality. Gandhi writes, "If your education is a substantial one, then it should spread its odour in the surroundings. You should spend a portion of your day-to-day life to serve the people around you in a practical manner".[57] Education will lead students automatically out to the community. But the attitude with which they approach the community should always be in a spirit of dedicated service in total selflessness. If that happens that will constitute on excellent foundation for spiritual life. What is required, then, will be a sublimation of these social values to the spiritual plain.

Methods such as those described above will be capable of developing spirituality in students. In the case of every such method certain norms are to be kept in mind in the process. The spiritual instruction should not turn out to be yet another routine subject like other disciplines. Unlike other subjects spiritual instruction or providing experiences in spiritual values is directly linked to the very ultimate goal of life and education. For this reason teachers and students alike should be convinced of the significance of the education for spiritual values.

Again every activity or method suggested for the development of spiritual values must create in the individual a lingering and intense consciousness of spiritual life: its aim, significance, the aspects of such a life and the methods of living it. Involvement in simple manual labour, for instance, can be done without any reference whatsoever to spiritual considerations. In the second case what makes the difference is the intense awareness that we help develop in the students. Paying a visit to a hospital and observing or lending a helping hand to any suffering patient at the hospital can turn out to be the best background for the concrete development and exericse of spiritual values in the individual at the level of consciousness. This may not be the case with a casual observer whose spiritual sentiments are not aroused by the observation.

In the development of a spiritual life in the student the very foundation will consist of the student's personal spiritual convictions. The education organised should lead the individual to this level. This spiritual conviction should be the ultimate aim of the instruction. Gandhi says, "If we are to become not animals walking on four legs, but human being who walk erect, then we should recognise the inherent discipline and control and we subject ourselves to these"[58] The formation of spiritual convictions cannot be imposed from outside. If this conviction cannot be developed in students then all the work that we may do in developing spiritual values will turn out to be useless as it usually happens in the case of training often given in religious institutions. Everything at our disposal should be done to prevent spiritual education from becoming a meaningless routine affair. It should not become like any other subject in the school or college.

Lastly spiritual education needs to be individualised wherever possible. Education in spiritual values is a matter of developing spiritual habits in the individual with a view to introducing transformation in his way of life and thinking. Hence a degree of observation of the individual becomes necessary. There will be tendencies to evade the spirit of this training and these tendencies will be contagious and easily influence others. For that matter a degree of observation of individuals becomes necessary. All these factors will help develop a spiritual life in students which Gandhi considered most essential.

References

1. An Autobiography, Intr.
2. Thekkinedath, J., *Love of Neighbour*, p.50.
3. *To the Students*, p.114.
4. *An Autobiography*, Intr.
5. *To the Students*, p.71.
6. *An Autobiography*, p.248.
7. *Mahatma*, Vol.1, p.68.
8. *An Autobiography*, p.383.
9. *Harijan*, 2 March 1934.
10. *To the Students*, p.252.
11. *Harijan*, 3 March 1946.

12. *An Autobiography*, p.357.
13. Jones, Stanley, in *Profiles*, p.134.
14. Durant, W., in Ibid, p.11.
15. Gunther, J., in Ibid p.47.
16. Gregg, R.B., in Ibid, p.168.
17. Holmer, J., in Ibid, p.127.
18. In J. Thekkinedath, *Love of Neighbour*, p.42.
19. Ibid p.177
20. An Autobiogrphy, p.383.
21. Jones, Stanley, in Profiles, p.134.
22. Young India 11 October 1928.
23. *An Autobiography*, p.382.
24. In J. Thekkinedath, *Love of Neighbour*, p.42.
25. Ibid p.177.
26. *An Autobiography*, p.383.
27. *Harijan* 18 February 1939.
28. *An Autobiography*, p.51.
29. *Harijan* 13 April 1940.
30. *To the Students*, p.182.
31. In J.Thekkinedath, *Love of Neighbour*, p.42.
32. *Mahatma*, Vol.4, p.40.
33. *Harijan*, 11 March 1939.
34. *An Autobiography*, p.118.
35. *Harijan*, 19 August 1939.
36. In J.Thekkinedath, *Love of Neighbour*, p.51.
37. *Harijan* 21 April 1946.
38. *Mahatma*, Vol.7, p.95.
39. *An Autobioghraphy*, p.383.
40. In J.Thekkinedath, *Love of Neighbour*, p.155.
41. Pillai, N.P., *Education*, p.21.
42. Ibid p.22.
43. Bhatia, B.D., *Philosophy*, p.126.
44. *An Autobiography*, Intr.
45. Pillai, N.P., *Education*, p.22.
46. *Towards New Education*, p.85.
47. Ibid p.31.
48. Pillai, N.P., *Education*, p.24.
49. *An Autobiography*, p.164.
50. Holmer, J., in *Profiles*, p.124.
51. *To the Students*, p.164.

52. In J., Thekkinedath, *Love of Neighbour*, p.179.
53. *To the Students*, p.164.
54. *Mahatma*, Vol.4, p.40.
55. *An Autobiography*, p.160.
56. *Harijan*, 13 April 1940.
57. *To the Students*, p.173.
58. Ibid p.183.

10

EDUCATION FOR PEACE AND TOLERANCE

1. Gandhi and World Peace

Gandhi in all his undertakings proved himself to be one of the greatest messengers of peace the world has witnessed and peace becomes the quintessence of his political philosophy. It is Gandhi's contributions to world peace that the world at large has aptly recognised in him. Gandhi showed the world not only the goal of peace but the supreme method of achieving world peace. George C.Mashall writes, "In his devotion to peace and tolerance of the brotherhood man, the Mahatma was one of those rare spokesman for the conscience of all mankind".[1] Peace and tolerance, for Gandhi, were the supreme means for the realisation of Truth and Love which were identical to the Ultimate End of man. Gandhi's spiritual, political, and economic tenets were permeated by the principle of peace. In the light of peace alone could the human being witness truth.

Gandhi developed his world-view against the background of a world of violence. Violence by the foreign rule, economic violence against the poor, political violence against the docon-trodden and underprivileged, educational violence against the illiterate and the backward and above all the violence of war and crime. Gandhi's message of peace took all its sharpness and sensitivity against this background of violence. He says, "What you gain by violence will be lost be greater violence".[2] Gandhi recognised violence as the root-cause of all evils and all evils are thus reducible to violence against the spirit of truth. Hence for him non-violence or ahimsa becomes the only path to truth and only solution to the problems of life-individual, social and national. Hence the great role of ahimsa in the framework of Gandhian thoughts. Thus non-violence becomes the identified with peace. Peace becomes the true and positive way to the realisation of truth.

Gandhian peace is an individual value. Just as truth and ahimsa begins with the individual and get realised in the individual, peace is a great value that should begin with the individual and become the basis for the development other social and psychological attitudes. Edmond Taylor remarks, "This has produced the great Gandhian personality, a combination of inner peace arising from a more total integration of all the elements in the personality than most men achieve".[3] The development of the spiritual personality takes place in total integration with the psychological attitudes. We find this integration revealed in the Gandhian personality. Peace becomes not only a goal but also a condition for self-realisation. Peace becomes the necessary condition for the spiritual development of the individual. For this reason the sages and rishis of ancient times desired total isolation in their encounter with God. Peace in the individual is identified with divine presence in the religions. For Gandhi peace becomes an individual value of great significance.

Peace becomes a great national goal in the Gandhian context. Gandhi said, "As long as India is not independent she is not in a position to contribute her share to world peace".[4] What Gandhi strived after was to establish the real peace in India, the kind of peace that will spread to the entire world . Gandhi's conception of Independent India meant an India solidly rooted on the principle of peace where truth and ahimsa reign supreme. Gandhi's world-wide acceptance and recognition are rooted on his peace full and non-violent revolution that he exercised in this country. Martin Luther King says, "With a small group of devoted followers, Gandhi galvanised the whole of India, and through a magnificent feat of non-violence challenged the might of the British Empire and won freedom for his people".[5] The non-violent revolution Gandhi galvanised set forever the light of peace that could guide the country in the right direction. It is this peace that Gandhi wanted Indians to enforce and develop because the very survival of the country depended on it. Gandhi wanted India to be a symbol of peace for the world because the great heritage of the country always symbolised peace. Gandhi wrote, "If India becomes free during my lifetime, and if I have the strength for it, I shall remain outside the official world and fulfill my duty of building a nation fully based on non-violence".[6] A nation based completely on non-violence only can enjoy to privilege of allowing the people to live of peace, truth and love.

Peace becomes an international goal in the framework of Gandhism. Today peace is the catch-word in international relations because the world has come to realise more than ever the vital role of peace in the very survival of mankind. At the time of Gandhi's assassination Earl Warren wrote, "The assassination of Gandhi removes from the world by a cowardly act a powerful force for world peace. Gandhi was essentially a man of peace".[7] The world recognised Gandhi's contribution to world peace in ways more than one. Gandhi professed his love of the British, the Americans and the Europeans as a whole at the same time he deplored the violent sophistication and advancement of the West. Gandhi loved the British but hated their ways. He writes recalling his role in the Boer War of 1899: "I felt that I demanded the rights as a British citizen it was also my duty to participate in the defence of the British empire". Based on this conviction Gandhi formed the Peace Corpse which consisted of 1100 members to provide relief work. Gandhi's love of the British was part of the great and universal drive he had for peace. Gandhi always set his eyes on world Peace as the foundation on which to build a world of truth and love. He says, "Once we accept truth and love as the foundations of our existence, then we have discovered the foundations of the unity of humanity".[8] The unity of humanity can be based only on the principle of peace as the necessary condition for the development of truth and love in the hearts of men. Gandhi saw the message of Christ as a unique expression of peace in the world: "I want the help of especially Christians to strengthen my conviction in non-violence because thousands of them believe that the message of Christ is the message of World Peace and good will".[9] Gandhism stands for international peace. It is only through peace that the world can move in the path of truth towards God.

Peace and national integration inherently correlated. So far as India is concerned national integration bears supreme importance because India's unity is a unity in diversity. Diversity in this country is indeed a great phenomenon. True peace in this country is possible only through the integration of these diverse political, social, cultural, religious and geographical elements that divide the country far and wide. Peace through national integration was one of Gandhi's foremost aims. Edgar P. Snow writes, "Gandhi never ceased to try to unite his countrymen and indeed with the whole world under the homely injunctions common to all faiths: individual perfection, tolerance, humility, love of nature (God), equality, brotherhood and cooperation".[10] Gandhi had the great foresightedness of envisaging an India united under one Nation flag not merely on the basis of political unity but an integration that would supersede all the differences under the supreme directive of truth and ahimsa. Keeping his eyes fixed on the ideal of peace and integration Gandhi said, "Hinduism must purge itself of untouchability, remove all distinctions of inferiority and superiority, and shed a host of other evils and shams that have become rampant in it.".[11]

Gandhian spirituality is founded on peace. Gandhi says, "In violence we exhibit not the spirit but the brute in us".[12] The spirit can be realised and nurtured only in a state of non-violence that is peace. All aspects of spirituality that can be practiced by the individual and can lead to God are based on peace in the individual as a condition for divine light. God's light in truth and love will shine on the individual only in a state peace. Spirituality is the realisation of truth and the vision of God through prayer, sacrifices and spiritual exercises that were so dear to Gandhi. He says, "Ahimsa is the only means to the realisation of truth.... A perfect vision of truth can only follow a complete realisation of ahimsa".[13] Peace is a state of complete non-violence in the individual, society and nation. Gandhian spirituality can be realised and developed only within the framework of peace that should reign in the individual. Where there is no truth there cannot be peace and where there is no love, again, there cannot be peace. Peace in the genuine sense would thus become the co-principle of truth and love.

2. Tolerance in Gandhism

Man's tolerance of one another's wrongs, tolerance and forbearance of social differences is fundamental to Gandhian thoughts. Tolerance is basic to the survival and progress of individuals, society and the nation. Dwight Macdonald says, "He practiced tolerance and love to such an extent that he seem to have regarded the capitalist and the garbage man as his social equal".[14] Tolerance is a fundamental Gandhian virtue that makes the Gandhian ahimsa a most potent thing. Tolerance becomes a refinement of the most powerful principal of ahimsa. In a country like India more than anywhere else tolerance becomes central value for difference reasons. India is a divided country with fundamental religio-philosophical and cultural separatism. This separatism is reflected most in our Hindu-Muslim and other communal rivalries and parochial tendencies. Gandhi saw that these communal rivalries would be a death-knell to the survival of this country. Gandhi's experiences after the partition immensely proved how malicious and terrible communalism in India could turn out to be. The Hindu-Muslim massacres after the partition compelled Gandhi to undertake a fast unto death, which he stopped on assurance from leading members of different communities that the bloody rivalries would be stopped at once.

Against this background tolerance is felt to be a very fundamental value in this country. Today tolerance is a constitutional value as an attitude fundamental to the democratic practices in this country. Tolerance and the fundamental rights are absolutely correlated. It requires tolerance on the part of one individual to recognise the democratic rights of another. It requires tolerance similarly to recognise the constitutional rights communities. This recognition requires forbearance which we call tolerance in this context. The rights of individuals and communities call for tolerance on the part of other individuals and communities. Here tolerance becomes a positive virtue and enters into the very realm of ahimsa or love. Martin Luther King writes, "We will return good for evil. We will love our enemies. Christ showed us the way, and Gandhi showed us how it could work".[15] Tolerance becomes love in its positive directions and Gandhi carries it to the logical extreme of loving one's enemies in line with the teachings of Jesus Christ. Tolerance as a constitutional value with reference to the fundamental rights takes the direction also of justice. It is merely allowing the other the necessary justice that he naturally deserves. Gandhi says, "My experience has shown me that we win justice quickest by rendering justice to the other party".[16] Tolerence becomes justice paid in equal measure to those who owe it under a given social set up.

Just like peace, tolerance becomes an individual value aimed at the development of the human individual. Relationship between individuals based on tolerance becomes fundamental to a spiritual society Gandhi envisaged. Differences in personal attitudes, aptitudes and endowements are basic to human life. These differences and the socio-economic status that becomes attached to these are part of socio-communal life. Individual tolerence becomes important when Gandhi wants these differences and the ups and downs to be forgotten in building a society based on truth and ahimsa. Dwight Macdonald writes, "It is true that Gandhi compromised with the rich, those untouchables of the class struggle, living at their villas. But he also compromised with the poor spending as much time with them".[17] Gandhi showed the world that tolerance was the key principle in mutual help and self-less service. This would mean accepting the enemy or the stranger with all the pitfalls that he usually has.

Tolerance becomes a social goal in Gandhian frame of social set up. Social development at all levels of interaction comes to be based on tolerance from this view point. If the tolerance of individual differences is significant in individual development, in the same token, tolerance is fundamental in social development. Social development is impossible without different communities interacting with each other. Conflicts and rivalries arise when it comes to the benefit of one community, perhaps, at the cost of another's inconvenience or loss. Tolerance plays a major role here in effecting a clear balance between such differences. Tolerance coupled with a sense of justice would prompt one community to accept the other and work for its development.

Gandhi attached such a great importance to communal tolerance with reference to Hindu-Muslim rivalries and problems of interaction. Gandhi always went out of the way to convince the two communities of the great necessity of mutual tolerance, even at the cost of his on life: "Being a Hindu himself Gandhi found it intolerable that other Hindus should be massacring the Muslim minority".[18] Gandhi kept on reminding Indian at large that the two communities are part and parcel of the very same nation. K.L.Gauba writes, "Whenever the question of separatism arose, Mahatma Gandhi and others, and the leading News Papers never hesitated to remind the Muslims that they belonged to the same race and nationality as the Hindus".[19] Ethnic tolerance was the unique solution for communal problems and Gandhi gave the highest priority to the value of tolerance within the framework of ahimsa. If truth is the aim at the individual, social and national level of life, then tolerance remains to be concurrent value along with peace for development at these different levels.

3. Educational Goal of Peace and Tolerance

Peace and tolerance are fundamental goals of education. Education considered from whatever viewpoint ends up in a rediscovery of peace at the very root of all formations and developments. Education aims primarily at helping the individual achieve a state of physical, psychological, social and spiritual balance or equilibrium. In other words the individual discovers, in the process of education, a self balanced in the right attitudes towards himself, society and God. This constitutes the state peace in the individual. It is a process of developing the self in these attitudes. The individual becomes capable of comparing and contrasting his own potentials and achievements with those of others not in a spirit of negative and unhealthy competition but in truth and live. This amounts to the development of peace within oneself. Peace in the right sense is not a negative state of lack of conflicts and problems within oneself. Peace is a positive and dynamic state of integrating in the right manner the diverse elements, conflicts and problems in the personality and obtaining a holistic state of quiescence. In Gandhi's own words this becomes a successful search for truth: "A successful search for truth means a complete deliverance from the dual throng such as love and hate, happiness and misery".[20] It is not the concellation of diverse elements but the harmony and integration of these elements that constitute peace in the individual as part of the development of his personality.

Education aims at promoting peace in the nation. Development of attitudes of peace in the individual leads to collective endeavours for peace in the nation. This has dimensions. On the one hand education ensures that the individual grows up in full awareness of the significance of peace at the national level, and on the other hand education attempts to direct this individual awareness to actual peace at the national level. Through the right orientations of educational content and methods and through the provision of learning experiences the awareness and a feeling of urgency for peace at the national level can be developed. Peace and tolerence go hand in hand. Peace can be regarded as the end and tolerance as the means and the method. Education should help students to price the value of peace and tolerance more than anything else.

Once gandhi was asked by a student: "What can studetns do to create Hindu-Muslim unity?" Gandhi answered, "The way is simple. Even if all the Hindus turn out to be hooligans and begin insulting you, you should not stop considering them your brothers in blood".[21] Gandhi had no excuses and compromises for his principles and his admonitions took an absolute nature. That show the level of greatness and the depth of sincerity he attached to these principles. Gandhi made it clear that education has vital role to play in developing peace and tolerance in all the affairs of the country, especially at all the levels of decision-making. The process of developing an intense awareness of peace permeates all levels and all aspects of education. It is not possible for education to have separate stream of 'peace education' along with other subjects and disciplines. But education should be in a clear position to integrate peace values with all other aspects of the curriculum.

Gandhi saw the evil practice of untouchability as a major obstacle to the practice and realisation of peace and tolerance in the real sense of the words in several parts of India. Untouchability reigned supreme even in the days of Gandhi and he remained conscious of its evil effects. He emphasised the role of education in creating the necessary wave against these evil practices: "National schools should be capable of spreading the message of charka, unite the Hindus and the Muslims, educate the untouchables and thus remove from schools the curse of untouchability".[22] The practice of untouchability grieved Gandhi to the depth of his personality. Education is the only solution of this practice if it is still persisting in any form in any part of the country. Ways in which one community considers another as inferior is another form of untouchability and this practice comes directly opposed to the ideal of peace and tolerance. Obstacles to the ideal of peace and tolerance crop up in different ways. Very often people fail to recognise that such ways have anything to do with the maintenance of peace and tolerance. Education has the sacred duty to safeguard the values of peace and tolerance from all such lapses that may occur in the individual, society or nation.

Education aims further at international peace, and tolerance at the level of nations. The Gandhian message of peace has gathered significance more than ever on the face of the growing arms race between world powers. The modern world has the ever growing feeling that humanity is moving towards a nuclear end. The nuclear holocaust has to be averted. Gandhi's efforts for peace in the world can be regarded as the only solution to divert such a holocaust. Norman Thomas says, "If ever men achieve a world peace, to no single man will it owe a greater debt than to Mohandas K. Gandhi". [23] Gandhian education recognises Gandhi's role in developing international peace and attempts to include the value of international peace and tolerance as an internal component of education. The very existence of the United Nations symbolises international peace and promotes all international peace negotiations. Studies on the UN has been made a vital component of the school syllabus with a view to developing an awareness of the problem of international peace in students. Again, education can attempt to synthesise the Gandhian teachings on peace with the efforts of the UN to render the knowledge of the students and their attitudes more powerful.

The education of the individual for peace and the formation of character are essentially correlated. Percy Nunn writes, "Nothing good enters into the human world except in and through the free activities of individual men and women: and that educational practice must be shaped to accord with that truth".[24] The shaping of the individual's character is the basic building-block in the shaping of the nation. Development of the basic peace-consciousness and an intense of tolerance at the level of the individual should constitute part of the process of character formation carried out by education.

Peace becomes part of personality development from all

perspectives. Peace-attitudes are part of the individual's spiritual personality in his attempts to move towards Truth as the ultimate Goal. Education for Gandhi is "the all-round drawing out of the best in the child and man-body, mind and spirit".[25] This 'best' for Gandhi is in fact 'the inner voice of Truth'. The strengthening of this inner voice of truth, as all of Gandhi's personal experiments consisted of, is actually the strengthening of peace in all its different perspectives. Gandhi says, "one person who can express ahimsa in life exercises a force superior to all forces of brutality".[26] Peace in the individual becomes the expression of ahimsa as peace and ahimsa are inseparable. A character well-founded on peace will exercise the attitudes of truth and ahimsa to others. Peace and tolerance provide a link between personalities of individuals within a given social set up. Peace at the individual level would thus become the flowering or blossoming of the personality. Based on this Gandhi tells students, "If your education is substantial, then it should permeate to the neighbourhood and exercise its influence".[27] The odour of peace in the individual cannot help permeating to outside the individual and exercise the right influence.

The East as a whole and India in particular stood for peace. It was the reflection of peace that the East has produced the World Religions. There is no religion in the world that does not stand for peace in the individual and peace in humanity. Peace is a treasured value for every religion. The contributions of India towards world peace is not sheer contemporary phenomenon but a traditional one. Being the motherland of three major world religions, it is most apparent that India stands foremost for this treasured value of peace. Indian culture thus embodies peace and tolerance as two great principles. Education which aims at the transmission of culture in fact transmits the value of peace and tolerence in the context of India. The right teaching of Indian culture will not be providing a puffed up concept or account of wars but of the great value of peace embodied in our culture. Education at the school level already spends considerable time in providing studies and experiences in Indian culture. This effort can be easily re-oriented to focus on peace so that the work will form a basis for the development of the right attitude of peace in students.

Education for peace and tolerance receives high priority in a world that is facing serious nuclear threat. Educational goals in all their diversities have a dimension of peace with reference to the individual, society and nation at large. These goals require a coordination to bring home the full importance of peace and tolerance. Peace is a value that should achieve integration with other values in education. Peace is an attitude that requires development along with other important attitudes to produce holistic personality. Peace becomes a principle that is capable of providing the necessary directions in the individual's attitudes towards himself, society and the nation. Education and Gandhism becomes a harmonious whole at the level of peace.

4. Educational Concepts of Peace

Peace is a concept in general education. As a concept peace forms part of the content of general education. As a traditional Indian concept peace has formed part of the content of all aspects of education. Languages in this country have sprung from the hearts of millions of our ancestors who loved and treasured peace and tolerance. These languages, both ancient and modern versions of them, contain countless expressions of peace whose analysis in the present context does not seem necessary. The Sanskrit term 'shanti' borrowed into all Indian language leads the human spirit to the very ultimate realms of human life. These concepts enable them to realise the value of peace and develop this value in day-to-day life.

In spite of all the representations of violence Indian literature in various languages include, peace and representations of peace has always been the ultimate value literature in this country attempts to project. No literature in any language is known to uphold violence for its own sake at the cost of peace as a value, whether individual or communal. Since literature as such is expected to cross the limits of communal and even national spheres, all good literature develops an overtone and sensibility that would lead us to the value of peace in humanity. Indian literature embodies this in all its dimensions and help Indians discover greater vistas of peace in the world. It is this literature, again, that must often becomes the content of education in India. If therefore efforts are made these is great scope of increasing the awareness of peace as a treasured value in education. Literature can be considered the best vehicle for perpetuating the concept and value of peace in a community because of the great potential of literature in representing life that would appeal most to the mind.

The concept of peace is also part of the content of science education. Science aims not at the destruction of mankind nor does it orient itself to purposes of violence. It is a fact that the world has been employing the inventions and discoveries of science and technology for purposes of war and destruction. It may also be said that most intense research into certain areas of science tookplace during the World Wars as well as it takes place as part of the arms-race by world powers. All the same no genuine scientist orients his genius for war and destruction. Science education has great scope for developing in the students great convictions regarding the peaceful applications of science and technology. These convictions are based on the fact that science and technology fundamentally aim at the progress of humanity and the strengthening of civilization as well as making this world a better place for man to live in.

Peace becomes a content of social sciences and culture studies. The teaching of social sciences at the school level naturally indulges the way India from time immemorial symbolised peace. The background of Hinduism, Buddhism and Jainism and all the religious innovations and movements emphasised peace as a principal value to be cherished on this land. They very social structure of this country is based not on rivalry but on peaceful co-existence as compared to the social structure of the West. Peace has been the most cherished value of several kings and emperors who ruled over this great land. The great principle of dharma or righteousness that govern all socio-economic interactions of traditional India is centered on peace and tolerance. Education through social sciences constitutes, thus, one of the most potent means of inculcating and developing in students a love of peace and tolerance. This value can be perpetuated in them through the variety of learning experiences that can be generated in the framework of such studies.

Peace becomes the content of Gandhian education more than in any other aspect. Gandhi's orientations in education have been fashioned after developing everything that would help the realisation of a whole set of related values, attitudes and perspectives. Peace is fundamental to these orientations. Gandhi's thoughts and personality become synonymous with the ideals of peace. Teaching Gandhism in one way or other, developing Gandhian thought through educational experiences would all amount to dealing with the concepts of peace and tolerance. If general education offers ample opportunities for dealing with the concept of peace, then Gandhian education becomes a field almost specialised in peace education. Gandhian education and peace education would be knit into a harmonious whole. It is because non-violence penetrates and encompasses everything in Gandhism, and non-violence would necessarily mean peace. Peace in the individual is a concept co-existent with truth and love. Peace becomes an attitude in which the individual can be given the necessary training. Gandhi's training and experiments in non-violence are for us a training in the supreme concept of peace. Peace in society is a cherished Gandhian value. When Gandhi envisions a non-violent society, that becomes a society well-grounded in the attitudes of peace, dedicated to the very cause of truth and love. Peace in Gandhism is a national concept because it is the only foundation for the nation to move to progress. In Gandhism, thus peace is everything, closely related to self-realisation.

5. Methods of Peace Education

1. The United Nations today constitutes the most supreme institution that functions at the very apex of all efforts for peace in the world. The UN has become the unique symbol of international peace and the hope of humanity especially one the face of an ever growing nuclear threat. Hence the very first method of peace education is to keep the students fully conversant with the aims, prospects and activities of the UN. The UN has quite a number of member as well as associated agencies like the WHO and the UNICEF. Students can get to know the activities of these agencies in detail. The spirit of the UN will be one of those important aspects which should control peace education in schools. Studies on the UN are already part of the syllabus for social science. But this is only casual and not powerful enough to develop a peace consciousness in students.

   Numerous activities related to the UN can be envisaged for schools and colleges. The conspicuous celebration of all the UN days in education institutions will certainly help foster a love for international peace on the one hand and the activities and the spirit of the UN on the other. These celebrations of the UN Days may be accompanied by different activities. The easiest that schools can organise will be study sessions, group discussions, talks by the staff or by guest speakers or other similar activities. Pictures relating to the activities of the UN can be collected on a regular basis and used systematically for small-scale exhibitions. As part of the UN studies, an understanding of the member-nations of the UN will be great help. An understanding of the cultural specifications of these nations and the vital contributions of these nations will provide scope for developing greater sympathy and understanding towards them.

2. Education for peace basically requires a development of the peace consciousness as a necessary atmosphere in academic institutions. This requires a general pattern

or framework of learning experiences, work experiences and co-curricular and extra-curricular involvements for providing an ever greater and well-organised awareness of peace. Efforts can be made to keep outside the scope of the institution violence of any form. Gandhi says, "We have to make this training school (the Basic school) a school for winning freedom and for the solution of all our ills, of which the primary one is our communal troubles. And for this purpose we shall have to concentrate on non-violence...... All problems are, therefore, to be solved non-violently".[28] By trying to maintain a sustaining atmosphere of peace students will in an automatic manner develop a sensibility of and sensitivity towards peace that slowly get embedded in their personalities. Like other Gandhian values and principles peace would constitute a symbol in the institution for the students to cherish. Violence in thought, speech or action will become a taboo against which every student will guard himself. All efforts must be directed this end of developing in the academic institution a lasting awareness and love of peace.

3. The use of peace-based materials in the school can be a method of peace education. Instructional materials of different types can be developed for students, in which the concept of peace can be coherently presented. These materials may be regular classroom study materials or additional reading materials which should have easy access to students. Students should be introduced to these materials in different ways such as providing additional reading hours or by motivating students to read them on their own finding their own time. These peace-based materials can again be in narrative fictional or descriptive form based on historical or fictitious events that can successfully incorporate the concept of peace. The success of these materials depends considerably on the way they are introduced to students. If regular study materials bear the message of peace, then these materials need to be presented most carefully so as not to miss

the focus on peace.

4. Peace consciousness can be developed as part of peace education through the method of culture studies for tolerance: Instead of developing a communistic and parochial attitude towards other communities and cultures, efforts can be made in education to promote peace-based culture studies. Considerable cultural interaction can be made possible at the level of education and promote better understanding between communities with diverse cultural experiences. A sense of acceptance and appreciation of the cultural concepts, cultural values and practices of other communities will make peace education a fruitful endeavour. As part of these culture studies tours and visits to culture centres, religious centres and functions of importance can be organised in such a way as to promote the value and urgency of peace and tolerance among communities based on Gandhian ideals. Inspite of ideological disagreements with the practices of other communities, students must have the necessary training to see things in a new perspective of peace and tolerance. It is most usual to be critical of others cultural practices only because these are just different and not opposed. Peace education enables us to overcome this tendency and see things in the new perspective.

5. Inter-religious experiences will constitute another method of promoting peace education. Gandhi says, "The communal unity is not confined to the Hindus and Muslims only, it extends to all, including the Englishman.....That is the message of non-violence".[29] Educational institutions will be able to provide students with religious experiences that belong to the different religions in our country. This effort must be based especially on those prayers, functions and ceremonies that have a universal, human significance and can be easily acceptable to members of other communities. Exposure to such religious services will enable students to develop a clear sense of sympathy attraction as well as

reverence for the religious viewpoints of other communities. These experiences can be chiefly in the form of simply prayer services and reading sessions based on scriptural texts that belong to the different religions. These sessions may be conducted by the staff and the students belonging to the school or by guest-participants who can be invited from the community. It is most important again that these experiences should develop the basic spirit in the them rather than merely add an item to the already burdened syllabus.

6. Peace education through a knowledge of the Red-Cross Society, Peace Corpse, the NSS and involvements in which ever of these possible will prove valuable at the school and college level. The international involvements of the Red Cross society in times of war would constitute excellent background for students to imbibe concepts and values of peace. The ideals, movements and the activities of the Red Cross should be studied and observed by a group of students in the school under the guidance of a teacher and present their observations and materials for the follow up of the rest of the school.

   The involvements of the National Service Scheme (NSS) provide today considerable help in developing the students' understanding of peace in the framework of social service. The NSS can easily lead students at the college level, where it is at present functioning, to the midst of the masses of people, get to know their problems and develop the values of peace and tolerance in them. The NCC at the school level may be oriented to the same mode of work. Keeping their eyes fixed on the integration, development and safety of the Nation, peace can constitute the foundation of every aspect of their valuable work. What usually happens is that violence and conflicts creep into these organisations in one form or other and destroy the very spirit for which they are intended. If we are in a position to safeguard these organisations against this danger they can be of great service to peace education.

Educational institutions may employ suitable methods of developing peace education which should be in total harmony with the working of the institution. In every subject, every material and in every activity we shall find a way of developing in students a deep awareness and sensibility of peace. Gandhi stood for total peace and tolerance: "The sun of ahimsa keeps away all the dark realities of hatred, envy and dislike. Ahimsa shines high up in the realm of education. No one can hide it like the Sun".[30] Gandhian education is basically an education for peace and tolerance that would clear the way to truth and love. The aims, the principles, the concepts and the methods of education can be oriented to develop peace in the individual as well as in the Nation.

References

1. Marshall, J.C., in *Profiles*, p.96.
2. *Harijan*, 10 February 1940.
3. Toylar, E., in *Profiles*, p.72.
4. *Harijan*, 3 February 1940.
5. King, M.L., in *Profiles*, p.216.
6. *Harijan*, 27 April 1940.
7. Warren, Earl, in *Profiles*, p.96.
8. *Harijan*, 18 February 1939.
9. Ibid 10 March 1940.
10. Snow, E.P., in *Profiles*, p.106.
11. *An Autobiography*, p.296.
12. Ibid p.256.
13. Ibid p.382.
14. Macdonald, D., in *Profiles*, p.110.
15. King M.L., in *Profiles*, p.191.
16. *An Autobiography*, p.136.
17. Macdonald, D., in *Profiles*, p.110.
18. White, M.B., in *Profiles*, p.89.
19. Gauba, K.L., *The Assassination*, p.8.
20. *An Autobiography*, p.261.
21. *Harijan*, 28 April 1946.
22. *Towards New Education*, p.21.

23. Thomas,N., in *Profiles*, p.166.
24. Bhatia, B.D., *Philosophy*, p.21.
25. *Harijan*, 14 July 1937.
26. *Gandhi*, M.K., in Profiles, p.45.
27. *To the Students*, p.173.
28. *Mahatma*, Vol.4, p.246.
29. *Mahatma*, Vol.7, p.96.
30. *To the Students*, p.146.

Select Bibliography

Abul Kalam Azad, (Maulana), India Wins Freedom. Bombay: Longman, 1959.

Acharlu, K.S. The Study of Mahatma Gandhi. Bombay : Foresight, 1985.

Adams, Don(ed.) Education and National Development. London : Routledge and Kegan Paul, 1971.

Agarwal, S.N., Gandhian Constitution for free India, Bombay : Padma Publications, 1944.

Agarwal, J.C., Development and Planning of Modern Education. New Delhi.

Ahluwala, B.K.(ed.) Facets of Gandhi. New Delhi, 1968.

Alexander, H. Social and Political Ideas of Mahatma Gandhi. Bombay, 1949.

Altaker, A.S. Education in Ancient India, Varanasi : Naul Kishore, 1957.

Ambedkar, B.R., Mr. Gandhi and the Emancipation of Untouchables. Bombay, 1946.

-do-, The Untouchables, New Delhi, 1948.

Andrews, C.F., Mahatma Gandhi's Ideas. London, 1949.

-do-, The meaning of Non-co-operation. Madras, 1920.

-do-, To the Students, Madras.

Athalya, D.V., Life of Mahatma Gandhi. Poona, 1923.

Avinashilingam, S.T.,Gandhiji's Thought on Education. New Delhi : Govt. of India, 1958.

Bandopathyaya, S.K., My Non-violence. Ahmedabad : Navjeevan, 1960.

Burns, M., India : Today and Tomorrow, London, 1937.

Basin, Prem, Socialism in India. New Delhi : Young Asia, 1968.

Basu, A., The Growth of Education and Political Development in India, 1898 - 1920. New Delhi : Oxford University Press, 1974.

Basu, Durga Das, Introduction to the Constitution of India. New Delhi : Prenctice-Hall, 1976.

Bedakar, D.K., Towards Understanding Gandhi. Bombay, 1975.

Benn, Stanley I and R.S. Peters, Social principles and Democratic State. London : Allen and Unwin, 1959.

Benoy, Gopal Ray, Gandhian Ethics. Ahmedabad : Navjeevan, 1931.

Besent, Annie, India That shall Be. Madras, 1940.

Biswas, A., Sunitee and R.P.Singh, The New Education Pattern in India. New Delhi : Vikas Publications, 1976.

Blang, Mark, Education and the Employment problem in Developing Countries. Geneva : ILO, 1973.

Bondurant, J.V., Conquest of Violence. Bombay, 1965.

Bose, N.K., Gandhiji : The Man and his Mission.Bombay, 1966.

-do- , (ed.), Selections from Gandhi. Ahmedabad : Navjeevan, 1963.

Bowles, Chester, Ideas, People and Peace.London, 1958.

Brubacher, John S., A History of the Problems of Education.New york : McGraw-Hill, 1947.

Burns, A., Colour Prejudice.London,1948.

Byles, M.B., The Lotus and the Spinning Wheel.London, 1948.

Chander, Jag Parvesh, Teaching of Mahatma Gandhi. Lahore, 1947.

Chatterjee, B.l., Gandhi. Calcutta, 1944.

Chatterjee, J.C., In Search of Freedom.Calcutta, 1967.

Chaudhary, Gopabundu, Gandhi and Utkal. Ahmedabad : Navjeevan, 1969.

Chaudhary, Ramnaravan, Bapu as I saw Him. Ahmedabad: Navjeevan, 1959.

Chaudhary, Ray P.C., Gandhi's First Struggle in India.Ahmedabad : Navjeevan, 1963.

Chattopadhyaya, S., Traditional Values in Indian Society.New Delhi : India International Centre, 1961.

Chirappanath, A.K., International Relations and Communal Harmony.In K.L. Seshagiri Rao and Henry O.Thompson (eds), World problems and human Responsibility : Gandhian Perpectives.New York: Unification Theological Seminary, 1988.

-do- Religion and Secu[illegible] India : A Christian Observation. In He[illegible]ompson (ed.), The Global Congress of the World [illegible]gions in South Asia. New York : Ibid.

-do- Modern Search for peace : Gandhian Way. In Journal of Gandhian Studies, (1978) p.168.

Cock and Cock, Sociological Approach to Education. New Delhi.

Cousins, Norman (ed.), Profiles of Gandhi.New Delhi : India Book Company, 1969.

Dantwala, M.L., Gandhism Reconsidered.Bombay, 1944.

Das, Desabandu, Way to Swaraj.Madras, 1923.

Datta, D.M., The Philosophy of Mahatma Gandhi.Madison, 1953.

Desai, A.R. Rural Sociology in India.New Delhi : Popular Prakasan, 1969.

Desai, Chitra, Sage of Sevagram.New Delhi: Barat Prakasha, 1952.

Desai, Mahadev, Gandhiji in Indian Villages.Madras, 1927.

-do- , The Gospel of Selfless Action.Ahmedabad, 1956.

Desai, M.P., The Problems of English. Ahmedabad : Navjeevan, 1964.

Dewey, John, Democracy and Eduation.New York : Macmillan, 1955.

Dhebar, U.N., Gandhiji, A Practical Idealist.Bombay, 1964.

Diwakar, R.R., Satyagraha in Action. Calcutta: Signet press, 1949.

-do- , Gandhi : The Spiritual Seeker.Bombay, 1964.

-do- , Gandhi : A Practical Philosopher.Bombay :1965.

-do- , Is Not Gandhi the answer.Bombay, 1966.

Dunkan, Ronald, Selected Writings of Mahatma Gandhi.London, 1951.

Durkeim, Emole, Education and Sociology.New York : Free Press, 1966,

Eapen, K.V., A Study of Kerala History.Kottayam : Kollett Publications, 1971.

Eaton, Janette, Gandhi : Fighter Without a Sword.New York, 1950.

Fischer, Louis, The Life of Mahatma Gandhi. New York, 1950.

-do- , Gandhi : His Life and Message for the World.New York, 1954.

-do- , Essential Gandhi - An Anthology.London, 1962.

Gandhi, M.K., All are Equal in the Eyes of God.Ahmedabad, Navjeevan, 1964.

-do- , My Experiments with Truth.Ahmedabad, Navjeevan, 1966 (repr.)

-do- , Basic Education. Ahmedabad: Navjeevan, 1956.

-do- , Bread Labour, Ahmedabad: Navjeevan, 1962.

-do- , Character and Nation Building. Ahmedabad : Navjeevan.1959.

-do- , Christian Missions. Ahmedabad : Navjeevan, 1957.

-do- , Conquest of Self. Bombay, 1943.

-do- , Constructive Programme. Ahmedabad: Nevjeevan, 1941.

-do- , Democracy : Real and Deceptive. Ahmedabad: Naveejan, 1961.

-do- , Discourses on the Gita. Ahmedabad : Navjeevan, 1960.

Gandhi, M.K., Ethical Religion. Madras, 1930.

-do- , Evil Wrought by the English medium.Ahmedabad : Navjeevan, 1958.

-do- , For Workers Against Untouchability.Ahmedabad : Navjeevan, 1958.

-do- , Glorious Thoughts of Gandhi, New Delhi, 1965.

-do- , God is Truth. Bombay, 1965.

-do- , Harijan, Ahmedabad : Navejeevan

-do- , Hindi and English in the South.Ahmedabad Navjeevan, 1958.

-do- , Hindu Dharma. Ahmedabad : Navjeevan, 1950.

-do- , Idea of Rural University, Sevagram 1954.

-do- , Indian Higher Education. Ahmedabad : Navjeevan (Harijan - 1938)

-do- , In Search of the Supreme. 3 Vols.Ahmedabad: Navjeevan, 1961.

-do- , Medium of Instruction. Ahmedabad : Navjeevan, 1958.

-do- , My Philosophy of Life. Bombay, 1961.

-do- , My Religion. Ahmedabad : Navjeevan, 1958.

-do- , My Socialism. Ahmedabad : Navjeevan, 1959.

-do- , My Varnashrama Dharma. Bombay, 1965.

-do- , Our Language Problem. Karachi, 1942.

-do- , Problems of Education. Ahmedabad: Navjeevan, 1962.

-do- , Rebuilding Our Villages. Ahmedabad: Navjeevan, 1966.

-do- , Satyagraha. Ahmedabad : Navjeevan, 1951.

-do- , Socialism of My Conception. Bombay, 1957.

-do- , The Role of Women. Bombay, 1964.

-do- , The Task Before Indian Students. Ahmedabad : Navjeevan, 1961.

-do- , Thoughts on Education. New Delhi : Ministry of Education, 1958.

-do- , Thoughts on National Language.Ahmedabad : Navjeevan, 1956.

-do- , To the Students, Ahmedabad : Navjeevan, 1949.

-do- , Towards New Education. Ahmadabad : Navjeevan, 1953.

-do- , True Education. Ahmedabad : Navjeevan, 1962.

-do- , Truth is God. Ahmedabad : Navjeevan, 1955.

Gauba, K.L., The Assassination of Mahatma Gandhi.Delhi : Jaico Pub. House, 1969.

Ganguli, A.N., Gandhi's Social Philosophy.New Delhi : Vikas Publications.

Gosh, Sudhir, Gandhi's Emissary, Calcutta, 1967.

Government of India, The Collected Works of Mahatma Gandhi, Vols.1 to 48. New Delhi : Publications Division, 1958.

-do- , Gandhian Outlook and Techniques.New Delhi : Publications Division, 1953.

-do- , India : Social Structure. New Delhi, 1969.

-do- , Welfare of Backward Classes. New Delhi : Pub. Division, 1963.

-do- , Report of the Committee on Religions and Moral Instruction.New Delhi : Ministry of Education.

-do- , Report of the Universtiy Education Commission.New Delhi, 1962.

-do- , Education and National Development.(Kothari Commission Report) New Delhi : Ministry of Education, 1966.

-do- , National Policy on Education (1986) New Delhi : Ministry of Education, 1986.

Gregg, Richard B. Self-Transcendence. London, 1956.

-do- , The Power of Non-Violence. Ahmedabad:Navjeevan, 1938.

Hiriyanna, M., Popular Essays in Indian Philosophy. Mysore, 1952.

-do- , Quest After Perfection. Mysore, 1952.

Holmer, J.H., My Gandhi. London, 1948.

Humayun Kabir, The Indian Heritage.London : Asia Pub. House, 1955.

-do- , Indian Philosophy of Education.Bombay : Asia Pub. House 1961.

Jack, Homer A.,(ed.), The Gandhi Reader. New York, 1961.

Jaffar, S.M., Education in Muslim India.New Delhi Idrah-I-Adabivat-I. 1972.

James, H.R., Education and Statesmanship in India, 1797-1910.London : Longman, 1911.

Jayaprakash Narayan, Socialism, Sarvoday and Demiocracy, Bombay, 1964.

Jesuit Scholars, Religious Hinduism.Allahabad : St.Paul's Publications, 1964.

Jones, Stanley E., Mahatma Gandhi : an Interpretation.London : 1948.

Jose, P.K., Foundations of Gandhian Thought.Calicut : Gandhi Peace Foundation, 1985.

Kaila, H., Mahatma Gandhi, New Delhi, 1960.

Kalekar, Kaka, Our next-Shore Neighbour. Ahmedabad: Navjeevan, 1954.

Karunakaran, K.P., Gandhi : Interpretations. New Delhi: Gitanjali, 1985.

Keay, P.E., Indian Education in Ancient Times. New Delhi.

Kher, B.G., The Pageant of life. Ahmedabad : Navjeevan, 1982.

Kher, V.B., (ed.) Social Sevice, Work and Reform, Vols.I to III.Ahmedabad : Navjeevan, 1976.

King, M.L., Strength to Love. London 1969.

Kochar, S.K., School Organisation. Ambala: University Publications.

Kopf, D., British Orientation and Bengal Resistance. Berkeley : Univ. of Caliphornia Press, 1969.

Kumarappa, J.C., (ed.) Towards New Education. Ahmedabad : NAvjeevan, 1951.

Laird, M.A., Missionaries and Education in Bengal, 1793-1837. London : Oxford University Press, 1972.

Law, N.N., Promotion and Learning in India by Mohammadans.New delhi, 1973.

Lott, B. Some Notes on the History of English in India.Hyderabad : CIEFL Bulletin, 1972.

Malkani, N.R., Ramblings and Reminiscences of Gandhiji.Ahmedabad : Navjeevan, 1972.

Mallik, Gurdiel, Gandhiji and Tagore. Ahmedabad: Navjeevan, 1961.

Mani, Mahajan P and K.S. Bharati, Foundations of Gandhian Thought. Nagpur: Dattsons, 1987.

Mathur, S.S., A Sociological Approach to Indian Education.Agra : VPM, 1966.

Mathur, V.S.(ed), Gandhiji as an Educationist.New Delhi : Metorpolitan Book Co., 1951.

Mayhew, A. The Education of India - A Study of British Education Policy in India, 1835 -1920. London : Feber and Gawyer, 1926.

Mazumdar, H.T., Mahatma Gandhi: A Prophetic Voice. Ahmedabad ; Navjeevan, 1963.

-do- , The Enduring Greatness of Gandhi. Ahmedabad : Navjeevan, 1982.

-do- , Gandhi versus the Empire. New York: Universal, 1932.

Mc Cully, B.T., English Education and the Origins of Indian Nationalism. Messachusetts (U.S.A.), 1966.

Menon, V.Lakshmi, Ruskin and Gandhi. Benares, 1965.

Merton, Thomas, Gandhi and Non-Violence. New York, 1965.

Miller, Rene Fulop, Dehumanisation of Modern Society (Lectures)Ahmedabad : Navjeevan, 1958.

Morgan, Arthur E., The Long Road. Ahmedabad : Navjeevan, 1958.

-do- , A Vision of Future India. Ahmadabad Navjeevan, 1957.

Munshi, K.M., Gandhi's Philosophy of Life and Action. Bombay, 1965.

-do- , Gandhi : The Master. New Delhi, 1948.

Mukalel, Joseph, The Educational Idealist in Mahatma Gandhi. *Gandhi jyothi.* (Bhagalpur) January 1988.

-do- , Gandhian Elements in the New Educational Policy. *Gandhi Marg* (New Delhi) September 1987.

-do- , Mahatma Gandhi's Concept of Religion : Prayer Vs Service. *Kerala Feature* (Trivandrum) March 1988.

Mukerji, R.K., Ancient Indian Eduation. New Delhi: Moti Mahal, 1960.

Mukerji, S.N., History of English in India, Baroda: Acharya books, 1966.

Nag, Kalidas, Tolstoy and Gandhi. Patna, 1950.

Naik, J.P., Educational Planning in India. New Delhi: Allied Publisher

Naik, J.P., Policy and Performance in Indian education, 1947-'74.New Delhi, 1975.

Nanda, B.R., Mahatma Gandhi. London Oxford, 1958.

-do- (ed.) Socialism in India. New Delhi: Vikas Publications, 1972.

Narayan, Shriman, Towards Better Education. Ahmedabad:Navjeevan, 1969

-do- , Education of the Future.New Delhi : S.Chand, 1973.

Naravane, V.S. Modern Indian Thought - a Philosophical Survey.Bombay : Asia Pub. House, 1964.

Narasimhaiah, C.D. (ed.), Gandhi and the West.Mysore : Universtiy of Mysore, 1969.

Natesan, G.A., Mahatma Gandhi, the Man and His Mission. Madras, 1932.

NCERT, Higher Secondary Education and Its Vocationalisation.New Delhi, 1977.

Nikam, N.A., Gandhi's Discovery of India. Bombay, 1963.

Nomani, Rushid, Textbooks for Secular India. New Delhi, 1970.

Nurulla, S., and J.P.Naik, A Student of History of Education in India, 1800-1961. Bombay:Macmillan, 1962.

Patel, Maniben, Letters to Sardar Patel. Ahmedbad:Navjeevan, 1950

Patel, M.S., The Educational Philosophy of Mahatma Gandhi. Baroda, 1974.

Patel, V.T., (ed.) Studies on Gandhi. New Delhi : Sterling Publicaitons, 1983.

Pathan, B.A., Gandhi Myth in English Literature in India.New Delhi : Deep and Deep, 1987.

Patwari, P.B., Reflections through Gandhian Angle.Ahmedabad : Navjeevan, 1982.

Peters, R.S., Ethics and Education. London: Allen and Unwin Ltd.1971.

Pillai, N.P., (ed.) Gandhian Literature : Education.Trivandrum : Gandhi Smarak Nidhi, 1965.

-do- , The Educational Aims of Mahatma Gandhi.Trivandrum : Kalyana Mandir Pub.

Polak, M.graham, My Gandhi : The Man. Bombay, 1950.

Prabu, R.K. (ed.) Gandhi and Children. Ahmedabad : Navjeevan, 1954.

-do- , (ed.) Truth is God. Ahmedabad : Navjeevan, 1955.

-do- , and U.R.Rao (eds), The Mind of Mahatma Gandhi. Ahmedabad : Navjeevan, 1967.

Pyarelal, Gandhian Techniques in the Modern World. Ahmedabad : Navjeevan, 1953.

-do- , Toward New Horizons. Ahmedabad : Navjeevan, 1957.

-do- , Mahatma Gandhi, Vol.I & II. Ahmedabad : Navjeevan, 1956.

Radhakrishnan, S. (ed.) Mahatma Gandhi : Essays and Reflections. London, 1949.

-do- , Mahatma Gandhi, 100 years. New Delhi, 1968.

Rajagopalachari, C., Gandhiji's Teachings and Philosophy. Bombay, 1963.

Rajendra Prasad, Constructive Programmes. Ahmedabad: Navjeevan.

-do- , Gandhi in Champaran. Madras, 1928.

-do- , At the Feet of Gandhi. London, 1955.

Ramachandaran, G., Promotion of Gandhian Philosophy. Mysore, 1966.

-do- , Educational Planning and National Integration.London : Asia Pub. House, 1965.

-do- , Education from Dewey to Gandhi. Ahmadabad.

-do- , and Mahadevan, T.K. (ed.) Gandhi : His Relevance to Our Times. New Delhi, 1967.

Ramajee Singh, The Relevance of Gandhin Thought. New Delhi : Classical Publications, 1983.

Ranji, Manni Tata, The Concept of Personality in the Educational Thought of Mahatma Gandhi. New Delhi :NCERT.

Rao, R.V., Gandhian Insititutions of Wardha. Bombay, 1947.

Rao, U.R., (ed.) The Way to Communal Harmony. Ahmedabad : Navjeevan, 1963.

Rao, U.S.Mohan, The Message of Mahatma Gandhi, New Delhi, 1968.

Richter, J.A., A History of Missions in India, New York :Revello & Co.1908.

Roland, Romain, Mahatma Gandhi. London 1924.

Ross, James S., Groundwork of Eduational Theory.London : Harp & Co., 1935.

Santanam, K., Gospel of Gandhi. Bombay, 1967.

Sarma, D.S., The Father of the Nation. Madras, 1956.

Satya Sundaram, Gandhiji as an educationist. Machilepattanam, 1970

Sen K.M., Hinduism,. Hardsmouth : Penguin.

Seshadri, C.K., English in India : A Historical Perspective.Baroda : M.S. University, 1977.

Sequera, T.N., Modern Indian Eduction. New Delhi: Oxford, 1967.

Shah, Gunvant, Gandhi for the New generation.Ahmedabad : Navjeevan, 1982.

Shah. S.M., (ed.), Human Settlements. Ahmedabad : Navjeevan, 1982.

Sharp, Gene, Gandhi Wields the Weapon of Moral Power.Ahmedabad : Navjeevan, 1960.

Sharp, H.(ed.), Selections from educational Records, Part I, 1781-1839 Calcutta : Bureau of Education, 1920.

Shirer, William, Gandhi : A Memoir., New York :Touchstone, 1979.

Sinha, S., Ahimsa Our Creed. Patna, 1956.

-do- , Indian Independence in Perspective. London 1964.

Srinivas ,M.N., Social Change in Modern India, Bombay : Allied Publishers, 1966.

-do- , India : Social Sturcture.New Delhi : Govt.of India, 1969.

Srivastava, B.D., Development of Modern Indian Education.New Delhi : Longman.

Taneja, V.R., Educational thought and Practice.New Delhi : University Publications, 1965.

Tendulkar, D.G., Mahatma, Vol.I to VIII. Bombay, 1960-1963.

Thekkinedath, Joseph, Love of Neighbour in Mahatma Gandhi. Always (India) : Pontifical Institute, 1973.

Thomas, P. Christians and Christianity in India and Pakistan.London, 1954.

Topa, Iswara, Ethos of Non-violence. Ahmedabad : Navjeevan, 1964.

Upadhyaya, J.M., Mahatma Gandhi as a student. New Delhi, 1965.

Vaizy, John, The Economics of Education. London :Macmillan, 1973.

Vakil, K.S. and S.Nagarjan, Education in India.Bombay : Allied Publishers, 1966.

Ved, Mitra, Education in Ancient India.New Delhi : Arya Book Dept., 1967.

Venkalarangaiya M.,Gandhi's Gospel of Satyagraha. Bombay, 1966.

Verma, I.B., Basic Education : A Reinterpretation.Agra : Shri Ram Mehra and Co., 1969.

Vinoba, Thoughts on Education.Varanasi : Akhil Bharat Seva Sangh, 1959.

-do- , Essence of Basic Education. Compiled by K.S.Archalu.Tanjore :Sarvodaya Pracharalaya, 1967.

Watson, Francis, Talking of Gandhi. London, 1957.

Weiner, Myron (ed.), Modernisation : The Dynamics of Growth. Washington : U.S.Information Agency, 1966.

Woody, Thomas, Life and Education in Early Societies, New York : Macmillan, 1949.

Yagnik, Indulal K., Gandhi as I Knew Him . New Delhi, 1945.

Zakir Hussain, National University.New Delhi, 1966

Index

Ahimsa. 61,139-40
Akbar. 44
All India Education Board. 100
Andrews. CF. 28
Arabic Language. 44
Aranyakas. 34
Aryanayakam. 100. 104
Ashramas. 36
Asiatic Society of Bengal. 41
Atman. 34
Auckland. 49

Basic education. 10.165-74
Bentick. 49
Bhagavad Gita. 34. 37
Bhagavan. 34
Bhakti-marge. 220-21
Bhatia. B.D.,. 28. 35. 112
Bowles. Chester. 12. 115.119
Brahmachari. 114
Brahmacharya. 36. 37
Brahman. 34
British System of Education. 10
Buck. Pearl. 15. 136
Buddha. 14. 43
Buddhism.42
Buddhist Education. 42-44. 170

Champaran Schools experiments. 94-98
- Difficulty to provide teachers. 96
- Education through sanitation. 97-98
- Untouchability. 94
- Village education. 95

Character formation in Gandhism. 198-202.
Charter Act of 1813. 48
Christianity influence. 52-58
Christ. Jesus. 52-55. 242
Craft Education. 165-74
- Broad based. 166-67
- Character development. 168
- Craft as principal for intellect. 171-72.
- Craft central education through charka. 172
- Craft centered education to develop problem solving. 172-73
- Craft manual. 168
- Development of mind. 167
- Importance to income of rural poor. 173
- Knowledge and mental development from life-experiences. 173-74
- Literary education. 171
- Literary education and. 167
- Manual work. 169
- Modification to British education system. 165.
- Moral development through handicrafts. 167.
- Need of the day. 166.
- Principals and values. 169
- Shortcomings in present day education. 165-66.
- Stress on learning of 172.
- Training of hand. 168.
- Truth and love. 170.

Curzon. 51

Davidson. Jo. 125. 199.
Descartes. 111.
Dewey. John. 60. 79. 104. 122. 123. 130
Dharma. 36-37.
Dhyana. 38-39.
Dickens. Charles. 122.
Discipline. 40-41.
Diwakar. R.R. 135. 219.
Durant. Will. 112. 216.

East. Edward Hydei. 48.
Educational idealism and pragmatism in Gandhi. 110-34.

Educational idealsim, 110-12
Absolute idealism, 110
Curriculum, 111-12
Spiritual nature of 111.
Educational pragmatism, 120-24
Life-experiences to 120-21, 123.
Moral training, 123-24.
Practical and Life problems in America, 120.
Pragmatism philosophy of education, 122-23.
Truth in, 122.
Foundation of Gandhian thoughts, 112-18.
Absolute values and truth, 115-16.
Emphasis on development, 117.
Gandhi vision of education, 113.
Indian philosophy and religious thoughts in, 112-13.
Mental development, 117-18.
Search for truth, goodness and beauty, 113-14.
Self-realisation, 114-15.
Spiritual society, 116-17.
Gandhian idealsim and educational practics, 118-20.
Craft, Centered education, 118-19.
Independent of thinking, 119.
Maturity and perfection of mind, 118
Self discipline, 120.
Stress on dignity of human personality, 119.
Pragmatism in Gandhian education, 124-82.
Child consciousness of social values, 129-30.
Concept of usefulness 127-28.
Craft, 124.
Development as a continuous process of experiment, 132.
Experiences around child from his point of new, 125.
Experiment in earth and water treatments 131-32.
Idealist with divine and spiritual, 129.
Life experiences, 124-25.
Social services, 130-31
Truth, 131.
Untouchability and caste diffesencies, 130.
Utility to curriculum, 128-29.
Work experiences, 126-27.
Education thoughts, 7, 30, 34-59.
Christian influence on education, 52-58
In ancient India, 34-41
Ashramas, 31
Dharma 37-38.
Dhyana 38-39
Discipline, 40-41
Gurukula system, 35-36, 39
Learning methods, 38
Learning of religious rituals, 39.
Literature on 34-35.
Manana, 38
Purusharthas, 36-37
Teacher - centered, 41
Training in craft and skill, 39
Vedic or Brahmanic education 35.
In medieval India, 41-46.
Bhakti cult, 45.
Buddhist centre of learning, 42-44.
Knowledge paths, 42.
Muslim education, 44.
Religious reactions, 42-46.
Western education in British India, 46-52.
Anglicists, 48-49.
Anti-Anglist education 52.
Creation of English speaking elite 50-51.
English as medium of instruction, 48.
English language of administration, 47.
Einstein, Albert 1, 15, 204.
Elizabeth 1, 46.
English language, 47-48.
Erikson, Erik A;16.
Experiments in education, 85-109.
Champaran school experiments 94-98.
Difficulty to provide teachers, 96.
Education through sanitation, 97-98.
Gandhi attempt to educate all, 95.
Primary education, 96
Village education, 95

Gandli's experiment with truth, 85-88.
As God, 86.
Course of time in, 88
Powerful motion, 87
Problem of discovery, 86-87.
Realisation of 85-86.
Gujarat Vidyapeeth, 101-03.
Gandhi fouded, 101.
Nationalist experiments, 98-101.
Against British system, 98-99.
Backward in education, 99
Basic primary eductation, 100.
Development of mind and soul, 99.
Importance of 100.
Phoenix settlement and Tolstoy Farm, 88-94.
Wardhe Education Conference, 103-08.

Ficher, Fredesril, 200.
Fischer, Louis, 13-15, 79, 124, 192.

Gandhian Studies - a rediscovery, 1-33.
Evolving national policy in education, 7-13.
International consesus, 13-19.
Rediscovery of 1-7.
Scope of 25-31.
Concept of labour, 29
Conscious of rural nature, 26-27.
Economics, 29.
Education, 30
Interdisciplinery learning and research, 206
Interdiscipinary role of multi-facial relevance, 31.
Nature of Gandhian thoughts, 25-26.
Peace Science, 30-31.
Political science approach, 27-28.
Religious philosophy of 28-29.
Scheme of Action, 26.
Ultramodernism and, 19-25.
Gandhi, Devdas, 77
Gandhi, Mahatma,
Einstein tribute to, 1
Father of the nation, 1
Leadership in freedom struggle, 4
Rediscovery of 1-7.
Gandhi Manganal, 89
Gandhi Rajiv, 9
Gauba, KL, 86, 194, 243.
Gnana-marga, 210.
Goals of education in Gandhian thought, 60-84.
Education and life-experences, 78-82.
Developing individual, 81.
Life experiences central aim, 79.
Primary means to achieve, 80.
Self-dependency, 81-82.
Various aspect to individuals, 79-80.
Education for social development, 70-74.
Character formation, 71.
Development of individuals, 70-74.
Development of Society, 71.
Value of social service, 71-72, 74.
Education for spiritual/moral development, 60-66.
Ahimsa, 61-64.
Character formation, 62-63.
Moral basis to character formation, 66.
Prayer, 65
Spiritual and moral personality, 61,64-65.
Spiritual personality, 64-66.
Spiritual principles, 61, 63.
Truth, 61-62.
Universality and eternal values, 62.
For knowledge, 66-70.
Communication of, 70.
Education for, 68-70.
Education reflect on human race, 67-68.
Holistic development of man, 67.
Learner, 69.
Primary education, 69.
Primary education, 69.
Process of brining change in human individual, 66-67.
For self discovery, 74-84.
Individuals, 74-76.
Self-discovery, 76-78.
Social attitudes, 77-78.

Grant, Charles, 48.
Gregg, Richard B, 4, 114, 199, 247.
Gujarat Vidyapeeth, 101-03.
Aims of 101-02.
Indian traditions, 102.
Service to village, 102-03.
Gunther, John, 4, 189, 217.
Gurukula system, 35, 42.

Hare, David, 48.
Harijan, 30, 93, 99, 204.
Hastings, Warren, 47.
Hegal III
Hind Swaraj, 89
Hindusim, 92.
Hindu Muslim communal rivalry,241
Hindu Vidyalaya, 48.
Hitler,101
Holistic education in Gandhism, 189-212.
Aspects of 189-93
Class room learning, 190
Develop personal qualities, 193.
Disintegration through specialisation, 193.
Individual's personality, 190.
Integrated approach to learning, 190-91.
Training in social attitudes, 193.
Values, 191-92.
Vocational education, 192-93.
Character formation, 198-202.
Altruistic or oriented, 199.
Humour and cheerfulness, 201-02
Peace formation, 200
Personal and spirituals, 198.
Personality formation 200, 202.
Self help, 200-01
Sense of direction in, 198-99.
Values, attitudes and aptitudes, 198.
For balanced development, 202-07.
Economic development, 204-05.
Individual personality, 203-04.
Knowledge and values, 206.
of individuals, 202-03.
Organization of attitudes, 204.
Political attitudes, 205.
Social attitudes, 205.
Vocation and information, 206-07
Liberal education 207-10
Capable of understanding, 208.
Freedom from bondages, 208-09.
Freedom from dependence on excess needs 209
Freedom from economic bondage 209-10
knowledge 210
Scope of personality, 208.
Traditions vs modernism in Gandhism, 193-98.
Educational tradtions, 194-95.
Integration between, 194.
Modernity for the better, 197-98.
Reformist in Gandhi, 196-97.
Religious traditions, 195-96
Sociological traditionalism, 196
Traditional beliefs, approaches and attitudes, 196-97.
Unity between the, 193-94.
Holmes, John, 16, 24, 77, 120, 125, 217, 226.

Indian Home Rule 89
Indian National Congress, 51, 52
International consensus, 13-19.
British and Americans firendliness to Gandhi, 13
Gandhian perspective for 18-19.
Gandhi's legacy, 13
Humility and simplicity, 17
Social reformer, 15
Symbol of unity, 14
To liberate truth and innocence, 15-16.
To rediscover impact of Gandhian principles and thoughts, 18
Universality of thoughts, 18
Vision enriching politics with ethics, 15.
Voice of Gandhi reflected world, 14.
Islam, 92.
Islamic education, 44

Jainsim, 42
James, William, 122.
Jones, E. Stanley, 55, 156, 193, 216.

Kant, 111

Karma, 36, 37, 45, 220
Karma Yoga, 42.
Kellenback, Hermann, 90,91, 93.
King, Martin Luther, 17, 18, 197, 239, 242.
Koran, 44
Kothari Commission (1966), 182, 185
Krodha, 37

Liberal education in Gadhism, 207-10.

Macaulay, 48-49.
Macdonald, D 205, 241, 242
Magna Carte of English Education in India, 49.
Mahabharata, 34
Manana, 38
Marshall, George c2, 237.
Marx, 29
Marxism, 143.
Mathews, Herbett, 13
Mehta, Ved, 115
Moksha, 3, 28, 36
Morality, 213.
Moral principles, 3-4
Mountbatten, 192
Mudaliar Commission 1953, 185
Muhammad Ghori, 44
Mukherjee, Radhe Kumud, 10, 80, 206
Muslim rule in India, 44
Musolini, 101

Nalanda, 39, 43.
Narayan, Sriman, 9
National Education Board, 100
Nationalist expert in education, 98-101.
National policy in education - early, 7-13.
  Attention to rural India, 11-12.
  Character formation, 11
  Drawbacks of British Education, 12
  Educational reconstruction, 10
  Fundamental characteristics, 9-10.
  Gandhian thought and practice on 7
  Train human potential at grass root level, 12-13.
  Vedic education system. 8
  Within framework of Indian Constitution 10-11
National service scheme, 254.
Need based education in India, 174-77
New Policy on Education 9, 30, 181-86.
New Testament, 55-56.
Nishkama Karma Yoga, 28-29.
Non-violence, 15, 135, 137-38, 250
Nunn, Perey, 23, 74, 75

Peace and tolerance, 237-56
  Educational concept of peace, 248-50
    Content of science education, 249
    Content of social science and culture, 249-50
    Non-violence, 250
    Violence, 248-49
  Educational goal of peace and tolerance, 243-48
    Charter formation,246
    Collective endeavours for, 244.
    East as a whole and India for, 247-48
    Hindu-Muslim Unity, 245
    Nuclear threat, 248.
    Personality development, 246-47
    Solution to holocaust, 246.
  Methods of peace education, 251-55
    Cultural experience, 253.
    Inter-religious experiences, 253-54
    Peace - based materials, 252-53
    Peace consciousness, 251-53
    Red Cross Society, 254-55
    United Nations, 251.
  Tolerance in Gandhism, 241, 47, 43.
    Communal, 243
    Individual, 242
    Social goods, 243.
    Tolerance and fundamental rights, 242
    Tolerance and love, 241
  World peace, 237-41
    Against violence, 237-38
    International goal, 239-40.
    National goals in Gandhian context, 238-39.
    Peace and national integration, 240
    Spirituality based in peace, 240-41.
    Truth and ahimsa, 238
Peace Corpose, 239, 254

Peace Science, 30-31
Persian language, 47
Phoenix settlement 88-90, 126
Pilate, Pontius, 15
Plato, 110, 111
Polak, 88,90
Prayer, 220-21
Public Instruction, 49
Purusharthas, 36-37
Purva-mimasa, 45

Ramanuja, 46
Ramayana, 34, 103
Red Cross Society, 254
Rediscovery of Gandhi, 1-7.
  Albert Einstein Tribute, to 1
  Champion of down trodden and poor in India, 5-6
  Comprehensive vision of 2-3
  Devotion to world peace, 2
  Gandhian political theory and solutions, 5
  His love of poverty ridden masses, 6
  India and World rediscovering, 6
  Jones on 1-2
  Moral principles, 3-4
  Political and religious tolerance, 2
  Religious thoughts, 3
  Spirit of interest in Gandhian thoughts, 4-5
  Thoughts, traditions and values, 4
Religious philosophy, 28-29
Roosevelt, Eleanor, 7
Round Table Conferenc,e 22
Rousseau, 103
Rowlatt Act 1919, 51
Roy, Raja Rammohan,48
Rudolph, S.H., 47
Rural reconstruction, 11, 177, 81
Ruskin, 88-90

Sabarmati Ashram, 87, 103, 106
Samkhya Philosophy, 45
Sanskrit, 47
Satyagrapha in Indian Education, 135-64
    Based on Ahimsa, 152-53.
    Based on character, 153.
    Based on love, 154-55
    Based on self denial, 155-56.
    Based on truth, 152.
    Skill or occupation, 153.-54
  As method of education, 146-51
    Ahimsa, 147
    Humility, 148-49
    Love, 147-48
    Social activities, 150
    Social justice, 150
    Sovereign remedy, 151
    Tolerance, 149-50
    Truth a way of life, 146-47
  As providing direction in education, 156
    Co-curricular, 159-60
    Curriculam, 157
    Discipline, 160-61
    Educational planning, 161
    Life-orientations, 159
    Material preparations, 158-59
    Life Orientations, 159
    Organising learning experiences, 157-58
    Self-dependency, 158
    Social redemption, 161-62
    Transformation of individuals, 156-57
  Educational goals and, 140-46
    Aims at develop of ahimsa, 144-45
    Aims at development of love, 143.
    Aims at development of social attitudes, 145
    Education in relation to 142-43.
    Education through non-violence, 143.
    Integral constituent of 140-41.
    Socio-centric by satyagraha, 145-46
    Truth achievement, 141-43
  Foundations fo 135-40
    Ahimsa, 139-40
    An end or goal, 135-37
    Non-violence, 138
    Passive resistance to, 136
    Principle of love 138-39
    Soul force, 136
    Truth and love, 136-37
    Truth and non-violence, 135, 137
    Truth synonym of God, 137-38
Schiller, 122

Self discipline. 2
Self-reliance. 2.15. 28. 30. 114-15
Sevagram. 119
Smriti literature. 34
Snow. Edgar P.. 113. 240
Socrate. 111
South Africa. 90. 136
Spinoza 111
Spiritual values and education. 213-36
  Developing. 227-34
    Conscientisation. 228-29
    Cultural studies. 232
    Health services. 232-34
    Orientation programmes. 229-30
    Prayer services. 231-32
    Self-help. 231
    Student literature 230
    Value centered syllabus. 229
  Nature of Gandhian morality. 213-16
    Morality and education. 213-14.
    Morality basic of economics. 214
    Morality foundation of religious beliefs. 213
    Moral principles in politics - 215
    Moral values control social life 215-16
    Truth and non-violence 216
  Spiritual values in education. 223-27
    Emotional development. 225-26
    Emotional values. 226
    Harmonisation of emotional life. 226-27
    Intellectual development. 224-25
    Mind and spirit development 225
    Thought of God. 223-24
    Truth 225
  Spiritual values in Gandhism. 216-22
    Bhakti-Marga. 220
    Concept of God. 217
    Concept of Prayer. 221-22
    Experiment with truth. 217
    Karma marga. 20
    Renunciation. 222
    Self realisation. 218-19
    Transcedents religious rituals. 217-18
    Truth and ahimsa. 219. 222
Sruti literature. 34
St. Francis of Assisi. 216
Supreme Reality. 2
Swaraj. 30. 35

Takshasila 39. 43
Taylor. Edmond. 2. 116. 139. 201. 238.
Templin. Ralph. 168. 197
Thomas. Norman. 17. 198
Thoreau. 10
Thurman. 145
Tolerance in Gandhism. 241-43
Tolstoy. 14
Tolstoy Farm. 87. 88. 94. 126. 167
Traditions vs modernism and Gandhi 193-98.
Truth 61. 88. 216. 219. 222. 225
Tulsidas. 103

Ultramodernism and Gandhism. 19-25
  Against Gandhi cautions 45. 24
  Automatisation. 23
  Consequences of 20-21
  Dehumanisation. 22-23
  Excess accumulation of physical comforts. 22
  Excess consumption of material goods. 21
  Holistic development. 19-20
  Human personality development. 19-20
  Individual benefits. 20
  Individual role in social scheme. 23-24
  Man's environment. 20
  Self destructive tendency. 24-25
  Use of cloths without restraint. 21-22
  Weaker passions. 21
U.N. 251
UNICEF. 251
Upanishads. 34
Urdu language. 44

Vaisheshika system. 45
Vandenberf. Arthur it. 11. 31. 197
Vedas. 34
Vedanta. 46
Vedic Education 10. 165-88
  Craft Education as basic education. 165-74
  National Educational policy of 1986. 181-86.

Agriculture and marketing, 185
Aims of 181-82
As part of Gandhian education, 186
Based on social service, 185
Bifurcation after secondary education, 183-84
Health services, 184-85
Implementation of vocational education, 183
Need to women and rural students 186
Objectives, 182-83
Prospects to women and rural students, 186
Rural University patterns, 181
To provide skilled manpower, 183
Need based education in India, 184-77
Continuous revisions of policies, 177
Eradication of literacy, 176-77
Human and material resources, 174-75
Mass education, 176
Problem -Oriented education, 175-76
Socio-economic needs, 174
Rural reconstruction, 177-81
Active participation, 180-81
Economic liberation, 178-79
Manual labour, 179-80
Process of enliving village life, 178
Self employment for village population, 179

Welfare to rural masses, 178
War and disarmanment, 70
Wardhe Education Conference, 103-08
Craft-centered and skill bases, 103-04
Free and compulsory education, 107
Gandhi's basic scheme, 107
Impact of training, 106
Medium of instruction, 107
Process of education, 108
Remuneration of teachers, 108
Role in primary education, 104-05
Self-supporting education, 106-07
Teaching of whole art and science as craft 105-06
Teacher - student ratio, 104
Warren, Earl, 239
Wellesley, 49
Wito, 251
Wood, Charles, 49
Wood's Despatch, 49-50
World peace, 2, 237-41

Yoga system, 45-46
Young India, 30, 36

Zakir Hussain, 100, 104, 106, 107
Zoroastrianism, 92